# THE MONGOL EMPIRE

OVERLEAF The Mongols – here seen setting fire to a captured city – were not the first conquerors to come out of the heartlands of Asia, but they were the best documented, their deeds recorded most notably by the painters and historians of Persia.

كه بنده معزول شد او بر سبيل بهانه حبك كرخان كه در بخارا نشست در آمد و نزد او رود و مير از آن خود بستاند و نام حبك الملك نهاد بر اينكه در آن بلاد كه آمده و فرستاده بوده و ديگر

باز باعزتى شد و لقب خود نوك كنك ده كرد كه معنى آن زبان ختايى سلطان عظيم الملكى باشد و از همه نقاضا با آن رأ بنه ماننده كه حبك كرخان اكثر

ولايات ختاى را برخود كرد و رواج كشت و النبان خان بقرار باقى بود و امراى هر يك از بندگان و ديگر مالكان مانده كه هم از آن جانب سلم كرده و در بندكى

ميسر مالكى را رواج كرده در آمده بودند و از ماننده ملوك طوايف براى خويش را حاكم و سلطان مملكتى مى ساخت و بعد از آن متع سال كه النبان خان

برجدذل با امراى نوكنك و سينجون محافظت شهرها بر دها رود ها كرد و بيش و بردست حبك كرخان ساوه

بهادر را به عنوبت بنك از بروم بروم خروج كه الملك شده بود و دستكشته با اتكى از مغول الزمانا ذل از حدود الزمانا بر آنجا زند و ان كوكر فراخنانى را كه

از النبان خان كه بخت الهى نشسته بروز و نيز رفته بود از شهر جرجا بروند كه آنجا بود كه آنجا بد كه آبحان النبان را برنده و ان شكر را بر دو رند و باطراق شهر را

كردند

و النبان خون چون مستقر در آن خان ات بنشنده بود كه شهر جرجنك بر نغار ثمانك و قوت النك و رعايا نام با نام ايذر يكى بام اينان از زنك

در يك بامى ولى ثينك فرستاده نامه و حورش شهر طالده و برند و با باتى كرده كه هزوردى سده نقير كه بزا رختانى آزا سيم كنيد و مردم از ده خطا ساير

كنكى خونشتن بر دارد چون جون با بناه رها برناه و دوان شده آمده شناى ماه شهر و تقله سور جو حبشناى رنته و ديگر بام رها با آبى كه ديگر رفته انده

انا سنبك ينى مسكنند حبك كرخان با بيان نا اسماده انده و درهاره هر دوزم مى آورند انه از بيان باز برنده حون نيت مى آمده ناه روى علونه شهر

على آنجا از غايت كرسنكى كه بشت آدمى مى خورند مى جورزده انده و مى خورده و قوت النك و حبنينا كمك كه النبان اورا بايرو به بشرجانكذه كه آشنده بود

ناخوه كرشده و اميد ديكر وابسته بام جرنك او جوكى نام و صبت اورا داشته دكله سنك برولات سنك مثل الملك النبان خان رنته و آن سنك نام سكه

با ساوقه نها در از فرستاده بود در شهر طالمه در بنده و باكبى سند حبنك كرخان فرستاده كه بدر حبنك كرخان شهر طالكذد

# THE MONGOL EMPIRE

## Genghis Khan:
## His Triumph and his Legacy

# PETER BRENT

Book Club Associates
London

This edition published 1976 by
Book Club Associates
By arrangement with
Weidenfeld and Nicolson

Layout by Juanita Grout

Filmset and printed offset litho by
Cox and Wyman Ltd, London,
Fakenham and Reading

# CONTENTS

## The House of Genghis Khan

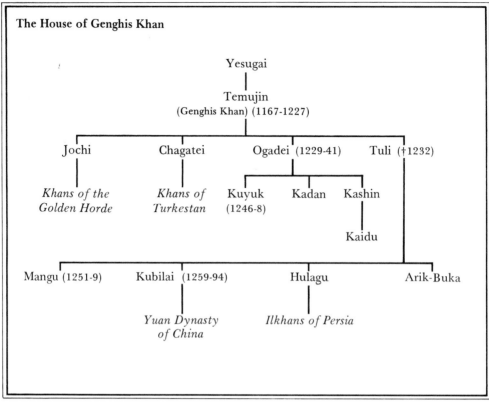

## Khans of the Golden Horde

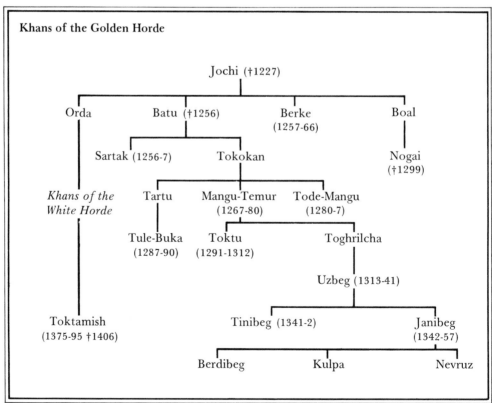

*Inclusive dates refer to reigns*

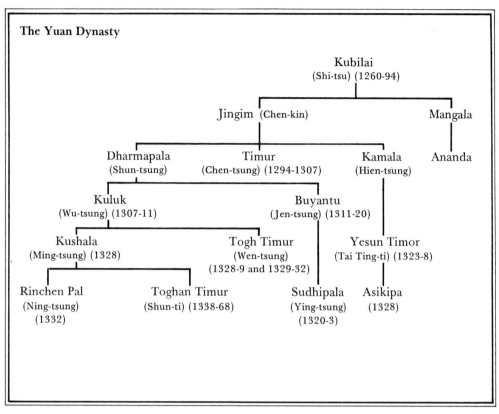

# The Yuan Dynasty

Kubilai
(Shi-tsu) (1260-94)

Jingim (Chen-kin)  Mangala

Dharmapala  Timur  Kamala  Ananda
(Shun-tsung)  (Chen-tsung) (1294-1307)  (Hien-tsung)

Kuluk  Buyantu
(Wu-tsung) (1307-11)  (Jen-tsung) (1311-20)

Kushala  Togh Timur  Yesun Timor
(Ming-tsung) (1328)  (Wen-tsung)  (Tai Ting-ti) (1323-8)
(1328-9 and 1329-32)

Rinchen Pal  Toghan Timur  Sudhipala  Asikipa
(Ning-tsung)  (Shun-ti) (1338-68)  (Ying-tsung)  (1328)
(1332)  (1320-3)

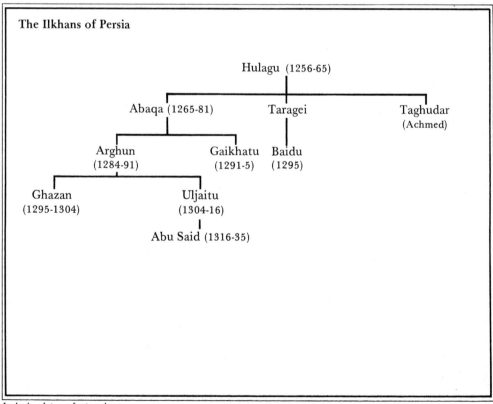

# The Ilkhans of Persia

Hulagu (1256-65)

Abaqa (1265-81)  Taragei  Taghudar
(Achmed)

Arghun  Gaikhatu  Baidu
(1284-91)  (1291-5)  (1295)

Ghazan  Uljaitu
(1295-1304)  (1304-16)

Abu Said (1316-35)

*Inclusive dates refer to reigns*

# Book One
# THE FOUNDING FATHER

# 1 SURVIVAL

It was a feast-day – the Day of the Red Disc, when summer's first full moon brings out the people in celebration of the season. On the banks of the River Onon the Taijiat, followers of the chieftain Targutai, assembled to the rattle of the *shamans'* drums. There was mutton to eat, one supposes, and beef because this was one of the major occasions of the year, and there was certainly *koumiss*, fermented from the whey of mares' milk, a drink that will have brought warmth and comfort even to those already happy to celebrate in the eyes of their gods.

The large tents of the Taijiat encampment will have stood empty, stretched white felt multi-layered and firm on its latticed wooden supports, the flaps down, each tent bright with its own stylized ornamentation of animal, bird or plant. The protective circle of wagons had probably been breached, some having been driven down to where the dark water whispered past the cries, the sudden boasts, the laughter of those feasting beside the tall fires. These, in their long surcoats and stubby felt boots, sat uncaring under that dark sky, the long canopy of the World-Tent above them, suspended from the Pole Star's central shaft. Or perhaps, staring up, they remembered other stories and saw the stars circling the firmament as horses tethered to that single, unmoving light. If there were gods, they knew that the *shaman* spoke to them and for them. His drum – its wood miraculously the wood of the Cosmic Tree – sounded in its rhythms his climbing footsteps as he mounted towards Bai Ülgän, god of the upper air and – under Tengris – the universe's greatest power. The people were contented; they were secure and for the moment with enough to eat, protected by the word of a strong chieftain, their grazing a certainty for one more season at least.

A young man sat at the edge of the feast. He was in his middle teens, already tall, with a broad forehead; the thin haze across his chin would grow into a beard the length of which others would remark on and remember. His eyes were keen, and in other places, other circumstances, his bearing had been noticed for its pride, for the particular energy it displayed. Here, however, where the light flickered and died, and the darkness stretched ready to encroach on the humility of those so far from the festival's centre, he could only sit, doubtless watchful, certainly in some discomfort. His neck was weighed down by, and his hands fastened to, a wooden collar. This, the *k'ang*, bowed his shoulders, chafed his skin, prevented him from lying flat and so had forced on him the weakness of the sleepless. To everyone who saw him, it marked out his situation – he was a prisoner.

His name was Temujin. Now he was nobody; but he had ancestors of note. His great-grandfather had been Kabul Khan, leader of the whole Mongol nation, a man who in his time had defeated an army sent from China by the Kin emperor, Holoma. That had been fifty years before. Kabul Khan had died by poison, some claimed, perhaps fed him by a Tatar agent (and the latter in turn paid by the Chinese, subjects of the Kin, to wreak their clandestine revenge). He had been succeeded by a cousin, Ambakhai Khan. A band of the Tatar warrior elite, the Juyin, captured him and sent him south to where the Kin, unslaked, had him unpleasantly done to death. He managed to leave behind him a message, however, demanding of those who followed him that they should revenge his capture and death: 'Though you wear all your ten fingers down until you have no fingers left, avenge me!' Mongols learned these words, passed them eagerly from father to son – they had taken them to heart.

To succeed Ambakhai, the Mongols chose another cousin of the same royal line, Kutula. He fought thirteen times against the Tatars, and at the end of this unlucky string of battles had nothing to show for it but repeated and damaging defeat. Under Kutula Khan, the nation languished, it broke into disparate parts, it lost its sense of itself. The Tatars pursued, killed, captured, robbed; the Mongol survivors, scattered, watched impotently from gullies and thickets, emerging at last to a world snatched from them. Their sad leader, Kutula, had been Temujin's grand-uncle.

Kutula's nephew had been a warrior named Yesugai. He captured a woman of great beauty and, as it turned out, of forceful character, a girl of good family; having chased off her betrothed, he married her with the blessing of his own relations. As befitted a prince, he too fought Tatars; during one of the many bleak battles in which Mongols unsuccessfully faced their neighbours, he captured a chief named Temujin Uge. When in 1162 he returned from war, his men leading this captive as a forlorn sop to the continuing sense of defeat that must have overwhelmed them, Yesugai found that he had become the father of a son. The boy had been born with his fist clenched about blood, certain sign of courage, battle and victory to come. Yesugai named him after the prince he had taken, Temujin.

Kutula Khan died. Yesugai gathered a following of his own, a heterogeneous collection of riders who had once been in the camp of Bartan Bahadur, Kutula's brother. They were all of one stock, that of the Borjigin clan, descended from a great chieftain named Bodonchar. Yesugai himself belonged to the line of elder sons who could trace their descent directly from that chief, so that in him strength, courage and intelligence combined with the blood inheritance to give his claim true substance. He was not a great khan, as Kabul Khan had been, gathering under his hand the energies of all the Mongol camps and tribes. He was one leader in a world from which unity had flown, in which enemies outnumbered friends and in which strength alone could hope to find alliance. The weak fell away, their men left them, their followers found other leaders, the tents in their camps grew fewer, the grazing for their beasts sparser. In the end such groupings were absorbed in the train of another chief, or disappeared under a sudden flight of arrows, to the swift throbbing of hoofbeats and screams of anguish that fell abruptly into silence.

When his son Temujin was nearly ten years old, Yesugai decided that it was time he became betrothed to some suitable girl. Taking the boy and a small party of warriors, he set out, his destination the camp of the Olkunut, from which Temujin's own mother had come. On the way, however, he came across another camp, that of a related tribe, the Onggirat. These were mountain people living not far from the territories of the Kin empire and maintaining with its rulers an uneasy friendship.

The Mongols, now as then, travel north to summer pastures, their felt tents or *yurts* folded for the journey, their flocks of sheep and goats tended by mounted herdsmen carrying the long pole with its looped end which is the Mongol lasso.

Their chief was named Dai Sechen and by appropriate chance he had a ten-year-old daughter, Berta. In slow and dignified debate, he offered this girl as a bride for Yesugai's son and, because Dai Sechen was a man of wealth and power, a valuable ally to have linked by a blood-tie to a ruling family in troubled times, Yesugai gladly accepted the girl. When he rode away, therefore, he left the betrothed boy in the Onggirat camp, a secure place in which Temujin could learn the skills of warrior and diplomat, and from which he could set out on the expeditions that would make his name in battle or the hunt. When he had learned, and grown, and married at last, he would return with his bride to the camp of his own people, strong and skilful in leadership's necessary tasks.

It is not clear how long Temujin remained with the Onggirat. One day, a cousin, from a different family, but of the same clan, the Qongqotat, rode into Dai Sechen's camp. Yesugai, he said, had felt the need to speak with his son and was asking for him. The request was unorthodox, but Yesugai was not a man one offended with impunity – besides, Temujin was his son and sons should obey their fathers. Dai Sechen gave his permission. Since Berta remained faithful to Temujin although it was four years before she saw him again, a steadfastness supported by her father, himself unswerving in his friendship for his young son-in-law, it must be supposed that Temujin at least remained long enough in the Onggirat camp to arouse such constancy. He was, on the other hand, a man who always drew to him the instant loyalty of the brave and the capable, so perhaps in his relationships time was of less importance than character. Nevertheless he had probably passed several apprentice years in the Onggirat camp – the date usually given for these events is 1175. In any case, all that Dai Sechen asked now was that Temujin should return swiftly to the tents of his bride and her people.

As they rode homeward, Munglik, the messenger, told Temujin the real reason why he had come: Yesugai had been invited to feast with a party of Tatars, courtesy had overcome reluctance and he had agreed to go; the Tatar *shamans* had exercised their skills and some potion, some powder, mixed with cheese curds or *koumiss*, had poisoned the Mongol chief. He lay dying and, racked by vomiting, trembling with pain and weakness, called for his son. They rode, one supposes, with the fierce rapidity of such horsemen in such an emergency, but all their speed was in vain. Yesugai was dead by the time Temujin reached his tents, and the boy, untried, unknown, found himself suddenly exposed to the harsh indifference of a world where only power brought security.

The camp broke up. It had held together for Bartan Bahadur and for his successor, Yesugai, but it would not hold while a boy gave the orders. The strongest chieftain was of the Taijiat tribe; his name was Targutai. When he drove off his people's wagons under his own leadership – and he would surely do so – many of the others would follow him. Temujin must have wondered how many; when the break came he saw – with what fury, what desolation of the heart one cannot guess – that it was nearly his whole camp. Security was hard to come by on those bleak steppes. There was no Great Khan now to hold the Mongols together, no unity of law or of

This picture of a Mongol archer leaping into the hunt comes from China, a country which knew Mongol ferocity well. It was the mounted archers, shooting on both the advance and the retreat, who were the core of Genghis Khan's armies.

concern. Each family tried to settle under the protection of some powerful lord. So, even if it was sometimes with reluctance, even if it was against the resistance of friendship and an ancient loyalty, most of the people set off behind Targutai's wagons. Temujin, whatever his feelings, must have understood the reasoning of those who were deserting him and his mother; in their place, he would have done the same. But the situation must have reinforced a lesson he had already learned – to survive, given his heritage and blood-line, he had to acquire the kind of strength that would tempt the strong into alliance and force the hostile into either acquiescence, neutrality or surrender.

He was the eldest son, the next in line to his father and the one whom his father had sent for on his death-bed, but it was his mother, Yulun, who was leader in fact of the remaining party. And it was a small party now – Temujin, his mother, his brother Kasar, two younger boys and a daughter; then Bektair and Belgutai, Temujin's half-brothers, whose mother had been another woman of Yesugai's; finally a handful of widows and old women with a clutch of infants between them, and a few loyal servants. They had been able to keep a small flock of sheep and goats, the animals owned by Yesugai when he died, their numbers few precisely because he had been the chieftain and so expected tribute from those who followed him. In short, they were bereft of friends, deserted and destitute, a handful of people – women and boys and old men – facing the tight-fisted indifference of Nature in this bleak land of mountain, forest and wide, wind-scorched plain.

The women, led by Yulun, bent to the task of food-gathering. In their baskets they brought back burnet, the roots of rushes and sedges, wild onions, juniper berries, hazel nuts, wild apples and bitter cherries, the fruits of the pine-tree, wild garlic and self-seeding millet. The boys hunted, now and then killing a vole or a steppe-mouse, or fished in the River Onon. In winter they were forced to kill some of their beasts, but food remained scarce. Bektair, older than Temujin and Kasar, sometimes grabbed for himself and his brother the few birds or animals that they were able to kill. Anger divided them when unity was their desperate need.

Kasar was becoming a notable archer, Temujin growing tall and strong. Intent on murder, they found Bektair on a small hill and came at him from two directions. Bektair, seeing their determination, sat, his arrogance turned to resignation. He asked them not to kill his brother, then folded his arms. Arrows thrummed briefly; then struck. Bektair was slung forward by their impact, dead as his head bowed. Yulun was angry, afraid perhaps that feud would follow, certainly knowing that they could not afford this bitter level of dissension. But there was no more trouble in their small camp; even Belgutai, it may be, accepted the justice of what had been done.

Targutai may have hoped that Temujin, left to the wilderness, would die. To kill him would lay the Taijiat open to the revenge of kinsmen; to allow him to starve, to expose him to the dangers of forest and steppe, brought with it no opprobrium. Everyone, after all, had to cope with such difficulties. But Temujin survived, and as such, vessel for the blood of Yesugai and Kabul Khan, was a possible focus for loyalty, an alternative loyalty to that – often grudgingly – offered Targutai. The latter knew that if Temujin could only show that he was worth following, there were many who would heed the demonstration and act on it. He resolved to capture Temujin, to hold him prisoner and so render him impotent. It would avoid a feud; if a little later Temujin died, people might have forgotten about him. It seems probable that it was reasoning of this sort that lay behind the Taijiat swoop on

Temujin's camp some time in the summer of 1182, by local reckoning the Year of the Tiger.

Warned by someone who remembered a previous loyalty, Temujin and the rest fled, but finally turned at bay with their backs to a cliff. That night Temujin rode cautiously out through the rough stockade they had made, then raced away down the darkness, swept forward on the yells of those who pursued him. The lumpy shadows of a copse, a thicket, opened for him, offered refuge, closed behind him. The Taijiat, reining in, waited for him to emerge. Time and hunger were their allies; later Temujin insisted that it was nine days before he attempted to evade their cordon. But he was weak, unsteady on his legs, both mind and muscle failed him; the Taijiat took him prisoner. Then they released his mother, Kasar and the rest, whom they had been holding in the meantime, and the little party – in who knows what bitterness? – set off up the valleys to where among the ridges and gorges of the mountains the headwaters of the Onon splashed and sang.

So Temujin had been placed in the *k'ang*, his arms spread, his head thrust forwards, a broken-winged bird tethered in the camp of those who feared and hated him. He had been forced to move from tent to tent, staying nowhere long in case his royal caste and powers of persuasion should tempt someone to help him. Even so, in the tent of Sorkhan Shira, a man who remembered Yesugai, he had found friends, especially Sorkhan's sons, Chimbai and Chila'un. They had even opened his wooden collar when he had stayed under their felt roof, enabling him to rest and sleep. But the weeks of captivity had been, one cannot doubt, a period of great anxiety; they would not have been, on the other hand, a period of doubt or brooding, for these were not in Temujin's character. It is certain that he had spent them waiting for the opportunity he must have convinced himself over and over again would arrive – the moment of laxity or confusion that would allow him to escape. And now, in this feast, at this point in the evening and at this place on the edge of light, he had decided that his opportunity had come.

He was on a tether, the other end held by a young man, one low in the camp's pecking order: who else would undertake the task of guarding a prisoner during a celebration? Temujin pulled away, jerked the cord from the other's hand, then flung himself forward and sideways as the other bent to retrieve it, his wooden collar transformed into a club. The blow smashed into the uncovered skull; the youth fell away and the dark night swung open like a door. Temujin ran, the river bank his guide. Before word spread in the camp that he had escaped, he had hidden himself in the stream, forcing himself into the darkness and moon-reflections of the water.

When the pursuit reached him, a long line of searchers stretching across the woodlands and the steppe, it was by chance Sorkhan Shira who walked the length of the bank, stared down at him and saw the faint, upside-down smudge of his face below the bank. He bent, spoke in a low voice, promised to say nothing. The search went by, its noise dwindled – then rose again as the line returned. But at last silence, the dark bank, the overhanging trees, and beyond them the empty miles, the valleys, the ridges and escarpments, the waiting mountains. Collared as he was, unweaponed and on foot, Temujin knew he had no hope of rejoining his mother. He climbed from the water, crept back into the camp; out on the steppe, watchful riders quartered the empty plain, but here no one expected him.

Again it was the sons of Sorkhan who persuaded their father to help him, untied his collar and burned it, hid him under the fleeces in the cart outside their tent. The family gave him food and drink and 'a straw-yellow mare with a white mouth' – they were all distinctive, all separately remembered, the clever horses of the Mongols. They gave him a bow and two arrows and saw him off, looking after him as he trotted carefully away from the camp; the watch for him had been lifted since it was clear that he had gone for good.

Temujin returned to the place where he had last seen his family. In the weeks that had passed their tracks had been obscured but not lost. For a skilful man, the marks of so many people's passing would take a long time to disappear. He followed them upwards, along the banks of the Onon and then westwards up the valley of the Kimurkha, until at its far end, snuggled under the burly weight of the hill Khorchukhui, he found his mother and his brothers, the tiny grouping of his people. He had survived hardship and capture, he had miraculously escaped Targutai, the strong chieftain, and as a result, unknown to him, his name had become the nucleus of a gathering legend.

Temujin led his little camp deeper into the mountains, to where the bulk of Burkhan Khaldun lifted its network of ravines towards the sky. Here, in what is now called the Yablonovyi Range, the rivers of this country, the Kerulen, the Tula and the Onon, begin their flow. Beyond the mountains to the west lies Lake Baikal. On its banks ranged the Barguts. To the east were the Tatar lands, and south of them the Onggirats, where Berta still awaited the return of her betrothed. To the south of Temujin's own people, the overall clan called Borjigin to which both he and Targutai belonged, the Kereits wandered to and fro across their grazing lands. West of them, between them and the Altai Mountains, could be found the tents of the Naimans and the Merkits. South of the Altai range, the great clan of the Uighurs grew fat on the eastern banks of Lake Balkhash. These and other clans and tribes lived as the Mongols did, grazing their herds, settling into crescent-shaped camps surrounded by protective wagons, then moving on when time, season and necessity demanded. Beyond them, south and east, were the great kingdoms: the vastness of China divided between the northern Kin and the southern Sung emperors. To the west of these lay Hsi-Hsia, established by the Tangut people in the eleventh century during their stand against the Sung dynasty that had ruled them until then. West again lay Kara-Khitai, founded by the survivors of the Liao, that passing imperial dynasty established, soon to founder, by the Khitan Mongol conquerors of China. Beyond them stretched the half-legendary uplands of Tibet, reaching to the knife-edged crags and blue-white snows of the Himalayas, the bulwark that imperfectly held at bay the southern world.

Of all these tribes and states Temujin must have had some knowledge; their names at least will have been known to him, and travellers, warriors and traders will have offered evidence for their existence. Of the Kin he must have known much, for his father-in-law, Dai Sechen, had reached agreements with them. The great emperors of China, after all, were the most potent force in this half of Asia and kept a wary eye on the Mongols to the north and west; they did not like to see concentrations of power there and, if any threatened, they would use bribery and skilful support, a little here, a little somewhere else, to bring about the turmoil that ensured their own comfort. For Temujin, the world was huge, hostile and designed to make him feel his insignificance. Yet he was free, he was known, he was born of a line of great chieftains. Perhaps these were after all days during which he brooded,

Ponies – tough, agile, often bad-tempered – provided that basis of all Mongol battle tactics: mobility. Genghis Khan's armies moved so swiftly that their opponents always vastly over-estimated their numbers. In peacetime, the horse was a Mongol's most precious possession. Babies learned to ride before they could walk; horse thieves were executed.

marking out the limits of his impoverished condition; or perhaps he stepped through his days, a hunter, intent only on the one day's game.

If so, a day came when his quarry turned out to be more dangerous, more complex, than vole or fish. Horse thieves rounded up the few beasts still left to the group and led them off; they must have thought that the camp, poor and thinly guarded, would be easy to pick clean. On the one remaining horse Temujin set out to pursue the thieves. Indomitable, he knew when the moment had come to end humility and turn to war – even if alone, with only courage and cunning to counterweight his solitude. In the event he was not to remain alone: four days out on the trail, he saw a young man whom he asked for information about the thieves who had preceded him. The young man had seen them; more, when he had heard this stranger's story, he gave him a fresh horse, mounted his own and, without farewells or explanations to anyone, rode on with Temujin. His name was Bogurchi, and his conduct tells one a great deal about the sort of man he was, and something about the kind of friendship and instant loyalty that Temujin could always inspire.

It was three days before they caught up with the horse thieves, creeping up to their camp, then galloping in, cutting the eight stolen horses out of the paddocked herd and moving them swiftly back, westward, towards Temujin's distant camp. There was pursuit, a line of riders stretching across the steppe, a cannonade of curses without doubt rising from them. The first of them came closer and closer to the two in flight; in his hand he balanced a stave with a noose of rope at its end – the Mongol lasso. A sudden flash of lifted hooves, Temujin's horse whirling, an arrow humming through the dusk, perhaps a cry; then flight once more. But not pursuit – the other riders were clustered about their wounded leader, all interest in the stolen horses gone.

So another tale was added to the complex of reputation that was slowly growing about Temujin's name. Thus it was with some pride that, Belgutai beside him, he at last rode back into the camp of Onggirats to claim his bride, the girl he had not seen now for four years. Dai Sechen was delighted to welcome him, and perhaps Berta too had reached an age when she would rather lie beside a husband than alone. There was a wedding feast, shortened by Temujin's haste to return to his own camp. The following day he set off, his bride with him, and to accompany her a small retinue. Temujin himself bore away Dai Sechen's gift to his mother – a tremendous and valuable cloak of sable, worth more perhaps than all the rest of his camp's possessions put together.

Temujin had a bride; he had his family about him, his tiny herd of horses, his small flock. It was a nucleus, but he needed to build on it, to create out of his intelligence and courage the kind of gravitational attraction that would draw to him the satellites he needed. He sent a message to Bogurchi – would his friend become his blood-brother, his *anda*? Bogurchi mounted and rode; in Temujin's camp on the banks of the Sanggur they swore their oath of brotherhood. Kasar, Belgutai, Bogurchi and Temujin – the camp's fighting force. The camp, nevertheless, had survived; if it were to continue to do so, it needed allies. Dai Sechen was tied to its people by the blood relationship of marriage; where would they find other friends?

Temujin moved his camp deeper into the fastnesses of mountain and stream, gave it into Bogurchi's charge, then with his brothers rode westwards to the land of the Kereits. Their leader was a man named Toghrul; years before, menaced by one of his many ambitious uncles, he had been forced to flee. Desperate, he had asked Yesugai, Temujin's father, for help. That politic Khan of the Mongols, seeing the chance to establish a friendly neighbour on his flank, became Toghrul's *anda* and, blood-brotherhood once sworn, took up its responsibilities and returned Toghrul to power. He had ruled ever since, his people accepting him more in resignation than with enthusiasm; time had, however, given him an aura of settled authority.

He was happy to welcome his old *anda*'s son, happier still when Temujin, calling him 'father', presented him with Dai Sechen's wedding gift, that sable cloak. It was, after all, as Temujin pointed out, a father's due to receive it. Toghrul was perhaps sufficiently dazzled by the value of the gift to believe Temujin to be a more powerful chieftain than rumour had suggested; in any case he made solemn promises of assistance: 'I will reunite your scattered people. . . . I will bring back to you your straying kinsmen.' Pleased with this, for the promises of kings were deposits in diplomacy's bank, to be called upon when needed, Temujin rode back to his camp. And there, soon after his arrival, he was offered the service of another friend – a young man of his own age, the son of a smith who had known his father years before; Jelmei thus became one of the camp's fighting men, another right arm to bear the early burdens of this people's struggles.

These struggles were now to be redoubled. When Temujin's father had captured his mother, it had been in defiance of law and convention: she had been on her way to the camp of her young husband, Chileidu, when Yesugai had stolen her away. Chileidu was the elder brother of Tokhotoa, and Tokhotoa was a chieftain of the Merkit. The stories beginning to be told about Temujin were now nearly his downfall, for it must have been through these that Tokhotoa heard of his whereabouts, of his weakness, of his precarious existence on the flanks of Burkhan Khaldun. He

called for aid from his kinsmen and rode to take vengeance for the wrong that had
been done to his family almost two decades before. Once more, then, Temujin was
in flight, this time with the Merkit warriors behind him. But the slopes and ravines,
the scree and scrubland of that high, broken country aided the fugitive. With the
men forced to scramble across the mountains for safety, the women and children
were as always vulnerable; when Temujin and the others finally came back to their
camp, it was to find it empty, their families taken, the tents burned, their few
belongings stolen or scattered. With Kasar and Belgutai beside him, Temujin rode
once more to the camp of Toghrul. It was time to draw on the account in which the
Kereit leader's promises had been deposited.

As it happened, history helped Temujin. When he was seven, Toghrul had been
the Merkits' prisoner and he held no happy memories of that time. So when
Temujin told him what had happened and how the Merkit had taken the women
and children, and ended with his appeal, 'We have come to you, Oh Khan, my
father, to ask you to rescue them, to bring them back to us', Toghrul needed little
persuasion. He agreed to march, and suggested that as an ally Temujin should
bring in the chieftain Jamukha. This man, as young as Temujin himself, was the
head of a clan, the Jadaran; he was also a sort of distant cousin of Temujin's, both of
them being descended from the great Khan Bodonchar, the founder of the whole
royal line. But, it was said, when Bodonchar took the woman from whom Jamukha
descended, she was already pregnant and it was not, therefore, the true blood of
that ancient chieftain that ran in his veins. Since many of the genealogies were
later written down by Temujin's friends, this may or may not be the truth. Certainly
as children Temujin and Jamukha had been very close, had indeed gone through
the ceremony of blood-brotherhood; now Jamukha was the head of his clan, chief
of a camp far more powerful than Temujin's, an ally of both Toghrul the Kereit
and of Targutai the Taijiat. Appealed to, he instantly agreed to help Temujin. 'We
will take this Tokhotoa by surprise, as if we came leaping through the roof-hole of
his tent. . . . We will overturn the shrines of his ancestors and destroy his people
until the place is an emptiness.' For most people, such sentiments were no more
than the rhetoric of warfare; Jamukha seems to have been among the few who
seriously meant what he said.

Toghrul rode out from his camp leading a force of two *toumans*. A *touman* was a
unit of men, at this time variable in number, but expected to act as one – it was, in
short, the Mongol regiment. During the great campaigns of Mongol expansion, a
*touman* was sometimes a fearsome ten thousand strong; at this time it would have
numbered a tenth of this, or even less. But one thing is certain – Toghrul's strength,
and Jamukha's, was far greater than Temujin's, with his five adherents. To match
them, he had to raise his first army. Now his reputation, which had earlier advertised his presence to the vengeful Merkit, became an advantage; given that he was
to ride in alliance with powerful chieftains, his standard was an attractive one to
follow. Men left their flocks, picked out their best horses and rode to the camp of
Temujin in quest of adventure, booty, animals and women.

Toghrul Khan was waiting for him when Temujin finally led his little force to
the meeting-place; together, the combined army, perhaps 1500 men, moved on to
where Jamukha awaited them, his impatience turning into a petulance not unusual
in him. But united the three moved forward, crossed the River Kilkho on impro-
vised rafts, their industry there observed by Tokhotoa's adherents. Warned, the

Merkit chieftain fled; when the Mongols struck his camp, it was to find only women and children under its felt roofs. There was pursuit, headlong, murderous, through the night. A covered wagon was seized, surrounded menacingly. Temujin, passing, called out forlornly the name of his wife. And timidly Berta clambered from the wagon into connubial safety. After this the Merkit were given a little respite. Tokhotoa rode on through the night, picking up in his flight one of the two chieftains who had assisted him, Dair Usun of the Uwas. They did not stop until they reached the lands about Lake Baikhal. The third chieftain, Khaghatai, stood and fought, only to go down to defeat and capture.

The Merkit women, the Merkit animals, the Merkit possessions were divided among the victors. Those who had taken a chance in following Temujin came home under the banner of a triumphant chief, each of them richer than when he had set out. They owed their new status to Temujin and it was with service that they would express their gratitude. While his power lasted they were his men without question. If he suffered defeat, they would reconsider their position, but as small men with their own security to look to, conditional loyalty was understood.

Temujin, for his part, discovered again his childhood friendship with Jamukha. Their blood-brotherhood was renewed in another ceremony; they were inseparable, exchanging gifts and 'sleeping under the same blanket', as the texts ambiguously inform us. Yet their very closeness posed problems for others on the plains – not those of jealousy, but those of allegiance. Here were two strong, young leaders, one with the larger following, the other with the right blood in his veins, both skilful and valiant in war. Small embassies came to the tents of each, there were quiet conversations, confidential meetings, a building-up of secrets. Winter passed, then spring and early summer. The Day of the Red Disc came round, Temujin's fateful anniversary of escape. The two young Khans were seen to speak, to separate, yet with no appearance of quarrel. It was the first day of their seasonal migration in search of summer pasture; the records say Jamukha, too near another tribe's camp and only half a day from the pastures he and Temujin had used all winter, wanted to settle where they were. It seems unlikely, and it has been suggested that one or other of them wanted now to be free, to loosen a little these marriage-like bonds of friendship. In any case the people of Jamukha stopped, while the column of wagons and horses and plaintive flocks that followed Temujin toiled on across the darkening steppe. The members of the nearby tribe, the Basut, panicked at this steady, yet almost certainly peaceful, advance, and fled to Jamukha's tents for shelter. Their abandoned camp was too tempting to be left untouched by the men of Temujin as they rode past it.

Temujin was alone now. He was once again the chieftain of a small collection of followers, not exactly a tribe, certainly not a family, yet united in their acceptance of his leadership. But he knew better than anyone how weak he really was, how tenuous in fact were the bonds between him and those he led. Boldly, he chose this moment to test the loyalty of greater men further afield: those who had sent messengers and embassies to him during the past months, who had murmured of their present dissatisfactions and their future hopes as the slow smoke lifted through the central chimney-hole of Temujin's tent, would now have to choose whether Temujin was really the leader they said they needed and were ready to accept. He sent riders out across the plains, the dark rays of his ambition stretching through the night.

A battle between Mongols and Chinese, as seen by a later Persian miniaturist.
The body armour, light and flexible, was reinforced by a coat of silk
below it. It is unlikely that the Mongols encountered battle elephants
so early in their campaign; when they did they defeated them with fire.

From the far corners of the Mongol pastures the riders came in pairs and in
parties, men of the Jalair and the Tarkhut, of the Mangqut and the Barulas, some
of them kinsmen of Temujin, like his cousin Onggur, others the relations of those
already at Temujin's side – Bogurchi's cousin Ogolai and Jelmei's two younger
brothers, one of them Subatei, soon to rise to great position. The Suldus sent men,
the Qongqotan, the Olkunut, the Ikireis and many others, petty chieftains arriving
with their own men spread in a galloping column behind them. The people of the
Baarin arrived with their wagons and their flocks, the greater prize because,
descended from that same consort of the legendary Bodonchar who had borne
Jamukha's ancestor, it was to him that they might with greater justification have

offered their allegiance. A chieftain of Jamukha's own clan, the Jadaran, arrived in pride and expectation; so did Temujin's uncle Daritei, one of the two brothers who had accompanied Yesugai in his capture of Yulun, Temujin's wise and adamantine mother, now revered by all.

This newly formed and heterogeneous group camped on the banks of the River Kimurkha; thus collected, they were like some unexpected planet arrived to unsettle with its gravitational pull the established order of a solar system. Soon they had attracted three most important satellites – the Jurkin, a people led by two grandsons of Kabul Khan; the camp of Khuchar Beki, a cousin of Temujin's whose allegiance was significant in that his father had been Yesugai Khan's elder brother;

Genghis Khan. He was tall, and remarkable for
the alertness of his eyes and the unusual
luxuriousness of his beard.

and the group led by Prince Altan, who belonged to an older generation, being the
son of Yesugai's predecessor, Kutula Khan. There was now, indeed, a plethora of
heroes and chieftains in the new clan, proud rivals all, men of ambition based on
blood, power and established wealth. None would serve under any of the others;
all might serve under Temujin, with his hereditary claim supported by present
success.

A council was called – among Mongols, leadership was decided by agreement.
From it, a deputation was sent to Temujin. The reports tell us that they now broke
into verse: 'We will make you Khan; you shall ride at our head, against our
enemies. We will fling ourselves like the lightning upon your foes. . . . If we disobey
you on the day of battle, take our flocks from us, our wives and children, throw our
worthless heads out on the steppe. . . .' If they did not actually use this rhetoric at

the time, it probably conveys what they said, and as usual a little more than they really meant.

Nevertheless, after Temujin had gone through the formalities of refusal, offering to each chieftain the honour that he knew the others would never permit him to accept, he graciously accepted the title of khan for himself. It must have seemed to him then that he had already travelled a long way in the period, less than ten years long, since he had been a desperate outcast, surviving on the berries his mother could gather and the small animals he and his brothers could shoot. He was in his early twenties now, surrounded by the white tents, the flocks, the horses, wagons and warriors of those who had sworn allegiance to him. It is not related whether he was surprised at this alteration in his circumstances, but when one considers his character, one rather doubts it. He was not the kind of person to be astonished at his own success; it would be his failures that would astound him – at least for the length of time it took him to learn their implicit lessons.

One last formality remained: it seemed necessary to his followers that he should be given some title that would demonstrate his new elevation. Since he did not rule all of them, he could not be called Khan of the Mongols. Finally they settled on the title by which he would be known; unfortunately, nearly nine centuries later there is a dispute over what that title may have meant. Some say he was now called 'Universal Ruler', others that his title came from a Turkic word meaning 'ocean' and so signified that he ruled the world, others more modestly that its derivation was a Chinese word meaning 'right' or 'correct' – the 'Rightful Khan'. Perhaps, others again have suggested, a new word was coined meaning 'invincible', so that he became the 'Invincible Prince'. It is not even certain whether it was here and now, or at Karakorum a few years later, that the title was bestowed. What is certain is that it was from the time when he was chosen as leader that Temujin used the name by which history has known him ever since: Genghis Khan.

Genghis Khan disliked the ostentation of power. He deliberately
retained his nomad customs all his life. Nevertheless, when
the situation called for it he too could seat himself on an ornate
throne under gold-embroidered canopies, thus striking awe and reverence
into his subjects, his client princes and ambassadors from abroad.

# 2 ACHIEVEMENT

Genghis Khan, like other chieftains, owned no land. That over which he had tentative suzerainty was bleak, hemmed in by the Yablonovyi Range to the west, the Khingan Mountains to the east and, to the south, by the Gobi Desert. The winters were hard, the cold shrivelling all life and comfort; only the Antarctic is colder than north-eastern Siberia, the plains and uplands of which lie to the north of the Mongol territories. Long seasons of snow and darkness stretched down from these near-polar fastnesses – and they were getting longer and harder. This was the thirteenth century, when the globe's ice-caps reached towards the temperate zones and once-fertile fields disappeared under glaciers or hardened into permafrost. In Greenland the changed conditions were destroying the last remnants of the Viking settlement; here, just south of latitude 60°N, which cuts through the tip of Greenland, the weather was bringing its own hardships.

In summer, however, the vast Eurasian landmass heats swiftly, now as then, and, where there are no rivers the soil dries and crumbles, all vegetation wilts. This was no land for agriculturalists to develop their skills. To the north, where rivers hiss through the valleys and ravines, forests of larch, birch, fir and aspen welcome the hunter, not the farmer. Between forest and desert lies the grass-ocean of the steppe, gleaming under snow in winter, flickering into a brightness of flowers in the spring, then slowly burning into the dun, khaki, yellow and pale-brown shades of late summer. Across the plains and woodlands, through the whiplash winds of the deserts, the travelling peoples of these lands made their constant way – Kereits, Merkits, Naimans from the Altai Mountains, Tatars from the Khingan range, and the many lesser tribes of the region. Among these stood the Mongols, grazing the valleys of the River Onon and the River Kerulen, unconsidered and unheard of.

From these unpromising lands previous invaders had spread terror both east and west as they sought to establish themselves in more amenable surroundings, or learned to exploit the hardness and the warrior skills their bleak environment had taught them. It was against a people centred here, the Hiung-nu or 'Northern Horse-barbarians' (the Chinese word for them indicative of their method and manner of warfare), that the Emperor Shih-huang-ti had ordered the protection of that complex and superhuman bulwark, the Great Wall. It was from here that some five centuries later what were perhaps the same people, the ferocious nomads we call the Huns, burst westward in a conquering drive that would pummel Europe into a new shape and a new era. It was the force they exerted that finally toppled Rome from its eight centuries of supremacy. It was from here, too, that the Turks (again perhaps descended from the Hiung-nu) had set out on the long,

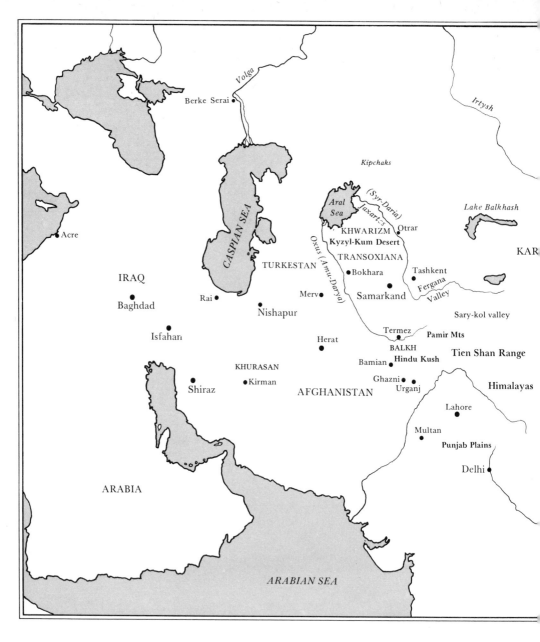

intermittent battering they were to give the world, those thousand years of repetitive warfare, from the sixth century to the sixteenth, that would see as its climax the fall of Rome's eastern capital, Byzantium.

The Mongols, however, were no more than distant cousins to success. They led lives which, though itinerant, were on the whole settled, unsurprising. They had seen others set off during the past ten centuries, moving westward along the grasslands, to disappear into fitful legend and forgetfulness over those inscrutable horizons that set such wide limits to their world. They themselves had continued perhaps for two thousand years the annual round of their lives, wintering in the north for water or in the south for warmth, moving in the spring to their accustomed summer pastures, the uplands grass where the heat was less fierce, or to the lusher meadows flanking some inextinguishable stream. These pastures were known,

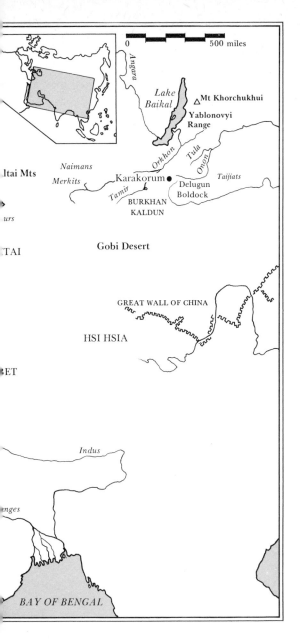

Coin struck by the Khaghan's mint in mid-thirteenth century. Peace and the rule of law in the lands governed by the Mongols produced a great upsurge in trade.

*Asia, including the Mongol Heartlands*

marked out by long usage, returned to year after year. When they travelled, they took down the smaller tents, mounted the larger complete on ox-carts; sometimes these were vast wagons twenty feet wide, with wheels taller than a man, drawn by two lines of eleven beasts each, the twenty-two straining at the traces, the vast cupola of the tent, its top half onion-shaped, riding behind them like some tethered balloon. When the tents were set down, they were quickly made serviceable, divided into two, with one section for the women and the skills of the kitchen, the other for visitors and friendship, the central fire sending a soft smoke up through the vent in the roof above.

In all this the Mongols were little different from the tribes who shared these territories. They had learned to survive, that imperative overriding all generosity, all squeamishness. They would eat mice, dead animals found beside the trail, even their own dogs or cats when times were hard enough – and times often were. If a man found himself alone and desperate, the snow a desert, its flurries like curtains hiding him from safety, he would open one of his horse's veins and drink the blood – but would make sure he sealed the wound when he had finished, for his horse was his key to the recesses of the steppe, the single factor that stood between him and an impoverished immobility. It was no more than pony-sized, this horse of his, but deep-chested, heavily boned and muscled; frequently evil-tempered, it was of an endless courage, able to subsist summer and winter on what it wrenched from the often inhospitable earth. It offered him the freedom of his world. As a result, Mongol and horse became a single, centaur-like entity. Babies rode before they could stand; when they grew up, sitting in the saddle was probably more natural to them than walking. While riding Mongols ate, slept, drank, argued and fought. As a result, horses became a symbol of prestige, marking out perhaps even more than women did the rich and the powerful; conversely, stealing them was among the most heinous crimes a Mongol could commit.

The people lived largely on what they owned, grew, hunted or found. From their cattle, sheep and goats they had the wool, furs and hides that clothed and armoured them. From the milk of mares and cows they made their curds, their cheese and their pale, harsh *koumiss*. The cereals they collected or occasionally grew were made into gruel or pounded into flour. When they killed or hunted, they ate well; what they did not need at once, they dried or smoked. They manufactured little or nothing, however: weapons, jewelry and fabrics percolated to them from markets in Samarkand and Bokhara, or trickled north-westwards from the established civilization behind the Great Wall of China. They were dirty, uncouth, loud-mouthed and foul-smelling. They were quarrelsome, and the lands they moved through were littered with the remains and the memories of a thousand pointless battles, a hundred thousand pernickety disputes. The rise of one brought the jealousy of another; the lush grazing of a rich clan brought down on it the retribution of the struggling; the decimation of a flock by winter would be followed in the spring by the decimation of those whose flocks had survived.

It was a hard world, watched over by a vast gallery of gods, minor deities and spirits, all descended from or answerable to the great Tengris. Bai Ülgän ruled the sky and air, Erlik Khan the underworld. The *shaman* was the intermediary between man and the gods, his vocation either hereditary, or sudden and particular to him. Ecstatic dream trained him, and his elders passed on to him their technical knowledge – the names of the spirits and what they did, the mythology and the genealogical descent of the clan and its leaders, the special language that kept shamanistic knowledge secret from the world. He would often have a particular relationship with one god and, at times of festival, he would speak in that god's name and with that god's voice.

These were the realities of the life led by those who now looked to Genghis Khan for protection and unifying energy: horses, movement, the extravagant cruelties of Nature, flocks, hunting, warfare and a supervisory spirit-world placated by the ambassadorial skills of the *shaman*, all bound by conventions of honour that were tough and unrelenting, and alleviated by passion, poetry and the occasional explosive self-indulgence of a feast. Into this age-old complex the Khan mixed a new ingredient – discipline. The Mongols had always been splendid warriors, but so had all their neighbours. Hardened by the stringency of their lives and rendered skilful by the demands of the hunt, all the steppe tribes could put into the field a horde of wild horsemen whose ferocity made them almost impossible to withstand. It was Genghis Khan who saw that it was not this that made an army. He was still a comparatively weak chieftain and if he wanted security, he would have to make the best possible use of his manpower.

It is very probable that Genghis Khan had already organized his earlier forces in a new and effective way, but he had hardly had enough time to develop his ideas of military structure to the full. Now, however, he set to work in earnest. He divided his men into *gurans*, or units of a thousand. These were then metrically subdivided into ten companies, each of ten platoons. Later, when his army grew, he would form ten *gurans* into that division of ten thousand men called a *touman*. These became the basic groupings that, in various combinations, made up his armies. He divided his horsemen into heavy and light cavalry, the former relying largely on their lances, the latter, who were perhaps twice as numerous, on their mobility and their skill with the bow. These last carried a bundle of javelins, the Mongolian lasso and a sword or axe, with a shield and helmet for protection; the heavy cavalry, however, wore complete body armour, of leather reinforced with metal, and carried a heavier sword or axe. Sometimes they, too, used their skill as archers – the Mongols were always fearsome with the bow, even when shooting from horseback. (Later Genghis Khan insisted on the further protection of a raw-silk undercoat for his soldiers. An arrow, when it struck, would carry the unpierced silk into the flesh; a wounded man's comrades could take the arrow out by pulling gently at the coat. Mongols as a point of honour did not abandon their wounded.)

At the same time as imposing discipline on his men, Genghis Khan selected those whose vision and commands would transform the aridities of training into the pounce and swoop of battle, the exuberant manoeuvres that would become the signatures of victory. He appointed these men as *orloks* or generals, picking for great office those who had stood with him through disaster and despair – Bogurchi, Jelmei and his brother Subatei; later there would be Jebei and Mukhali, as well as Sorkhan Shira and his sons, who had helped him three vital times during his escape from Targutai's camp; Kasar, too, the famous archer, the brother who had suffered and fought with him from the beginning, now became one of his great lieutenants. To keep himself informed of what the far-flung units of his army, the far-flung tribes of his people, were doing, and to pass to them his own wishes, Genghis Khan finally organized his communications system. This was based on the 'arrow riders' – men who bandaged their bodies against the harsh blows and aching fatigue of hours of hard riding before setting off across the steppe, changing horses as weariness caused mount after mount to slow and falter, eating and sleeping as they rode and covering huge distances in a matter of hours, their endurance a byword, their speed unparalleled in the unmechanized, pre-electronic world.

While establishing his military strength, Genghis did not neglect diplomacy. He sent messengers to Toghrul and to Jamukha; the first welcomed his new status, the second accepted it without recognizing even for a moment that it placed his erstwhile *anda* above him. But grazing rights, as so often, made overt the latent rivalries of the steppe. Jamukha's brother Taichar drove off horses that he said were grazing on his lands; their owner, a follower of Genghis Khan, rode to recover them, Mongol-style, flat on his back along his racing horse's spine, his arrows flying as though from a whole company of archers, circling the darkness beyond Taichar's

Approaching Pekin from the west, travellers passed through
the Great Wall by the Chü-yang Gate. Mongol ambition, however,
carved out a broader and bloodier route.

camp-fire, then riding off to collect the stolen horses. He left behind him the dead
body of Jamukha's brother, an arrow in his back.

Righteous fury fuelled Jamukha's campaign. He called kinsmen to his aid and,
with this gathered army, fell upon Genghis Khan. The latter, though warned, was
hardly ready, nor was his army past the first stages of training. Jamukha drove
him back, up the ravine-split sides of the valley of the Onon. But the new army
held, its morale remained high, and Jamukha turned from the dreadful task of
pursuing it through mountains, sacking instead the camp of a neutral tribe (precisely because it had kept its neutrality) and boiling alive seventy of its leaders.
Such behaviour was not calculated to keep his allies happy – there are levels of
ferocity that frighten friend and foe alike. Two clans defected from his forces to
those of Genghis Khan, helping to lift still further the confidence of those only half-
defeated men.

It was therefore as an intact force that Genghis Khan's variegated followers
went into the years of peace that now settled over these plains and valleys. The first
event of note, proclaiming, albeit implicitly, the new status of Genghis Khan, was
the arrival, unexpectedly from the south-west, on emaciated camels, half-crazed
from lack of water, starving and destitute, of Toghrul, his father's old friend, the

chief of the Kereits. Chief no longer, however – one of his brothers, recalcitrant in his ambitions since that day so many years before when Yesugai had restored his *anda* to his place, had once more swooped in usurping fury and driven Toghrul out. At the head of a Naiman army, raised during his own exile, this man, Black Erke, now proclaimed himself Khan of the Kereits; desperate, Toghrul, despite his years, had fled beyond the Altai Mountains, then swung south and east, through the lands of the Uighurs and the Tangut, to arrive at last among the tents of the Mongols. Genghis Khan treated him with the utmost respect, then gathered his own army and gently rode with him towards the pastures of the Kereit; Erke fled without battle and Toghrul was restored – an old debt had been repaid, an old alliance made apparently more secure than before.

To the east, meanwhile, other trouble was brewing in which Genghis Khan was eager to involve himself. In 1198 the Kin emperor needed allies in his effort to subdue Megujin, a powerful Tatar chieftain. The messengers he sent to Toghrul, who was well known to him, also called at the camp of Genghis Khan. For the Mongol leader they represented an opportunity to overwhelm his father's killers. Together with Toghrul's forces, he rode down the valley of the Ulja, on the banks of which Megujin's Tatars had dug themselves in. Where the valley broadened, the Chinese commander, Wanyen Siang, had his troops deployed. Megujin, as Genghis had forecast, was caught 'in a pair of pincers'. Crushed, his men driven to the water's edge, he died. Toghrul was given the title '*Wang*', which means 'Prince', by the grateful Chinese; the Mongols from then onwards always called him 'Ong Khan', their version of the word. Genghis, for his part, was also graciously given a title – *Chao-churi* or 'Deputy Commissioner for Peace in the Border Marches'. But this was not to be his greatest prize, for it was while looting the Tatar camp that he found and took for his mother – a habit of his with promising orphans – a small boy wearing a nose-ring whom Yulun named Shigikutuku. When he grew up, he would be that rarity in a land of itinerant warriors, a man of calm and genuine wisdom, a far-sighted man, under the Khan the people's law-giver.

It was always Genghis Khan's gift to see and reward merit, even when it lay hidden behind the sullenness of a prisoner. Soon after the Tatar campaign, he fought and bitterly defeated his neighbours, the Jurkin, who had not only refused to help him in battle but had made trouble for his camp during his absence. Sacha Beki and Taichu, the brothers who led them, were captured and made to answer in fact for the oath they had sworn at his election – they were beheaded, and their black heads were flung out on the steppe. But though they were sons of enemy clansmen, he now took into his own service the youth Mukhali and his brother; at the same time, he accepted as his aide another young man of the Jurkin, Borokhul.

The days of vast conquest, however, still lay in the unimaginable future. It was a present threat that concerned the Mongols of Genghis Khan's camp – Jamukha had been elected Khan of the Mongols by a *kuriltai*, a meeting of chieftains, held on the banks of the River Arguna. After spiteful deliberation he was given the title Gur Khan, 'Sole Ruler', a challenge in itself since he was still a vassal of the ageing Toghrul, the Ong Khan. Using this as a diplomatic weapon, Genghis Khan rode out together with the Kereits to put down Jamukha's threat. The armies met among the woods and valleys of Koyitan: at once rain swamped the ground and melted valour; perhaps the *shamans* had overdone their invocations. The armies separated, but morale in Jamukha's following, which had expected easy victory and which was

in any case much more heterogeneous, much less committed, than the Mongols and
Kereits opposite, seeped away with the flow of the rainwater. Chiefs packed their
tents and led their people back to distant homelands. Jamukha turned against his
erstwhile supporters; his army diminished even as Genghis Khan watched. It
was a sort of victory, though no arrows had sung across that air.

Pursuit began; but Ong Khan, old and happy to see his younger neighbours at
one another's throats, soon returned to his own camp. Out of expediency, or
perhaps for ancient reasons of his own, it was Jamukha's allies, the Taijiat, whom
Genghis Khan decided to follow, driving them down towards the River Onon, on
the far bank of which they turned and stood. Battle lasted the length of the day,
and ended indecisively, though with Genghis Khan established in a bridgehead
on the Taijiat side of the water – and with a deep wound in his neck. All night his
attendant Jelmei sucked the wound, for among Mongols premature clotting was
believed to be harmful. (In effect such treatment meant that the wound was constantly cleansed, preventing the sepsis that was in those days probably the greatest
danger.) In the morning, though weak, the Khan stood armed and ready, his men
beside him, the hard day ahead – to find that in the night he had been made the gift
of victory. Deciding that with the enemy on their side of the river there remained
little hope of success, the Taijiat had crept quietly away. Once again, the swift
pursuit hallooed about the slopes and valleys; men fell or were captured. Women
were dragged, screaming or stoical, to their new tents. It was during this fast-
moving chase and capture that Sorkhan Shira and his sons were brought to Genghis
Khan and pardoned for their necessary service to Targutai. So the last of what
would be the 'Four Coursers' joined his leader – Chila'un, the old man's eldest son,
who had befriended the imprisoned Temujin so many years before.

Genghis Khan now had, complete and terrible, though not yet at their fullest
power, the four great commanders who undertook for him all the most difficult
tasks, the men he sent when the odds against success were vast and almost overwhelming, whom he always expected to win and who would so rarely disappoint
him. His *anda*, Bogurchi, Chila'un, the son of Sorkhan Shira, Mukhali the Jalair,
and Borokhul – Genghis Khan's Four Coursers.

Another man now taken into the Khan's service and later to rise to leadership
was an archer who had earlier and from a great distance shot Genghis Khan's
horse from under him. When Genghis Khan asked who had so nearly killed him
this young man stepped unhesitatingly forward. Renamed Jebei (which means
'Arrow'), he became one of the Mongols' most successful *orloks*, sign of Genghis
Khan's magnanimity and prescience. And he chose another Taijiat, Naya'a, as an
officer, for the curious achievement of letting the chieftain, Targutai, go free. But
the code was clear and Genghis Khan always abided by it – a man did not betray
his chief. He could change his allegiance openly; he could not turn and use his
privileges against the man who had granted them. Whenever the followers of the
Khan's enemies tried to curry favour with him by bringing him the body, dead or
alive, of one they had sworn to serve, he would immediately order their execution.
Such treachery damaged the very structure of Mongol society, based as that was on
hard leadership willingly accepted.

OPPOSITE A *kuriltai* or council: to debate great issues, and most
importantly to decide the succession of the Khaghanate,
the Mongol leadership would meet in assemblies like this.

A Persian impression of Genghis Khan in battle against the Tatars,
the warrior people responsible for the death of his father.

Genghis Khan now set out on another campaign against the Tatars, determined
this time to destroy them. He won his battles, herded together great flocks of
prisoners, but during this war lost two of his followers – not through wounds, but
by defection. Three great leaders, Altan, Daritai and Khuchar, leaving off the
chase after the fleeing Tatars, rounded up instead their enemies' untended flocks.
Angry at having his orders disobeyed, Genghis had these hapless sheep and goats
taken from them; Daritai, perhaps understanding the need for discipline, submitted to this, but the other two led their people into a sulky independence. The
many prisoners, meanwhile, were summarily disposed of – measured against the

hub of a wagon wheel, those taller were beheaded, those shorter were taken into Mongol service, being young enough to learn a new allegiance.

Again warfare beckoned, and still in this same Year of the Dog. Ong Khan had been fighting and defeating the Merkit while Genghis Khan had dealt with the Tatars. Now the two chieftains united against the powerful Naimans, a people divided between two Khans, the brothers Bai Bukha and Buyiruk. The latter, chief of the southern Naiman, seeing Mongol and Kereit out against him, fled to the far slopes of the Altai Mountains. Implacably Genghis and Ong Khan followed, finally brought him to bay beside Lake Kishil-Bashi and defeated his army, though unable to capture him. On their homeward march the two allies, ostensibly jubilant at their victory, found themselves one dusk faced by a force of the northern Naiman. Morning would see combat renewed; they settled for the night, their watch-fires leaping across the darkness, the splintered flames marking their battle lines. But at dawn, as the fires paled and died, Genghis Khan could see that behind those lit by Ong Khan's men no one now stood in readiness. Under their cover, the old man, his acclaimed father-surrogate, had quietly left the field. He had become a devious, paranoid ruler, so obsessed with the possibility of others' treachery that he no longer hesitated to betray anyone. Jamukha had suggested that Genghis Khan was negotiating with the Naiman – perhaps it was true. In any case his men were restless, having had no profit from their long pursuit of Buyiruk. In the night he had led them homeward.

Alone, Genghis Khan embraced prudence. He pulled back his disciplined forces, brought them in a body to and through the mountains. The Naiman, with a choice of enemies to follow, decided against attempting battle with the well-trained Mongols. It was Ong Khan's forces, particularly the camps of his son, Sanggum, who felt the weight of Naiman fury. Ong Khan, beset, reconsidered the past, then resurrected it: he called on Genghis Khan for help. The Mongol, his sworn allegiance a matter of personal honour, responded by sending his Four Coursers on their first mission. Sanggum was rescued, the Kereit saved; Ong Khan, in his delight and gratitude, now renewed what he had already shown he valued little – his oath of father–son relationship with Genghis.

Seeking to make this alliance even firmer, Genghis Khan, now in his mid-thirties and with sons of his own, thought that his eldest, Jochi, might usefully take as his betrothed one of Sanggum's young sisters, while in reverse a Mongol princess was offered to Sanggum's son Tusakha. But Sanggum, jealous perhaps of this son-by-vow, this over-successful 'brother' by whose forces he had had to go through the humiliation of rescue, loftily refused his permission. 'When one of our women goes to them,' the Mongols' *Secret History* quotes him as saying, 'she stands in the corner by the door, gazing constantly at the place of honour on the far side. When one of their women comes to us, she sits in the place of honour looking towards the corner by the door' – as a result of which reply, the *History* tells us, 'the love in Genghis Khan's heart for Ong Khan and . . . Sanggum diminished a little.'

This setback, however, slight as it seems, was enough to have widespread repercussions as news and gossip leap-frogged over those unquiet plains. Jamukha was meeting, far to the west, such disaffected ex-vassals of Genghis Khan as the over-proud Altan and Khuchar, as well as a number of the Mongol's enemies. Most importantly, however, he welcomed among the new conspirators the uneasy Sanggum. It was through his determination, his forcing the old man to choose between son and 'son', that Ong Khan himself was brought into this alliance. And it was Sanggum who, preferring the economies of treachery to the waste of war, baited a trap for Genghis Khan by now apparently acceding to the Mongol leader's marriage plans.

Happy, even if a little surprised at this change of mind, Genghis Khan set off for the Kereit betrothal feast, not suspecting that death was to be its principal guest. On the way, however, he stopped at the tents of that Munglik who years before had led him to his father's death-bed; when he heard the story, the old man, survivor of a dozen devious campaigns and plots, was properly suspicious. Persuaded,

Genghis Khan turned for home. With assassination thus averted, the conspirators had nothing to lose by open pursuit. They decided to set off at first light, in order to cut off Genghis Khan before he could reach his camp. But now the devious were to be out-manoeuvred – two horse-herds, aware of what was planned, rode through the night, to warn Genghis Khan and make their own fortunes (each would in time command one of Genghis Khan's *gurans*).

The Khan fled, then rallied. South of Burkhan Khaldhun, somewhere in the wide crook of the River Kerulen, he collected his forces – men of the Uru'ut, of the Mangqut, fine fighters, steadfast in his service since that first day when his column had toiled past the halted wagons of Jamukha. Now, in this place, its location lost to us, although its name, Khalakhaljit, is still remembered, they grouped themselves about the Khan and, strong in the discipline they had learned, awaited the far larger army of Sanggum and Jamukha.

The Jurkin in the van, that army surged across a spur of mountain, down a slope. Arrows bridged distance, then more heavily the javelins; swords and axes rose, caught the light, swung downwards, out of sight; then rose once more, their metal dulled. Khuyildar, the Mangqut chieftain, whirled his mount in combat, lifted his shield too late, fell wounded; about him his men stood in linked defiance, beat back the Jurkin, finally carried their wounded leader to safety. The Uru'ut advanced, their formation solid, a wedge driven into the failing cohesion of their enemies. Sanggum, attempting to redress the balance of the battle, rode forward in fury; an arrow took him in the cheek and it was the Kereit tribesmen who now strove in rescue.

At nightfall Genghis Khan withdrew, but in orderly fashion, as always. To have survived was victory enough. Next day he awaited pursuit, but Ong Khan, his son wounded, had lost his eagerness to fight. Nevertheless Genghis Khan's situation remained precarious; he sent out messengers to ask for help, but one by one they returned with news of evasions, refusals and hesitations. Jamukha and Ong Khan on one side, Genghis on the other – the men of the steppes, traditionally and necessarily on the side of the big battalions, had lost their confidence in the Mongol leader. Less than three thousand people remained in Genghis Khan's camp.

On the banks of Lake Baljuna, Genghis Khan pastured his horses, tended his wounded, nursed his pride and considered his future. The Onggirat had joined him, but overtures he had made to his new enemies had been rejected. He needed an opportunity to alter defeat into attack – and one day, in the bedraggled, dust-covered figure of his brother Kasar, opportunity arrived. Kasar had evaded Ong Khan, but it was only after a tortuous search, a journey that had long outrun his supplies, that he had stumbled across his brother's track. Without hesitation, Genghis Khan saw the possibilities in this situation. He sent two of the men back to Ong Khan, their message that Kasar, disillusioned, unable to find his brother, was now anxious to join his camp. Ong Khan, happily feasting his own success in a golden tent, sent his favourite Iturgen as a guarantee of welcome and safe-conduct to the place on the River Kerulen that Kasar had suggested as a meeting-place. For Iturgen this was a death sentence; Kasar himself struck off his head. At the same time it gave Genghis Khan the information he needed about Ong Khan's whereabouts, and about the confident disposition of that devious chieftain and his men.

The Mongols came out of the hills and grasslands like an encircling fire. Before

Archers like this could keep up a constant and accurate flow of arrows while
riding at full tilt across country. The age-old skills of the Central Asian
horsemen are said to have originated the legend of the centaurs.

them shimmered the light and shade, the streams and abrupt outcrops of the Gorge
of Jer. Among those cliffs waited the wide crescent of Ong Khan's camp. This was
the moment and the place that would decide Genghis Khan's power: if he lost now,
all his support would vanish. If he won, he would have broken for ever the bonds of
his allegiance. Three days and nights of ferocity later he had his answer: Ong Khan
and his son had scuttled through the Mongol cordon, but the Kereit had been
smashed. The Khan 'shared them out on all sides to be stripped of their possessions
and to be enslaved. . . . After he had dissolved the people of the Kereit in this way,
he passed the winter in the mountains.'

Ong Khan was killed on the edge of the Naiman territories; his son, betrayed by his remaining follower (whom Genghis Khan beheaded for this treachery), turned to banditry and died in that trade, still young, but useless, bereft of hope and honour. The Mongol clans and tribes, seeing so clearly the wind of history, submitted one by one to their obvious leader. Only the northern Naiman, perhaps uncertain of this new power to the east of them, decided that it should be put down. Warned by the Onggut, Genghis Khan set off to face this latest threat.

It was during this campaign that he founded what would become one of the most feared military units in history, his own personal guard, almost as close to him as his own brothers, the walls that secured him, the constant foundations of his safety and strength. There were seventy appointed for duty by day and eighty by night – at least at this first founding of the unit; later, it would number a thousand men, this *guran* being commanded by his 'Arrow', Jebei. Around him he retained for the security of his headquarters a hand-picked *touman*, ten thousand sons of chieftains, the sign and the reward of the countless separate acts of allegiance that made up his network of power.

The chief of the Naiman, Tayang Khan, as the Chinese called him, or Bai Bukha, after a morale-sapping hesitation, marched along the River Tamir to its confluence with the Orkhon, crossed that, then swung carefully eastward of Mount Nakhu. Genghis Khan, warned of his arrival, set up his field commanders – Kasar leading the main force – and issued his orders in the military code he had perfected: order-of-march would be 'thick grass', battle order would be 'the lake', battle method would be 'the gimlet' – the phrases seem more reminiscent of the *I-Ching* than Clausewitz.

Less intelligently, Tayang Khan arranged his forces across the foothill slopes of the mountain, the Mongols below him. Had he attacked in this battle of Chakir-ma'ut, the position would have favoured him; had he dug in, he might have defended it, since he had the superior numbers. Instead, half-hearted to the last, he let his army be pushed backwards, and backwards again, skirmishers recoiling on their own lines under the weight of Mongol assault, the heavy cavalry of Genghis Khan cutting their disciplined way into the resulting confusion, Kasar, the Four Coursers of the Khan, his young brother Otchigin all heroes in the attack, their weapons again and again hammering in the lesson of Naiman presumption. Near the very top of the mountain Tayang Khan at last stood and fought. As so often in his life, the effort came too late – by the time he had mustered just a little resolution, the moment for it had long passed. Wounded, he was taken and soon after died. His son Guchuluk fled, to find a refuge at last with the khan of the Kara-Khitai – whom he would reward with treachery and usurpation. Another to flee was Jamukha, the ubiquitous rival, who had once again leaped at an opportunity to aid in the destruction of his blood-brother – and once again had seen that opportunity snatched away.

The Merkit remained, the sole true rivals to Mongol power, a power that had shown its strength in the battle of Chakirma'ut against even so established a people as the Naiman. So Genghis Khan rode north, and in a disciplined action on the steppes of Saari he destroyed them. The Merkit chieftain, Tokhotoa, fled with his sons; implacably, Genghis Khan followed, to the foothills of the Altai and the forbidding edge of winter. In the spring of the following year, 1205, he finally caught up with them; on the far side of the mountains, the remnants of the Merkit had joined with those of the Naiman in a last attempt to halt this new force, which had grown up almost without anyone's noticing. Predictably their stand was smashed, and Guchuluk, who had interrupted his westward journey for this gesture, could do nothing now but continue it. Tokhotoa died, but his sons fled on, bearing his severed head. Subatei, vast in girth, yet to grow even vaster in reputation, took up the pursuit as Genghis Khan himself turned back. It would be another year before Subatei returned, having killed the Merkit princes on the River Chui, far to the north.

There remained a last rival, the only name still to stand against the legend Genghis Khan had become on the steppe. Jamukha, in flight, represented a continuing danger – Genghis Khan himself had come out of the wilderness and destitution to his newly achieved estate. But Jamukha's followers had never been as steadfast as had Temujin's in the old days, nor could Jamukha ever inspire the same loyalty. His five remaining attendants fell on him one evening, bound him and brought him to Genghis Khan. If they expected reward, they underestimated their new patron's rectitude. He had them beheaded, one after the other, while the bound Jamukha watched in sombre satisfaction. And then Genghis Khan displayed once again his occasional astounding magnanimity – he offered Jamukha a renewal of their old friendship. But Jamukha, with a stern nobility of his own, rejected it. They were no longer equals: 'When the whole world attends you, what kind of prize would I be as companion? . . . I would be like a louse in your neck-band, a gnat in your leg-wrappings. . . .' He compared his past and his present with that of Genghis Khan – he had had neither the advantages nor the success of his friend and rival. 'Therefore I am inferior to my *anda*, who has been so favoured by Heaven.' But he had a final request – to be put to death without his blood being shed, for in Mongol belief the soul resided in the blood. With some sorrow, and yet one suspects not without a measure of relief, Genghis Khan agreed. Jamukha was wrapped in a great carpet and, thus protected, was crushed to death. He was buried in a high place, an honour reserved for the great and heroic. With his passing the last obstacle was removed from Genghis Khan's path.

In the next year, 1206, the Year of the Tiger, all the clans and tribes of the steppes, the endless families and loose, confederated camps, made their laborious way, in a flurry of flocks and a frisking of horses, to the watershed of Delugun Boldock, where the River Onon has its beginnings. The felt tents gathered, they stood in vast circles, they became a town, a city, a suburb-fringed megalopolis. It was the *kuriltai* of the People of the Felt Tents – all the people, the steppe-dwellers, the nomads of that vast region, come to offer the only allegiance that now promised them security. They had come to see Genghis Khan elected the Khaghan, King of Kings, Khan of Khans, Ruler of the Steppes. A new force had arisen, based on an unprecedented unity and centred on a single blazing, yet eminently practical, intelligence. It was an event that should have made the world nervous; far away, in the imperial palace of the Kin, it is true that a note was made in the annals, a line or two to show that the Empire was not asleep. Yet asleep or not, it dreamed, and if the world felt alarm, it was no more than a twinge, a passing spasm. Then its attention wavered; later, it might have cause to regret its unconcern.

# 3 TRIUMPH

**W**ho was he, this Khan, sitting on the threshold of history in his great white tent, its wooden pillars bright with gold, his nine-tailed standard flicking in the cool upland winds? He was tall, it is said, with a noble beard and eyes that were described as like a cat's. He was, clearly, a man of resource and resolution. He was not afraid of hardship himself, nor of inflicting it on others. He was cruel, when diplomacy demanded it, magnanimous when he could see the profit in it. He had smashed the Kereits, because their treachery had to be punished in a manner all would remember; he had pardoned the defeated Naimans, had handed back their weapons, married the widow of their chieftain, accepted one of their princesses as wife for his son Tuli, in this way settling his western frontiers with friends. He was a man who could not read or write, but when his men captured the Uighur scribe, Tatatungo, Tayang Khan's chief minister, he learned from him the significance of a royal seal and the value of writing; Tatatungo became his own Keeper of the Seal, the teacher of his children and the children of the *orloks*, and the channel through which the Uighur script became that of the Mongols. He was a man who despised the urban culture of his Chinese neighbours and the mercantile culture of the Islamic lands far to the west; at the same time, he was often to use those who had their roots in these civilizations as his own advisers, and he would show a religious tolerance that makes the Christian Europe of his day seem barbarous by comparison. Yet he was ruthless: the destruction of cities, of territories, of whole peoples, seems never to have caused him a moment's concern. His loyalty to those who served him, and those who entered into friendship or alliance with him, was absolute; his vengeance on those who broke their obligations terrible.

Unlettered, untutored, come from poverty and blighted hope by way of force and fantasy, his empire resting on the inspired giving of one sable coat, he had nevertheless a world-encompassing vision. From a long line of swift, improvisatory tacticians had sprung this one colossal strategist. And yet the question remains – was he ambitious for conquest, at this moment, with the many peoples of the grass-lands gathered about his tent in unified commitment? Were his conquests piece-meal, each based on its own logic, yet each one setting the next inevitably in motion? For the moment, perhaps, as Gokchu, the 'Trusted of Heaven', Gokchu the *shaman*, proclaimed him Khan of all the peoples, and as the princes of those peoples carried him on a sheet of black felt towards his throne, he was content. He was the 'God-sent', uniter of nearly half a million people, lord of another million and a half, overlord of the steppe from the Altai to the Khingan, utterly dominant, his status marked by the gifts of the great chieftains piled before him – brightness of gold,

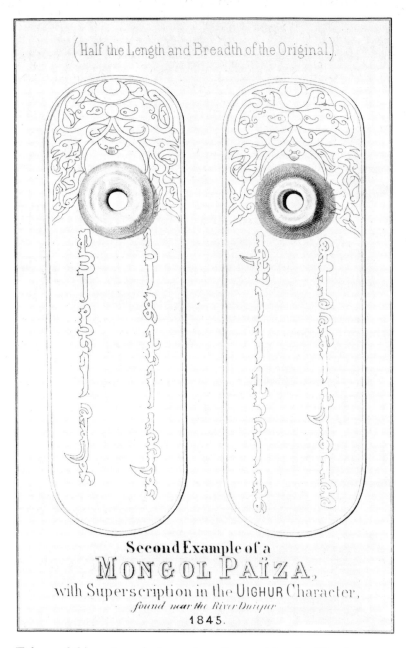

Second Example of a
MONGOL PAÏZA,
with Superscription in the UIGHUR Character,
*found near the River Dnieper*
1845.

Tokens of this sort marked out those favoured by the Khaghan.
The script is Uighur, adopted by the illiterate Genghis Khan
to make possible a Mongol administration.

dark radiance of furs, glitter of silks, brilliance of brocades. The hundred cauldrons of the feast raised an obeisance of steam to the sky, that sky whose blue would by his decree henceforth be part of the name of those he led: the Koko-Mongols, the Mongols of the Blue Heaven. But it may be, too, that despite his forty or so years of age, he glanced once or twice towards the women where, in placated state, sat the only person he seems ever to have feared – Yulun, his mother.

While the people were still gathered and the weeks of feasting passed, the work of organization began. It was now that he gave Tatatungo, his Uighur adviser, the task of writing down the *Yasak*, that code of laws that he proposed for the Mongols. Stating, 'There is equality', it was to apply to everyone: 'Each man works as much as another. . . . ' These laws have survived only in fragmentary form, but ranged from matters of detail, like the prohibition against washing in a running stream or against cattle drinking from a well – probably simple measures of public hygiene – through such moral precepts as the one urging men not to be drunk more than three times in a month, to matters of State – for example, the death penalty was decreed for any prince or *orlok* discovered in communication with a foreign monarch. The *Yasak* also included such general exhortations as the commandment to treat all religions with equal respect. The laws limited the ruler as much as the people – he should take no grand titles, but be known simply as Khan; he should not seize the property of a man dying without heirs, but see that it went to those who had looked after him; his soldiers should not be less than twenty years old. On the other hand the people should supply the Khan's needs from their surplus, and each tribe was obliged to send for his use horses, rams, milk and wool or woollen goods; and any man who left the military unit to which he was assigned was to be executed. Regulating all functions and duties, the *Yasak* bound the Mongols into a single controlled unity. Of great importance historically was the law laying it down that on the death of the Khaghan (a title Genghis, of course, never used of himself) all the princes of the family should gather in a *kuriltai* to decide on the successor. The obligation to do this became a political focus of an intensity affecting not only Mongols but also at times their most distant neighbours.

To administer these laws a judge was needed, some man whom all could trust, whose uprightness and disinterestedness would be manifest to everyone. Genghis Khan picked Shigikutuku, grown into a man from the gold-braceleted orphan he had picked up so many years before among the tents of the defeated Tatars. It was he who, under the Khaghan, was responsible for the new ideals of honour and disciplined conduct that now spread astonishingly among these unlettered and superficially uncivilized tribes. Violence, robbery and theft all diminished, as did adultery, considered among these many-wived patriarchs to be a crime equal to any of the others. This was partly due to the stringency of the new juridical procedure: only those were found guilty who had been caught red-handed or had freely confessed. It may be that this diminished not so much the incidence of crime as that of criminals caught and punished, but it seems indisputable that for the ordinary tribesman, travelling across those endless pastures with his tent, his wagon, his family and his flocks, a new peace now brought him comfort.

Petty wars and the sudden, ferocious raids of neighbours disappeared. Banditry almost vanished. Disputes either no longer arose or were settled by discussion and law rather than by force of arms. Part of the reason was that, at this first gathering of his people, the Khaghan, who now had suzerainty over lands that stretched for a thousand miles east and west between the mountains and for six hundred miles northwards from the Gobi Desert, decided that the time had come to apportion once and for all each tribe's grazing lands. In order to base his decision fairly, he first ordered a census of his peoples' tents. It was now, too, that, faced with the need to know everything that happened in his domains, he extended and perfected his system of messengers, the 'arrow riders' who drove their horses and their own bandaged bodies to and beyond the point of total exhaustion as they thrust on, hour after hour, day and night and day again, from the ends of his vast territories.

To release his men for war (Genghis knew where his power lay) he gave women new and far-reaching responsibility over everything the family owned. Their bodies, on the other hand, belonged as before to their husbands; to take a lover was to court death as well as pleasure. The men, for their part, had at all times to be ready for war; their chieftains were to use peace as periods of training and the hunt as their training scheme, seeing to it that their men were prepared at any time to reach for weapons and horses and gallop away to the Khan's battles. It was the men's responsibility to see that their weapons were always keen, their bow-strings ready to be tautened, their quivers full of good straight arrows. It was the women who had to make sure of the rest of the war equipment – the sheepskin cloaks, the riding boots with their felt overshoes – and who saw to it that saddle bags were always filled with dried milk, curds and *koumiss*. The *touman* of one tribe would then link with that of its neighbours into an army group, to which the Khaghan would appoint an *orlok* as commander. Because these groups knew one another and trained together, they answered swiftly to the orders they received. As to those orders, they were passed through a permanent committee of trusted leaders, what may be termed a general staff, and administered by lesser officers. Ordinary laws were enforced by a sort of police force that kept the highways safe and saw to it that lost or stolen beasts were restored to their owners – and also that such thieves as still took the sheep, cattle, camels or, perhaps worst of all, horses of their neighbours were punished, as the law decreed, by death.

There was another aspect of military organization, however, which Genghis Khan understood early, and understood more clearly than many of the other great commanders of history. He realized that the only useful decisions were those he took when he knew all the facts. Information was, as much as manpower, the raw material of victory. He gleaned what he could from travellers, allies and prisoners; for the rest, he established from the beginning a far-flung web of spies, a tentacular stretching out of his power that neither Gobi Desert nor Great Wall could thwart. In the country of the Kara-Khitai to the west, in the Tangut state of Hsi-Hsia to the south and in the great bureaucracy of China to the south-east, his informants watched, noted and, from time to time, sent him what they had learned.

Meanwhile, as his peace settled over the steppes, his power increased. The Uighur khans accepted him as overlord, transferring their allegiance from the oppressive rule of Kara-Khitai, and the tents of his own camp became a focus for the caravans of traders. It might have seemed that he could rest and be content. But Genghis Khan, whose father had died by Tatar poison because of an enmity long encouraged by the Chinese, knew that the enormous, complex, ancient and overwhelmingly powerful civilization which watched from the far side of that Wall would, sooner or later, decide to move against him. Everything he heard told him that the Mongols would be scattered before the might of the Kin as the sand was flung aside by the bitter winds of the desert. He could not fight them – or was not yet ready to. His armies trained, but they lacked the experience, the confidence, the technique necessary. Where were they to learn these? Thoughtfully, he looked southward.

The Tangut were originally a semi-nomadic people, mainly Tibetan, but adding to themselves over the years many Chinese and even Tatars. Their wars with the Chinese and the Khitans (those cousins of the Mongols whose earlier successes had dwindled to the despotism of Kara-Khitai) had resulted in their establishing them-

Mongol women ride as skilfully as the men.
The laws of Genghis Khan set out the rights
and duties of the sexes in a society
where women sometimes attained great power.

selves in their own vast tract of land, to the west of the Kin. There, they developed
a complicated script derived from the Chinese, they translated the works of
Buddhism, of Taoism and Confucianism, they established learning, a network of
market towns, a system of fortifications and a bureaucracy – they were, in effect,
adherents of the culture of China, differing from their neighbours only in the com-
parative rawness of their own borrowed civilization. Two centuries are not much
to set in the scales against two millennia. For Genghis Khan, however, the similarities were tempting – Hsi-Hsia would be the training ground on which his armies
learned to cope with the might of the Kin, when the time came for that might to
be tested.

There was a further pressure on the Mongol leader to attack his neighbours –
the need to placate his followers. Success was the cement that tied together such
empires as his. He had reached his new elevation on a long trail of unlikely victories.

Each one had given those who followed him both plunder and the secure feeling that comes from being on the winning side, under the protection of a strong ruler. But such feelings are volatile and need to be renewed at constant intervals. Genghis Khan, having destroyed all enemies among his fellow-nomads, had now to discover new ones among the settled nations beyond the steppes. It was only among these, too, that there lay ready for plucking the kind of plunder that would energize his half-sated followers. He was discovering what other leaders had found out before him, and others not yet born would learn – that the ready acceptance of the ruler by the ruled depends upon a degree of happiness which only an increasing scale of rewards can bring. In this lies the debauchery of conquest.

In 1207 Genghis Khan led a force southward across the Gobi Desert, digging temporary wells to keep both men and horses watered. He arrived on the borders of the Tangut state in sufficiently good condition to defeat the army sent against him and to capture a number of villages and small towns. Then he appeared before the ramparts of Volohai. For the first time in history, a Mongol army was faced with the problems of a siege. They proved insuperable. The men of the steppes, used to fast-moving mounted warfare, to the ranks and columns and sudden, savage groupings of the open battlefield, found that the assault on such prepared positions led only to an endless drain of life and of morale. In a force where every man felt himself by tradition free to depart if the tide turned against his leader, where for centuries armies had been loose confederations of equals, the mood began to turn against the Khaghan.

Genghis Khan, however, was a man of devious and inventive cunning, not only a man of force. He now informed the commander of the fortified town that he would lead his men home if he received tribute – one thousand cats and ten thousand swallows. One imagines the startled debate within the walls; one knows the out-come, for the curious payment was made. Now the Khan set his Mongols to work, tying tufts of cottonwool to the tails of these beasts, setting light to them and letting them go in one terrified, flickering stampede through air and over land. Like sparks blown by a gale, birds searched for their nests, cats for their haunts. Beyond the walls, smoke arose, first here, then there, soon in a dozen places, in a hundred – the whole town blazed. And while the garrison fought flames, the Mongols took their citadel. Despite the jubilation of his men, the Khaghan understood very clearly that he had come to the end of what was immediately possible. There was only a limited number of tricks that would cause the surrender of fortified towns; the only real method was to learn the techniques of siege warfare. He demanded an annual tribute of the King of Hsi-Hsia, and after hesitation that monarch politically agreed to pay at least the first instalment. There is no doubt, however, that he intended on some suitable occasion to regain the full value of it by force of arms. Able nevertheless to claim a victory, Genghis Khan withdrew.

There now began an astonishing extension of Mongol military skill. These wild cavalrymen of the plains, their competence as warriors learned in hunting and in inter-tribal skirmish, their wars swift and full of movement, now settled to learn the

Genghis Khan sits in state, surrounded
by attendants. Even in luxury, he remained
a nomad, however – his palace is a tent
and outside it fly the yak-tail
banners of a khan.

موریتای بزرک جنکیزخان نومی سیده باید بضب فرهود ولبت جنکیزخان رو بمقدر
کث وعزیمت اوجنک ببروق بادشاه کیه مه امان وکردن بزرق جان بمذکورا جون مبارکی وفرخی ماربس مال که بسال یوزرائدموافق
بار رجب سنه ابین وسبعنا بهجری درآمدیم درا وابدبضلها رجنکیزخان فرهود مانوفی نه باید سید بهای که زنده ومعیی باعطبت
موریتای نمدل ساخت ودر ان یوزبلنابی لتب بزرک جنکیزخان یبروی مزرکزنده وسبارکی بیجت بنشت

حكايت

وستادن جنكيز خان سوبداى بهادر را بانكو حكم نوم ملكت و آخر

long-drawn skills of siege-craft. The flexibility of mind shown by their leader –
astonishing enough when one considers how many commanders have ended by
beating their heads against the stone walls of tradition – had to be matched by their
willingness to take seriously the lessons he wanted to be taught. What had sand bags
and giant wicker shields, what had scaling ladders and battering rams to do with
the battles they had learned to fight? Nevertheless, at Genghis Khan's command,
each tribe assembled a siege-train and practised how to employ it. Indeed it was now
that the central core of the Mongolian military establishment was founded, a force
of officers who were constantly active, either in the field or in training. They were,
in essence, a professional corps, for they spent a large part of their time in either
honing or deploying their skills. It was they who made the final difference between
the Mongol forces and the largely amateur, *ad hoc* armies of their near and distant
neighbours. Genghis Khan's was the mind that conceived this unprecedented
military academy, and his the authority that made it possible.

For all their long-term interest in sieges, the Mongols had by no means lost their
more traditional abilities. Under his eldest son, Jochi, Genghis Khan sent an army
westwards, confident of its success even if he did not ride with it himself. Since Jochi
had as his lieutenants Subatei and Jebei, he had reason for his confidence; Naimans,
Kirghiz and Merkits in turn would endorse by their surrenders and defeats this
view of Mongol competence. When Jochi returned his gratified father placed under
his rule 'the forest-dwellers'. In this way a dynasty was founded in the kingdom of
Kipchak, north of the Aral Sea, which would have its repercussions on European
history.

For two years Hsi-Hsia paid tribute to the Mongols: the third year's instalment
did not come, a sign that the Tanguts no longer feared Mongol wrath. In this they
proved over-optimistic; as before, the army they sent against Genghis Khan and
his eighty *toumans* was swept aside. It was the walls of their cities on which they now
relied. This time, however, Volohai fell quickly, and not even the Great Wall, a
long spur of which stretched eastward across the Tangut domains, could hold up
the Mongol advance. The Tangut army tried to rally, then fled into the capital,
Hoang-hsing-fu, on the Yellow River. Genghis Khan took a leaf out of Chinese
military practice and began to dam the river, hoping thirst would drive the
garrison to surrender. Men of the steppe, however, were not practised engineers;
the dam burst, flinging a surge of released waters upon the besiegers' camp. The
result was stalemate, with the Hsi-Hsia sovereign locked within his walls, but
Genghis Khan unable to defeat him. Though the countryside lay open to Mongol
plunder, the country remained unbowed. The Khaghan proposed peace; the King
of Hsi-Hsia was pleased to accept the offered terms. There was a ceremony of some
splendour, after which the Tangut ruler found himself not only more firmly Genghis
Khan's vassal than before, but also that lusty autocrat's latest father-in-law.

It was when Genghis Khan was on his way home from this campaign that a
delegation from Pekin came to see him. They brought him news of a new Kin
emperor, Wei-Shao. It was customary for the lesser princes outside the Wall to

The camp of Genghis Khan. No one was
permitted to pitch his tent before that
of the Khan, whose view remained
uninterrupted clear to the horizon.

In addition to their mounted archers, Mongol armies had units of
light and heavy cavalry carrying throwing javelins, and lances
and sabres for hand-to-hand combat.

bend in ritual obeisance at the name; Genghis Khan spat. 'If an idiot can become
the emperor, it is hardly worth kow-towing to his messenger,' he said. The Chinese
ambassadors reported this to a furious Wei-Shao. An army was dispatched, but
balked at the vastness of the steppes. They attacked the hapless Onggut instead,
then crumbled under a Mongol counter-attack by Jebei. In his golden fastness,
however, the new 'Son of Heaven' had had enough of unruly barbarians. As far as
he was concerned, he said, there was peace on the north-western frontier. When the
General of the Wall brought insistent news of Mongol preparations, he was thrown
into prison. What are mere facts, after all, to an emperor who has made up his
mind?

It must have been something of a shock, therefore, when reality rudely altered
imperial convictions. Yet not as much of a shock as all that, perhaps, for when the
200,000 men of Genghis Khan's army drew near to Pekin in that year of 1211, there
were after all armies ready to meet them. In the event, however, they made little
difference. Genghis Khan had prepared well. He had called to his service every
fighting man within the 600,000 square miles of his domains, he had mobilized
every ally, pressed into use every available mount and wagon. To guard his own
territory he had left behind no more than two *toumans*; the twenty marching with
him he had divided into three divisions under the *orloks* Mukhali, Subatei and
Jebei, these three army groups comprising the two wings and centre of the main
force. Before all these a deadly crescent of scouts travelled swiftly, a vast fan that saw
everything, marked each suitable camp site and executed every potential spy. This
enormous force marched from the River Kerulen across mountain and desert,
450 miles, to arrive at the gates of China without a casualty.

The ponderous armies of the Kin moved to defend their capital, for the line of Mongol advance led directly towards that sacred city. Then, abruptly, the invaders vanished. Days passed without the arrival all had feared. Suddenly news came from Shan-si Province – the Mongols had crossed the Great Wall (with the secret help of Onggut mercenaries) and were ravaging the rich towns and harvests of that land. At the same time, Jebei with his column began a campaign of harassment against the armies gathered to defend Pekin. Although in this way beset, they nevertheless left the fortified defence lines of the Pekin plain and marched westward and upward, through the guarding escarpment that protects the fertile plateau of Shan-si. As the enormous columns – some have estimated the Chinese army at half a million men – wound out of the passes and on to the flatlands, Genghis Khan struck. Jebei, swifter than his adversaries, attacked the rearguard at the same time. Arrows seemed to roof the world as the Mongols stretched and loosed, stretched and loosed the strings of their short bows. The foot-soldiers of the Son of Heaven broke. The massed and disciplined horsemen of the Khaghan struck them, destroyed them. The lands of the Kin lost their main protection.

Now Genghis could safely split his forces. He and his son Tuli besieged Ta-tung-fu; Jochi, Chagatei and Ogadei, his other three sons, took an army each and whirled through Shan-si, reaping the harvest of their victory. Jebei, meanwhile, took his group eastward to reconnoitre the best route to Pekin. But before Genghis the walls of the invested city held, day after day, week after week. His sons, having gathered in what Shan-si had to offer, struck across the mountains to Chi-li Province. Here they too found themselves thwarted by their inability to overrun well-fortified towns. The Mongols, for all their training and preparation, were still mobile soldiers of the steppes. When Jebei took and held a weakly defended pass that led straight down to the plains of Pekin, Genghis Khan raised his siege, sent his 'arrow riders' to his sons with the command to join him, and led his combined forces, laden now with slaves and colourful booty, to the very walls of the Kin capital.

The artifacts of China, like this
stoneware vase made during the
period of the Sung dynasty,
fascinated the nomad Mongols.
Many of them, however, despised
the urban culture upon which
Chinese arts and crafts were based.

Despite the appearance of physical and dynastic solidity presented by Pekin, its rulers were in fact no more entitled to its throne than was Genghis Khan himself. It was only a hundred years before that the Jurchen, a people of the far north, had swept aside the Khitan emperors of the Liao dynasty and established themselves in these northern provinces. They had attempted to reduce the southern empire, ruled by one of China's traditional lines, the Sung, but had been halted by a defence of the Yangtze that had involved the startling use of gunpowder. After that, cultural infiltration and administrative necessity had combined to make the Kin rule more and more traditional, more and more Chinese. Despite Jurchen efforts to preserve their own less refined culture, they had succumbed to the religion, the philosophy, the bureaucratic daintiness, the science and mathematics and – most emphatically of all – the love of theatre of their vassals. It was therefore to all appearances a wholly Chinese monarch who now glowered from behind his walls at the assembled Mongol hordes.

And what fortifications they were, these ramparts of the most strongly defended city in China. Genghis Khan rode to and fro, marvelling at the task that faced him. Eighteen miles of walls for him to survey, forty feet high, fifty feet wide at the bottom and tapering to forty at the battlements. Before these ramparts lay three deep moats; nine hundred towers overlooked them. The four main approaches to the city were each defended by a complex and well-stocked fortress. Nothing he had envisaged when he had first prepared his siege-trains had been on a scale like this! When after a month the grasslands of the Pekin plains began to fail under the demands of almost a million horses, he decided to take his Mongol booty into winter camp.

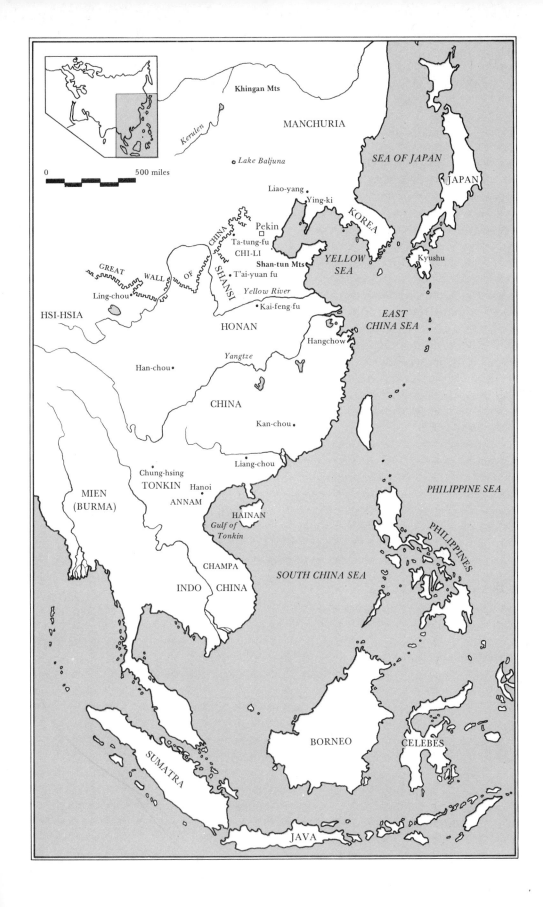

Khingan Mts

MANCHURIA

*Kerulen*

○ *Lake Baljuna*

Liao-yang •
• Ying-ki

SEA OF JAPAN

JAPAN

0    500 miles

KOREA

Pekin □
• Ta-tung-fu
CHI-LI

Kyushu

CHINA

GREAT    WALL    OF

SHANSI

**Shan-tun Mts**

• T'ai-yuan fu

YELLOW
SEA

Ling-chou •

*Yellow River*

EAST
CHINA SEA

HSI-HSIA

HONAN

• Kai-feng-fu

Hangchow

*Yangtze*

Han-chou •

CHINA

Kan-chou •

Liang-chou •

PHILIPPINE SEA

Chung-hsing •
TONKIN    • Hanoi
ANNAM

MIEN
(BURMA)

HAINAN
*Gulf of
Tonkin*

PHILIPPINES

CHAMPA

INDO    CHINA

SOUTH CHINA SEA

SUMATRA

BORNEO

CELEBES

JAVA

His army was already beginning to move, although he himself was not yet sure where he intended to settle for the cold season, when to his surprise a delegation arrived from Wei-Shao. If its purpose was to discover the state of the Mongol armies, it played its hand with an un-oriental clumsiness. The general who led it, offered the Khaghan's hospitality, was soon telling more than he learned. Perhaps what he knew disturbed him, and what disturbed him he had to discuss – even with an enemy. Because, as he pointed out, the Jurchen emperors were hated by the people, the true Chinese dynasty of the Sung awaited the chance to attack them from the south, while to the north-east the last of the Khitan princes looked for the chance to restore his family's Liao dynasty. The emperor was beset, his position was shaky and – across the centuries one can hear the new slyness in the tone, the sideways flicker of glances – even the general himself, outcrop of the Liao line, would be prepared to help the Mongols if it meant the restoration of Khitan rule.

Genghis Khan, fortified by what he prized most, inside information, marched northward, to place his camp between the Kin and the Khitans. The position had its own bonus, for in crossing the double barrier of the Great Wall he picked up the vast brood-herds of the emperor's stud farm, which had supplied the horses for the Kin cavalry and would henceforth supply his own. Gathered from the grazing land between the walls, their departure crippled the mobility and power of Pekin's armies. Throughout that winter of 1211–12 the Khaghan laid his plans, sent out his emissaries, evaluated their reports, followed these with instructions, promises and praise, weapons of diplomacy that he could always wield as expertly as he could his sword and bow.

In the spring the Khitan rose. Genghis Khan marched again across devastated Shang-li, only to discover that Chinese energy had repaired its defences. Once again he bent to the repetitive routines of a siege, investing Ta-tung-fu a second time. Jebei, in the meantime, had been sent to support the Khitan revolt in the north. In Shang-li, however, Mongol arms were flung back by the Kin defences as remorselessly as granite flings back the waves. The rudimentary siege-craft they had practised proved too unsophisticated against the multiple walls, the cunningly placed towers and the weaponry of this great civilization. Desperately Genghis Khan himself led an attack, storming towards the wall with all the ancient Mongol fervour. Nothing availed, neither precept nor example; hurled back, wounded by an arrow, he turned for the north again. He had been defeated; for the Mongols of old, this would have been the end of the war. For the hordes of Genghis Khan, however, newly disciplined and differently enthused, setback led only to reconsideration. Beyond the Great Wall, they got to work, teaching themselves and learning from their Chinese captives more and different techniques of siege warfare.

Meanwhile Jebei faced a similar problem in the Khitan territories. In the field his *toumans* were a match for the Chinese. But walls – in this case those of the eastern capital, Liao-yang – proved too much for him. He, too, camped uselessly below them, led assaults, watched his men dwindle in numbers and their morale sink. But Jebei had his own methods, Mongol methods. As though come to the end of his resources, or summoned elsewhere by enemy or edict, he moved abruptly away from the city, leaving his camp and its baggage abandoned. For two days he steadily withdrew; on the second evening, his men freshly mounted, he raced back to the city, covering the distance in that single night. Dawn saw his riders burst

through their own dust-cloud to fall on the bewildered garrison, come out to loot
the silent tents of their departed besiegers. Before they could retreat, they were
destroyed. Immediately, the Liao prince proclaimed the Khitan independent and
himself a vassal king under the protection of Genghis Khan.

The year turned, and spring brought renewed warfare. There was now a solidity
in Mongol resolution, a determination and a skill against which no wall seemed
proof. One after another, the fortified towns of the north fell to their assaults.
Pressure on the emperor increased; more and more Khitan commanders altered
their allegiance, as politically, too, Genghis Khan was gaining the day. And at the
very centre of Kin rule, in the Pekin palace itself, the rottenness appeared. The
eunuch general, Hu-sha-hu, turning on his master, captured the capital and murdered him. But if Genghis Khan thought that he now had friends beyond those
walls who would open the citadel's great gates for him, he was soon disabused:

Mandarins play Go, an ancient game of skill which remains popular today.
The urbanity of Chinese life was disrupted by the ferocity of the Mongol
invaders, but in time the conquerors too came to submit to its attractions.

setting a new Kin emperor, Hsuan-tsung, on that turbulent throne, the energetic eunuch thrust towards the Mongol advance, caught its columns at a river ford and flung them back in disorder. Lame, heaved from place to place in a wheelchair, Hu-sha-hu waited for the flanking attack he had ordered, and which would have completed the destruction of the Mongol armies. It never came; the hesitations of that attack's commander, Kao-chi, saved Genghis Khan. The Kin soldiers were not to have a second chance of victory.

Rescued from Hu-sha-hu's wrath by the new emperor's intercession, Kao-chi tried to rectify his earlier mistake, but no valour could bring him back the victory he had so carelessly let go. Pushed back again and again, fighting at last among the very houses of outer Pekin, he turned in his despair on the man he knew would this time have him executed for his failures. His soldiers rushed Hu-sha-hu's house, caught and executed the general and then moved on to surround the palace. Faced with the twisted, blood-stained head of the dead eunuch, Hsuan-tsung accepted the inevitable and made Kao-chi his new commander-in-chief – no enviable post with Genghis Khan once more under the walls of the capital.

These political preoccupations among his enemies, and the continued imperturbable barrier presented by those enormous walls, seem to have angered the Khaghan. In any case, he divided his forces into three great army groups that swung outwards from the capital, tearing the wealth from the heartlands of the Kin domains. The Mongols now had no truck with sieges; faced by a walled town, invariably defended by peasants gathered from the surrounding countryside, they would round up the women, children and old people who had been left behind and drive these forward at the head of their advance. In a land that held the old in the highest regard, where family ties were always strong, no garrison would raise its hands in a defence that might harm their nearest kin. It was at this time, too, that terror as a positive weapon entered the Mongol armoury. Those towns that surrendered at once were spared bloodshed and plundering; those that fought were ruthlessly destroyed. Ninety fell to Genghis Khan. Only eleven centres held out, desperate, stubborn, isolated.

For six months this pillaging, this scything down of a country, continued without respite. In the spring the armies assembled again outside Pekin. Once more those wide ramparts stood against Mongol ambition, their intransigence apparently endless. The *orloks* wanted one culminating victory, but their Khan knew it was probably beyond them; if not, it would lead only to their being themselves beset within those vast fortifications. Victory would turn into imprisonment. And the Chinese, as the Mongols had learned in a hundred different engagements, had fire and explosives, catapults and siege-engines, which their opponents could not match. Nevertheless, pressed – and perhaps in his heart not averse from making the attempt – he let his battalions loose, only to see them flung back with appalling losses. An outlying fortress fell to his forces, then was retaken. Those Mongols who swarmed to the foot of the very walls themselves found they were being taken in the rear as by-passed garrisons sallied to cut them off. His earlier certainties thus bloodily confirmed, Genghis Khan suggested to the emperor that, his provinces devastated and his capital beset, he might be glad to make peace. After hesitation and discussion, Hsuan-tsung agreed.

Three years after he had crossed the Gobi Desert on this huge enterprise, Genghis Khan was able to leave China, his triumph, if not total, sufficiently complete to have altered for his lifetime the relations between Pekin and the people of the steppes. A new bride marked this alteration, a daughter of the previous and unfortunate Emperor Wei-Shao. Behind his bedraggled but exuberant column marched thousands upon thousands of prisoners. Before making himself ready to recross the desert, he weeded from these the artists, scholars and craftsmen who might be useful to him as practitioners or teachers; the rest he killed.

As he waited for the summer heat to decline and the Gobi to become passable, however, Genghis Khan learned that Hsuan-tsung, the Golden Emperor, had moved from Pekin to the southern city of Kai-feng, beyond the Yellow River, further than the Mongol columns had hitherto penetrated. If there was one thing more than another that displeased the Khaghan, it was the thought that his word was doubted. He had taken his tribute of horses and craftsmen, of ivory and silk, and he had agreed in return to leave northern China. Now, as if afraid, the emperor had moved his capital, and had set himself up beyond the barrier of the river, a secure area from which he might perhaps mount a counter-attack in a year or so.

Under the *orlok* Mukhali, Genghis Khan sent an army to the help of the Khitans, now once more beleaguered by treaty-defying Kin forces. He sent Subatei with another army eastwards to Manchuria and Korea. A column was sent southwards to help a detachment of the Imperial Guard, Khitan warriors who in fear of arrest and execution had mutinied. Again it was before Pekin that a rendezvous was arranged between this southern force and the army under Mukhali, who now became supreme commander. Under the pressures of this second Mongol campaign, northern China fell apart. Provinces and even cities declared themselves independent; their rulers became royal overnight. Meanwhile eight hundred communities fell to Mukhali's columns, some razed to the ground, others spared to be administered by Chinese governors acting under Mongol orders. For there were many Chinese now prepared to serve the only clearly apparent power in those lands; even Jurchen warriors joined those Khitans and Chinese who now fought in the Mongol ranks.

Under the Prince Wan-yen, Pekin as always stood firm. Within those awe-inspiring walls, however, famine and disease worked for the besiegers. There had been little time to replenish the city's supplies in the short period of peace between the two Mongol investments. To the south, one relieving force after another was met and broken by the Mongol armies. The defenders' morale sank; the survivors turned in their extremity to cannibalism. Wan-yen proposed an attempt to break out through the encircling Mongols; his plan rejected, he killed himself. The garrison turned against its masters, looting those they had once so staunchly protected. Wan-yen's successor fled, having at least the courtesy to take his mistress with him. In May 1215, quite peaceably in the end, guided by a Kin officer, five thousand warriors under Mukhali marched through the gates and found themselves at last within those walls where Genghis Khan had never, would never, set foot.

He had taken stock of these city-dwellers, and he did not like what he had discovered. They were too wrapped up in property, were too soft, too devious, too far removed from honour. They had a certain cleverness, but their tricks could be learned; if not, their craftsmen could practise them for Mongol masters as they had for the Kin. They had neither the nobility nor the toughness of fibre that made them in his eyes the equal of the Mongols; there should be no alliance with them, as there had been with the peoples of the steppes. But one meeting of great significance would come out of the capture of Pekin. For weeks the caravans, laden with fabrics and with gold, with brocades and jewelry, set out one after the other north-westward towards the desert and the tents of Genghis Khan, waiting at its edge. With them marched an endless stream of the wise, the talented and the accomplished. Among these was Yelui Ch'u ts'ai.

Twenty-five years old and Khitan by birth, Yelui Ch'u ts'ai was an administrator; in the Mongol lists of the captured he figured as a sage and astrologer. He was tall, quiet and dignified, despite his youth. Noting his family connections with the Liao, Genghis Khan exclaimed that through the Mongols his house had been avenged. But Yelui Ch'u ts'ai replied, calmly, that for three generations his family had served the Kin: 'I would be a liar and a fraud if I now became the enemy of my father and my Emperor.' Genghis, a man who valued loyalty perhaps above all other feelings, at once responded to his prisoner's manifest nobility. As he had done so often before with prisoners he respected, he at once offered this Chinese sage a position – as his personal astrologer. Soon this was amended, and Yelui Ch'u ts'ai became his personal adviser, his principal minister.

Yelui Ch'u ts'ai combined nomadic ancestry with Chinese culture: he had the vision of both the man of the plains and the man of the cities. It was he who said: 'The Mongol Empire has been won from the saddle – it cannot be ruled from the saddle.' At the Khaghan's side, and at the side of his son, Yelui Ch'u ts'ai always argued against destruction and for the long-term view – a razed city paid no taxes, a depopulated land could bring neither tribute nor trade, a decimated people were no help in war. And magnanimity brought its own long-term rewards. It was to Genghis Khan's credit that, despite the bitterness of many jealous rumours (all without foundation – Yelui Ch'u ts'ai was poor when he died, leaving only books, musical instruments and a cabinet of medicines), he always trusted his Chinese adviser, always listened to him, always understood what he said, and often did as he suggested.

The Kin emperor, from the safety of his southern seat, hoped for peace. The Mongol leader offered it to him – as King of Ho-nan and therefore the Khaghan's vassal. The rejection of these terms led to skirmishes; finally Genghis turned his back on China and returned to his own headquarters on the River Onon, leaving Mukhali with some forty thousand men as his representatives in all the lands from Manchuria to the Yellow River. Matters in the west seemed to be demanding the attention of Mongol diplomacy or Mongol arms.

When the Naiman had been broken, their prince, Guchuluk, son of Tayang Khan, had found shelter with the Kara-Khitai. He had married the grand-daughter of their Gur-Khan, then repaid hospitality with treachery: in 1211 he drove his benefactor from the throne. To the crime of usurpation he had added that of tyranny, persecuting the Muslims under his rule (through his wife's influence, he had become a Buddhist convert). Muslim chiefs, disturbed, appealed to the Mongols for help; Guchuluk, for whom Genghis Khan was nothing more than his father's hated killer, riposted with torture and execution. For Genghis Khan, loyalty his brightest virtue, the Muslim appeal was a command. Summoning Jebei from Korea, he sent him westwards with two hundred thousand men. His orders were to reopen the mosques and proclaim religious tolerance for all.

In a world ruled – under Tengris, the Ultimate Lord of All – by a multitude of gods and spirits, one deity more or less mattered little. Mongols were always

The Mongols believed in religious toleration and, under
their rule, many sects flourished side by side.
In China, Buddhist priests and monks came to wield great
influence, especially at the expense of the Taoists.

relaxed about other people's worship, and saw no threat in permitting the practices
of Nestorian, Muslim, Buddhist, Tibetan Lamaist, Taoist or Confucian beside that
of their own *shamans*. The promise of tolerance was therefore no empty one, and the
Naiman people rose to it. The Moslems were a majority; in every town where Jebei
appeared, they overwhelmed the garrison and flung open the gates. On the orders
of the Khaghan himself, the Mongols stole nothing, raped no one, drove away no
man's flock. Guchuluk, not for the first time, stood, fought, lost and fled. High on
the Pamir Mountains, in ravine and snow-field, he tried to lose the hunters Jebei
sent after him. In vain – cornered by their skill in the valley of Sary-kol, he died;
his head was taken east to the Onon, accompanied by a thousand of the white-
muzzled horses of the region, the only plunder taken during the campaign. With
China humbled and Korea a vassal in the east, with Hsi-Hsia paying tribute in the
south and the Liao kings his dependants, with Jochi scattering the recalcitrant
Merkits and bringing the weight of Mongol power to bear on the Kirghiz and the
Tumats of the north, with the Uighur willing allies and Kara-Khitai under
domination in the west, the world's horizons had rolled back again for Genghis
Khan, and everywhere he saw himself victorious.

But the world held rivals all the same, and Mongol success in Kara-Khitai had
brought Genghis Khan face to face with one of them. To the west now lay the lands
of the Khwarism-Shah Muhammad II, the Turkish ruler of what was known as the
Khwarismian Empire. This had been expanding since the turn of the thirteenth
century; much of what is today Persia, Afghanistan and Pakistan lay within its

borders. Now its ruler faced the monstrous bulk of the new Mongol empire across the imperturbable eddies and windings of the River Jaxartes, the Syr Darya, making its way down to the Aral Sea. Genghis, aware of the size and wealth of his new neighbour, and that Mukhali was still engaged with the Kin far to the south-east, made no warlike move. On the contrary, he sent a delegation and a conciliatory message, its friendliness strengthened by the many presents that accompanied it.

There are questions about what occurred next. Was Muhammad made angry by the implied superiority in Genghis Khan's 'I regard thee as my most cherished son'? Sons were their father's vassals – Muhammad, a man both narrow and arrogant, looked up to no one. Was Shah Muhammad responsible for Genghis Khan's second caravan of friendship led by a man named Ukhuna being waylaid and killed, or was it the work of Inalchik, his local governor at the frontier town of Otrar, an officer known for his suspicion of the Mongols? After all, in 1218, when the Caliph Nasr of Baghdad had joined with the Nestorian patriarch of that city to ask Genghis Khan's assistance in their defence against Muhammad's invading armies, the Khaghan had replied, with smug severity: 'I am not at war with Shah Muhammad.' Now he sent an embassy to the Shah in his capital of Samarkand, demanding that Inalchik be sent to him for punishment. There is a suggestion, however, that there had been spies in that massacred Mongol caravan; in any case, Muhammad refused point-blank, executed the Khwarismian who had led Genghis Khan's delegation and shaved his two Mongol companions before sending them back. 'You have chosen war,' Genghis Khan remarked; by the autumn of 1219, the Mongol armies were marching west towards the River Jaxartes.

By now the fifteen *toumans* of this army, 150,000 men, were battle-hardened, their experience honed by constant training and their expertise supported by detachments of forcibly recruited Chinese engineers. As the years of conquest passed an unexpected variety of engines and weapons would supplement Mongol courage and mobility, the khans' and *orloks'* swift strategic sense and the ruthlessness of their tactics. Some have said that they not only flung fire and great rocks from their enormous catapults, they used flame throwers and even explosives. Certainly the techniques of siege-craft they had learned with such difficulty before the endless walls of China were theirs to apply against any fortification that stood in their way. The mining of saps, the building of towers, the advance under wicker shields, the hurling of pots of flaming naphtha from those catapults, the filling of moats and the thunderous ramming of gates were now among the Mongol skills of war. But they had not forgotten the abilities and weapons with which they had begun; horse and rider were still the basic unit of their fighting force, the bow was still their most potent weapon, shooting first the light arrows that flew across distance like swarming bees, their whistling hum full of a meaningful menace, then the heavy, armour-piercing arrows as they closed, to scatter and destroy the cavalry facing them; and it was still their curved sword that at close quarters slashed its way to victory.

By now, too, the Mongol armies had perfected their approach to pitched battle – two ranks of spaced squadrons of heavy cavalry stretched wide and menacing in the van, three ranks of mounted archers ranged behind them, ready to whirl through, shooting, the arrows like a dark fountain before them, then wheeling and retreating, still shooting over their horses' rumps, letting the next wave through.

When the enveloping crescent of archers had created its worst destruction, the heavy cavalry charged. If work remained still to be done, there was always a corps in reserve, aching to join those actively engaged. Signal flags kept flowing the orders and information that Genghis Khan knew to be the life-blood of an effective army; at night lamps or blazing arrows had the same task. Conversely, what in modern times has been called 'disinformation' was liberally supplied to the enemy: feigned retreats, dummies on horseback or sitting by camp fires to confuse estimates of Mongol forces, smoke screens lifting from burning vegetation behind which a column would strike out in some unexpected direction – these were the stratagems that would bewilder, confound and eventually destroy those who took the field against the Mongols. And when, their armies broken, they took to flight, Mongol pursuit was remorseless and implacable. What Genghis Khan wanted to teach his enemies was that resistance was hopeless, that the attempt to mount it would be punished with the utmost cruelty. Only swift and willing surrender would elicit magnanimity – survival hung on instant submission.

This was the army that now, for the first time, set its face in all earnestness towards the west. Late in the summer of 1219, a column of Mongol riders swung southward, burned and pillaged along the lower reaches of the Jaxartes, then, having protected the main army's flank by this manoeuvre, withdrew northwards again. Muhammad, persuaded by this as by the logic of geography, disposed his forces along that river, holding a line between the Pamirs and the Aral Sea. But Jebei had discovered an alternative route. That winter, disregarding all hardship, under his and Jochi's leadership some thirty thousand men struggled through the deep snow that lies at 13,000 feet, through the snowstorms that scream across the seams and outcrops of those regions, through searing cold and the debilitating cramps of starvation, relentlessly making their way towards the green fields and laden trees of the valley of Farghana. They had found a pass, at the point where the Tien-Shan range meets the Pamirs, that would bring them down into the water-fed plains of Transoxiana and so open the route to Samarkand and Bokhara.

Now for the first time one of the great heroes of Islam's Middle Ages steps into the story: Jelal ud-Din, Shah Muhammad's son, who led an army against this unexpected Mongol force. The *orlok* Jebei wanted to avoid combat, but Jochi disdained a politic retreat; the *toumans'* withdrawal, when it came, was a ruse. Turning, they fought, attempting to enfold the Khwarismian army from the higher ground. Despite their efforts the day ended in stalemate and, leaving only their camp fires to hold the enemy, they pulled back during the night into the mountains.

Genghis Khan now sent further orders. Muhammad was in Samarkand, pleased with the victory over Jochi's army, yet carefully looking to his capital's defences. He was to be by-passed by Jebei, who had once again to strike across the grain of the country, clambering on through the Pamirs to descend on the headwaters of the Amu Darya (the Oxus in classical times, simply the Amu in today's Soviet Union). Once again Jebei's column marched up into the snows. Jochi, meanwhile, with reinforcements of five thousand men, swung away in a more northerly direction towards Khojend, on the Syr Darya (the River Jaxartes), a city east of Samarkand, south of Tashkent. Its governor, Timur Melik, withdrew into his central keep, a fortress on an island in the river. At almost the same moment, Chagatei and Ogadei, Jochi's brothers, appeared with a vast horde outside the gates of Otrar, a city which, under the threatened Inalchik – who had, perhaps, been the cause of all this trouble – settled down to a desperate defence. They at least had nothing to hope for from Mongol magnanimity.

Now, with those two sieges in progress, Jebei struck, west of where Muhammad waited. Desperately the beset monarch sent reinforcements to the valley of the Amu Darya, where the dreadful smoke of Mongol depredations rose above every town and village in their path, a heavy curtain that hid from view the southern mountains. Beyond these, in Afghanistan and Khorasan, new armies were being raised; if Jebei captured the valley provinces, Muhammad would be cut off from his own reinforcements.

While these desperate battles were in progress, holding the fate of his dynasty and state in balance, Muhammad received news that must have seemed to him incredible. Far to the west, come as if out of the skies after which he had named his people, Genghis Khan himself had appeared at the head of a ravening horde. How had he got there? Where had he come from? The answer was the same as so often before – the Mongols simply did not recognize the impassable. They had crossed the Kyzyl Kum Desert, a fearsome tract of land south of the Aral Sea, their army led by suborned Turkish guides – 'that knew not clean from unclean', as the Muslim historian Javaini takes the time to point out – and were now, from this unexpected quarter, seething towards Bokhara.

In battle, the Mongol leader liked to give his enemies an escape route, the better to cut them down as they fled. Now he did the same. Bokhara's garrison fled through the gate left so helpfully unguarded. In the open, the Mongol horsemen struck. Some twenty thousand men had been left to defend this great trading city; almost to a man they perished miles from the safety of their ramparts. To quote Javaini once more: 'When these forces reached the banks of the Oxus, the patrols and advance guards of the Mongol horde fell upon them and left no trace of them. . . .' The people, thus untended, surrendered. Soon the Khaghan himself was addressing them: they had committed great sins, he told them, assembled apprehensively in the great summer prayer space before the town, listening with the strained attention of the condemned to his interpreter. 'If you ask me what proof I have for these words,' he said, 'I say it is because I am the punishment of God.' When he had finished haranguing them, he appointed tax-gatherers, group by group, and so began the hard bargaining of conquest: 'Your money or your life!'

War, not booty, was his main concern, however. He forced the stubbornness of the last citadel with fire, he burned by accident or design much of the rest of that gracious city of gardens, trees, cool houses, craftsmen and rich merchants, he forced the population to smash their own defences and fortifications, to fill in their moats and dykes. When the work was done, Bokhara posed no further threat to the Mongol advance. Genghis marched on towards Samarkand. In Khorasan a refugee, asked to tell what had happened in Bokhara, replied with admirable succinctness: 'They came, mined, burnt, killed, plundered and left.' It was the authentic voice of those who had experienced the Mongols.

In Samarkand Shah Muhammad could see nothing but enemies wherever he looked: Jochi east of him, Chagatei and Ogadei to the north, somewhere to the south the rampaging forces of Jebei and now, advancing ominously from the west, Genghis Khan. His outlying fortresses fell one after the other. In Khojend, Jochi stretched a causeway to where Timur Melik still held out. Timur fought back with catapult and boat-borne sallies, then fled down the river. The Mongols had laid a

Mongols watch the departure of the inhabitants of captured Balkh. These citizens were fortunate – they capitulated without resistance. Using terror as a potent weapon, Genghis Khan ordered that where his forces were opposed, the enemy's defeat should invariably be followed by massacre. Only instant surrender guaranteed mercy.

chain across the stream, but the desperate flotilla rode over it, broke through it, escaped. Soon Timur Melik was speeding southwards to join Jelal ud-Din and the army he was raising. At Otrar it took five months for the garrison to break. Every man was killed or taken prisoner and, once a prisoner, made a slave. Inalchik fought to the end; nothing else was left to him. When the walls were breached he retreated to the citadel. When the citadel fell, he fought the invaders floor by floor. On the roof, his last arrow gone, he flung tiles down on his pursuers. But he was taken, and brought to Genghis Khan; molten silver was ladled into his eyes and ears and he died at last in the contortions of his pain.

Muhammad fled, although Genghis Khan, now thoughtfully contemplating Samarkand's inhospitable walls, did not hear of it at once. Remarking, 'Walls are as strong as the courage of their defenders,' he sent Jebei, Subatei and his son-in-law Toguchar with one *touman* each in pursuit of the fleeing Shah, then set himself to invest the vast city. Behind its walls and towers, half a million people cowered, their riches useless, their trust placed of necessity in the strength of stone and the courage of their hundred thousand Turkish defenders. Trust was to have short shrift. It did not take long for the Mongols, their armies now combined outside the gates, to smash their way into the city. The garrison attempted to break out, but was held, cut down, the survivors finally swept back. Then the citizens turned on their protectors; sometimes old cruelties come home to roost – seven years earlier Samarkand's own Khan, Osman, had been treacherously killed by Shah Muhammad, a crime that the people had not forgotten. Seeing no point in further resistance, thirty thousand Turkish soldiers defected to the Mongols. Genghis Khan, who had a way with traitors, ordered them to be executed to the last man. The rest of the garrison shut itself in the citadel, while the citizens under their own leader, the Sheikh-ul-Islam, flung open their gates to the invaders. Had the Mongols not lifted oppression from the backs of the Muslims of Kara-Khitai? Why should they not prove equally generous now? The Khaghan, a man who used fear and gratitude as his personal weapons, responded by giving the fifty thousand Muslim families their freedom. The remainder of the population, which had tried to resist him, he had driven out on the plain. He picked out artists, artisans, labourers, warriors willing and able to serve under his standard; the rest he had killed. In a fountain of flame, the citadel fell. So Samarkand was captured, a city and a fortress that the whole country had expected to hold out for a year. Genghis Khan, with terror, diplomacy, energy and discipline, had taken it in three days.

Far to the south, Muhammad and his pursuers played their deadly game of hide-and-seek. The Shah fled to Balkh, then to Merv. To him it must have seemed as though he were only a step or two from the edge of some constantly crumbling cliff; even as he left Merv, he learned that Balkh had surrendered without so much as a token resistance. Genghis Khan's policy was reaping its harvest. The whole country had heard of how the Muslims of Samarkand had been treated, of how those who had remained in the lands that the Mongols now administered found themselves in the firm but far from unkind grip of an unbiased justice. Everywhere religious tolerance offered a new security to an area criss-crossed by a multiplicity of faiths. People who had suffered under the sometimes capricious and always feeble rule of the Khwarismian Shah found themselves secure again for the first time in years.

The fair-minded ordinances that brought Genghis Khan the approbation of his new subjects were largely based on the counsel of Yelui Ch'u ts'ai, his attendant sage. But the orders that put them into operation were those of the Khaghan, and they applied to everyone. In order to turn the people against the Shah, he had insisted that the three *toumans* pursuing Muhammad should neither kill unnecessarily, nor pillage. Those who surrendered were to be treated with generosity; only those who resisted were to feel the fury of Mongol retribution. All obeyed – until his son-in-law looted a town that had already surrendered to Jebei. A common soldier brought the Khaghan's icy sentence: reduction to the ranks, his *touman* to be merged with that of Jebei's. It was as a ranker, one cavalryman among others, that Toguchar died outside the walls of Nishapur.

> Genghis Khan rides into battle. He was not only a brave
> leader, but also one of great resource. Almost invariably
> his forces were outnumbered; almost invariably some
> unexpected manoeuvre more than redressed the balance.

واشان انیز برند و بکر یزانند و ان صفاف غایت مردی و ان صفاف عایت مرد و ماه ار بود خالی هسور مین هولان جلد خسلیرچان لهجویتان دابان لردوهیم
شورست و نامداران غتای وحی رجه دراز خیک ست شذ نذ

وحسنگک خان آز آنجا کاسیاب و کام از پاز کشت و خرابرهنگ ان کا اورا کونه بنی و مبرده بر سیند و کنیاز نجه بندی نوریسند له دریش جم

His death was in vain; the town stood firm, and had in any case seen the fleeing Muhammad depart three weeks before. Westward the Shah hurried, half-offering to fight, toying with the command of this force, then of that, finally travelling on again, leaving in his wake demoralization and a trail of swift surrender. Near the city of Rai (not far from today's Teheran) thirty thousand Persian troops at last gave Jebei and Subatei battle. The Mongol tactics of arrow flight and charge broke them; it was the people of Rai who paid the price in loss, rape and murder. Westward again, to Hamadan, where pursuers at last caught up with pursued – but without actually realizing that they had done so. A skirmish, a Mongol patrol swooping down on a cavalry detachment, the whirr and thrum of arrows, a white horse fleeing, its rider bowed in the saddle, blood blackening his sleeve – the Shah had been wounded, nearly caught, but had escaped again.

His route was northwards now, to the shore of the Caspian and beyond. It was on a small island that he settled, his last empire this tiny circle of earth and scrub, death his palace, his poverty so dire that he had not even a shroud to wear as he entered it. Coming so soon after his forces had threatened the Crusaders of the West as they struggled in the Mediterranean basin, his death let loose a zig-zag flight of rumours across Europe. Prester John, the legendary emperor, the hidden Christian, the elusive joker in the worn Crusader pack, had struck after all. Risen in glory and might from his secret domains in the heart of Asia, he had lifted pagan pressure from the warriors of the True Faith. The hallelujahs of delight were heartfelt; it would be some time before Europe realized how misplaced they were.

It was January 1221. Genghis Khan, in the meantime, had been using the attack on Termez, a city on the Amu Darya, as a laboratory for the new and bigger siege-engines perfected by his son Ogadei. It took eleven days for the garrison, cowed by the stones and flaming pots of naphtha flung at them over the walls, to surrender. Yet it was not only war that occupied the Khaghan – he listened moodily to the views of the Muslim *mullahs*, then reiterated his belief in religious tolerance. 'Under my rule everyone may pray to any god he pleases,' he decreed – adding, however, that his were the only secular laws to be obeyed. At Yelui Ch'u ts'ai's prompting, he sent for the Taoist sage, Ch'ang-Ch'un, an elderly recluse living in the Shan-tun Mountains; the invitation forced the hermit out into the world on a journey that took him from eastern China to the plains of Persia. ('I am old and infirm and fear I shall be unable to endure the pains of such a long journey,' he wrote to Genghis. 'Public affairs and affairs of war are not within my capacity. . . .' But the Khan's emissaries made him travel nevertheless.) The interest Genghis took in the sage was not entirely philosophical, however; Ch'ang-Ch'un was one of the most respected seekers of the *tan*, the philosopher's stone, which was believed to hold the secret not only of the transmutation of metals, but of immortality itself. As it happened, both these old men, wise in such different ways, were to die in the same month; it is unlikely that the Khaghan's anxiety over the future of his family and people, which had first prompted him to ask the hermit's advice, had been to any extent allayed.

'I am the punishment of God,' Genghis Khan tells the inhabitants of Bokhara after the capture of their city. He speaks from the pulpit overlooking the open space cleared for summer prayers. Their garrison of twenty thousand having been cut down almost to a man, one may assume the people heard his sermon with great attention.

What is clear is that in the tone of that invitation we can discern across the centuries something of Genghis Khan's great charm, his proper pride and proper humility, his awareness of himself and of his limitations.

I hate luxury and exercise moderation [he wrote]. I have only one coat and one food. I eat the same food and am dressed in the same tatters as my humble herdsmen. . . . In the space of seven years I have succeeded in accomplishing a great work, uniting the whole world in one empire. I have not myself distinguished qualities. . . . But as my calling is high, the obligations incumbent on me are also heavy and I fear that in my rule there may be something wanting. To cross a river we need boats and rudders. Likewise we invite sages and choose assistants to keep the empire in good order. . . . I implore thee to move thy sainted steps. Do not think of the extent of the sandy desert. Commiserate with the people in the present situation or have pity upon me and tell me the means to preserve life. . . .

Thus the Khan of Khans, the Emperor of the Steppes, ruler of northern China, overlord of Korea and Manchuria, conqueror of all the lands between the Yellow River and the River Oxus, to an old monk dwelling in holy solitude on the slopes of a remote mountain range.

Not that Genghis had forgotten the war. He had sent his three oldest sons west-ward to the Khwarismian heartlands, south of the Aral Sea and east of the lower Amu Darya; to watch them and report on their accomplishments and deportment, he sent Bogurchi as their chief-of-staff. Clearly he was thinking seriously about the succession. At the same time he took to heart one of his own ordinances: 'When there is no war raging, there shall be hunting; the young shall be taught how to kill wild animals so that they become used to fighting. . . .' He organized a huge hunt that occupied the Mongol army for four months and was reported in awestruck terms by its Persian observers.

The method was simple in theory, horrendously difficult in practice. A vast outer ring was marked out, called the *nerkeh*. Here the drive began; bit by bit every animal within this area was driven inwards, despite every hazard of terrain and without a single man being allowed to use a weapon. Only when an incredible accumulation of game had been herded into an inner ring, the *gerkeh*, was a kill permitted. By then, nervous, furious and desperate, the tigers, the great boars, the leopards and bears they hunted were as dangerous as any human enemy who might meet them in the field. In the meantime their manoeuvres across scrubland or scree, through forest and ravine, had sharpened their skills both as horsemen and as tacticians.

To the west, Jochi and Chagatei were quarrelling. Genghis Khan immediately placed the gentler, more diplomatic Ogadei, a drinker, a convivial man, but keenly intelligent, over both of them. His conciliatory skill soon brought about peace in the Mongol camp. While his sons' war thus continued, the Khaghan demanded the return of his most valued lieutenant, Subatei. Wrapped like an 'arrow rider', this corpulent commander covered 1200 miles in just over a week, changing horses every 35 miles and eating and sleeping in the saddle as he made his non-stop charge across the plains and plateaux of Persia. What the Khaghan wanted was information, and the sort of analysis only the experienced eye of an *orlok* could make. Subatei told him about the western state of Khorasan, assured him that no Persian army was active there, nor was there any sign of the only enemy force now being spoken of – the levies being raised by Jelal ud-Din in Afghanistan. In Iraq, further to the south-west, wealthy and heavily populated,

Yuan period drawing of a Mongol with his horse. The pony's tail
is bound and leather stirrups await the rider. These gave Mongol
cavalry a steadiness in the saddle which the knights
of Western chivalry never matched until they, too, adopted them.

there were no reports of military activity either; even if an army was being raised
there in the Shah's cause, it would have a difficult time reaching Khorasan, since
the route was open only in spring and autumn – winter was too cold and summer
too dry.

But the *orlok* had other news, too – raiding beyond the Caspian, his men had discovered a completely different race of men, a people with long, narrow faces, light
hair and round blue eyes. In order to see them better, and to explore the lands that
lay to the west of Kipchaks, Subatei proposed returning to Mongolia by travelling
west and north around the Caspian, before swinging eastward again. These were
the regions Genghis had long ago given to Jochi, the lands west of the River
Irtysh, and so he agreed to Subatei's plan, stipulating only that his journey should
take no more than three years. For Genghis was pleased with the information his
*orlok* had brought him. With no army poised anywhere in Persia to launch an attack
against him, he was free to move his own forces wherever he wanted – even on a
reconnaissance into Europe.

In Khwarism itself, the city of Urganj had all this while held out against Mongol
attack. Ogadei had tried to use his siege-engines, but the land was flat and feature-

less, here in the delta country of the Amu, and there were few suitable rocks. He tried to storm the walls, but was bitterly repulsed. Sallying forth, the garrison trapped a detachment of three thousand Mongols and left not one of them alive. Ogadei ordered the river to be diverted, but the townsfolk dug wells and so kept up their water supply. In the end fire decided the day, a punishing barrage of blazing naphtha. After seven days of fighting, street by street, the city fell. Most of the population was slaughtered, and when the fires had died down the river was once more diverted. Sweeping through the burnt and battered town, it flushed out the last dazed survivors from their cellar hiding places.

Elsewhere, and especially in Khorasan, the narrowness of human nature now faced the Khaghan with new opposition. The Muslims, convinced in their religion, began to express their resentment of the very tolerance that ensured their own freedom of worship. Since they were manifestly right, such acceptance of their beliefs was only proper; that it should extend to others seemed to them a crime against God. Everywhere, they arose in desperate insurrection. In response Genghis launched his son Tuli in a war of extermination. Thriving towns with populations of tens of thousands were stormed, burned, annihilated. Young women were enslaved, artisans were conscripted, the healthy males were turned into coerced shock troops, men who had to fight in the Mongol van or be cut down by those who followed them. His siege-train had three hundred catapults hurling stones of up to a hundredweight, seven hundred mangonels dispensing the searing naphtha in its pots, three thousand mobile launchers sending burning arrows into the roofs of the beleaguered. Merv held out against him for three weeks, Nishapur for three days. In Herat he uncharacteristically spared the population; when it rose again after his departure, Genghis sent another army, remarking icily to its commander: 'Since the dead have come to life, I command you to strike their heads from their bodies.' When the Mongols finally marched away, forty tattered survivors were all that crept from the ruins. Yet its garrison alone had numbered a hundred thousand men.

When, outside the fortress of Bamian, invested by Genghis Khan during his own campaign in the foothills of the Hindu Kush, he learned that his favourite grandson, Chagatei's son Moatugan, had been killed, his revenge was so terrible that even a century later nothing grew and no one lived in a valley once noted for its beauty and fertility. (When Chagatei returned from his campaign, the Khaghan sternly asked whether he would obey his every command; on his knees Chagatei swore he would. 'Your son is dead,' Genghis said. 'I forbid you to weep and complain.' Chagatei never did.)

Jochi, still offended at having had Ogadei elevated above him, withdrew northwards once the Khwarismians had been subjugated. But the really bad news came from the south. Jelal ud-Din had appeared with an army at Ghazni, in Afghanistan, and had defiantly destroyed a large Mongol detachment. Genghis sent the just Shigikutuku against him, but for once a Mongol force found itself facing a commander both resolute and competent. The luxury of inferior numbers that the Mongols could usually permit themselves brought them to grief on this occasion. Setting dummies on his reserve horses, the *orlok* tried to make his thirty thousand men look more. Jelal ud-Din, after an initial hesitation, refused to let himself be deceived; for the first time in this campaign, a Mongol army had to flee. Perhaps the tide might have turned then and history been altered, but Jelal ud-Din was a tactician, not a strategist. He wasted time on celebration – included in which was the torture of Mongol prisoners – and allowed himself to be drawn into the disputes of his chiefs. When Genghis Khan and his three sons approached across the mountains and valleys of Afghanistan, he began to withdraw.

Cornered at last, with the Mongols in a half-circle about his levies and the Indus at his back, Jelal ud-Din had to fight – and almost won, although this was one of the few occasions when a Mongol army outnumbered its opponents. He struck with energetic savagery at the Mongol centre; as it staggered, threatening to break, Genghis Khan riposted with one of those moves that, by their very unlikelihood, displayed his genius as a commander. He sent ten thousand men over mountains that appeared to give the Khwarismian flank complete protection. Struck in this unexpected manner from the impossible direction, Jelal ud-Din's army reeled. The Mongol centre rallied, attacked with recovered courage. Yet again Jelal ud-Din charged, leading the last seven hundred men of his own guard, all that remained to him; desperately he took back the colours that the Mongols had captured. Genghis Khan had ordered that he should be taken alive, but heroes are difficult game. Whirling about, he raced for the edge of the low cliffs that overhung the river. Without hesitation, horse and rider leaped outwards into air. How high was that famous leap, remembered over centuries in poem and story? Some say twenty feet, others fifty, others seventy; it hardly matters. It was high enough, and the bravery of the escape was recognized at once by all who witnessed it, for the Khaghan himself gave the order to stop shooting, the Khaghan himself prevented his men from taking up the pursuit. Jelal ud-Din had earned his safety. 'One cannot believe,' Genghis remarked, 'that such a father could have produced such a son!'

Jelal ud-Din fled into India, leaving behind him the collapse of his father's empire. Sullenly, with occasional uprisings, the people accepted their fate, although it took the massacres at Ghazni, Herat, Merv and Balkh to convince them. A Mongol column marched into India, capturing Multan and Lahore, but the heat of the Punjab plains drove it back again into the mountainous north of the country. By this time, however, it was the summer of 1222 and Genghis Khan had a new pre-occupation – his visitor from China, Ch'ang-Ch'un. One senses through the stilted accounts and cool translations the monarch's pernickety concern, his curiously anxious respect for the philosopher. Having expressed his gratification that Ch'ang-Ch'un had accepted his invitation after he had refused those of both the Kin and Sung emperors, he ordered a meal for the sage. No sooner had his visitor eaten than Genghis posed his first and most important question: 'Have you a medicine of immortality?'

Li Chi ch'ang, the disciple who accompanied the Taoist hermit, records Ch'ang-Ch'un's reply: 'There are means for preserving life, but no medicines for immortality.' The philosopher seems on the whole to have been somewhat unforthcoming with the monarch – perhaps out of a genuine indifference, perhaps to hint at the unwisdom of Genghis Khan's impatience, perhaps to display his own irritation at having been dragged so high-handedly across Asia. It was in any case much later, installed in Samarkand, that he took up again the tutoring of this imperious, yet curiously humble, monarch. Asked by Genghis how he might ensure the permanence of his empire, he mentioned the fragility of whirlwinds, the transience of storms. 'If neither heaven nor earth can achieve permanence, how much less can man do so?' As to government, it was a task of delicacy and balance, 'like the roasting of small fish. . . . Only one who is just to all his subjects is a good ruler'. Gratifying though it is to be addressed by a noted sage, and catholic as Genghis was in his religious and philosophical attitudes, one suspects that for all his politeness he was beginning to feel a little cheated.

Taoism had long been known for what he had invited Ch'ang-Ch'un to teach him, the techniques of avoiding death. He had imagined this to be a medicine; in fact, of course, what was involved was a profound spiritual and physical self-discipline. Only in contemplation could the adept become aware of the essential oneness of the universe, the very essence of the single path: the Tao itself. The wise and the happy, therefore, allow the Tao free play by avoiding action – the best governors, in short, are those who reject the direct business of governing. Genghis Khan, establishing his local overlords and tax collectors (incidentally exempting the Muslim *imams* for the first time from all imposts), is unlikely to have considered this doctrine to be of any great practical value.

Nevertheless, although Ch'ang-Ch'un wanted to go home, the Khaghan insisted that he should remain to teach his doctrine to his sons. He called a *kuriltai* – the first that had no precise military significance – and beside the Syr Darya awaited his offspring in a magnificent camp. Much of his new state had been unwillingly put on, for he had little taste for the garnishings of power; the thing itself was perhaps too real for him to enjoy its masks. Others are different, as Yelui Ch'u ts'ai understood very well; it was at his prompting that Shah Muhammad's golden throne stood in a gold-adorned pavilion of silk and brocade. For ordinary people power exists when it manifests itself with a theatrical brilliance and it was necessary that everyone should realize the extent of Genghis Khan's achievements, the resonance of his majesty. For the Khaghan himself, however, other matters were more important – Ogadei arrived, and Chagatei, but Jochi, with apparent stubbornness, sulked in the north, his messages telling of illness, an inability to travel. As a gift he sent twenty thousand of the dappled horses of Kipchak, but Genghis wanted to see him, his eldest son.

Subatei came back from the west with tales of battle, victory and arduous journey – and with the sadder news of the death of Jebei, Genghis Khan's long-time lieutenant, won to loyalty from the ranks of the enemy, named 'The Arrow' after the shot that nearly killed the man who became his master, himself dead now, not in battle but of fever, somewhere to the west of Turkestan. There would be worse news, however. Genghis Khan's disappointment at Jochi's absence turned to anger, to a white fury. If duty could not bring him, arms would. He began to prepare for war, whisper of internecine campaigns to come. A new message forestalled him: Jochi had died, sick, weak, fading in his tent.

For two days the Khaghan sat alone in his great pavilion. Perhaps Ch'ang-Ch'un might have comforted him, but the Chinese ancient was already homeward bound, his will to return greater even than that of Genghis Khan's to keep him. The Khaghan's sorrow was deepened by the injustice of his recent anger; now he remembered his son's pride with fondness. He must also have pondered mortality again and the problems of his succession. It was wearily that he set out, eastward, homeward, cheered only when, on the very frontiers of Mongolia, he met his two youngest grandsons, proudly celebrating their first kill as hunters: Kubilai, Hulagu, the first nine and the other eleven, their names to clang in history at the two ends of Asia, but for the moment still children puffed with delight at their exploit. He smiled, and rubbed their thumbs ceremonially in the blood of the hare and the hart they had killed. Perhaps he saw once again the future stretching away through the centuries, his dynasty assured.

In the east, the Mongols' war continued. Mukhali had died in 1223, but his son Buru continued as commander of his *toumans*; his father's sole regret as he died was that he had failed to take the Kin emperor's southern capital. 'That is left for you to do,' he told his son. Genghis Khan, however, had a task he thought of much greater importance. When he had first set out to avenge Muhammad's treatment of his envoys, he had sent for aid from his allies and his vassals; the King of Hsi-Hsia had refused, the only one to do so. He had replied with impertinent logic that if the Khaghan's own army was not strong enough to fight his wars, perhaps he had better not fight them at all. Now, although that King had died and another sat on the throne, the time had come to make the response such a reply deserved. Nor would it be a moment too soon – the Kin too had a new Emperor, Shu-hsu, under whom resistance had stiffened; soon, it was said, he and the disaffected King of Hsi-Hsia would come to an agreement.

Only a year of rest had passed for the army and its Khan when Genghis, now over sixty, led out 180,000 men. In his last campaign in Hsi-Hsia he had made the mistake, which he hoped that his accompanying sons and grandsons would take to heart, of ending the fighting before his enemies had been beaten to their knees; now that sin of omission would have to be rectified. He was injured, perhaps in a skirmish, more probably in a fall, but rode doggedly on. No urging to turn back could move him. Every day since the campaign against Shah Muhammad had begun, he had remembered with fury Hsi-Hsia's betrayal. Nothing now would prevent his revenge.

Confusing his Tangut enemies by this time taking a different route across the Gobi Desert, he erupted out of the wilderness on the country's north-western borders. In March 1226 he took Etsina; a few weeks later his forces were in Kan-chou, then in San-chou; within months they had overrun much of the fertile areas and were in Liang-chou, to the east. Autumn was settling on the land now and the thin winds sharpened their cutting edge in readiness for winter. The Mongols approached the Tangut capital, Chung-hsing. Ying-li, sixty miles south of it, fell to them; when they laid siege to Ling-chou, less than twenty miles away, Genghis Khan, who had been resting with some of his forces, once again took command.

Winter hardened the landscape. The rivers stilled under steely ice. Snow hurled down on mountain gales. The King of Hsi-Hsia sent an army of three hundred thousand men south, to relieve the siege of Ling-chou. The Mongol army retreated, as though overawed by such strength set in the field against them. Encouraged, the Tangut cavalry swept forward – they would clutch now at the victory that had for so long eluded them. They struck out across the ice-field that was the winter version of the Yellow River. But temerity and civilization undid them. Their horses were shod; on the ice metal found small purchase. Tangled, tumbling, slewing from side to side, the Tangut horses halted in their charge. And while they hung there – one can hear the yells curl through the freezing air, see the steam rise from the nostrils of beast and rider – the unshod ponies of the Mongols whirled without hindrance across the treacherous surface.

The Tangut turned for their own bank – but too slowly and too late. Even as they tried to rejoin the horrified ranks waiting there, a new whirlwind struck. A second

Winter, hardening the plains and
freezing the rivers, gave the armies of
Central Asia great mobility.
Here a force is seen crossing the Jaxartes.

force of Mongol cavalry had swung wide and across the ice; now it swept, darker than any blizzard, into the Tangut army's flank. Hammered sideways, unit after unit recoiled, each breaking before being forced upon the next, all giving ground, disorganizing all formation, their confused attempts to disentangle themselves, to turn, reform and fight, only compounding their confusion. And as they swung and veered, a directionless welter of men and animals and weapons, survivors from the detachments that had been sliced open and dismembered far out on the ice were hurled upon them by the Mongol charge. A moment later, that charge itself was on them. All order vanished. Turning this way and that, stampeding through their reserves, assailed from every direction, the Tangut army died.

The King of Hsi-Hsia fled into the mountains; in the plains and valleys he had left, the smoke of his people's tribulation rose from every town, every village. Whole populations scattered, scrambling for refuge, hiding in the wilderness of foothill and scrubland, then clambering higher, into the crevices and black ravines of their mountains. Pursued, they were cut down. Their crops bent under a storm of hooves as Mongol riders destroyed their harvest. Trapped in an upland fort, their king died, his fall a symbol of their own.

The new Tangut ruler, Shidurgo, held out in his capital, proof so far against Genghis Khan's most advanced siege-engines. Ogadei, meanwhile, had been moved south, to face the Kin; another Mongol force subdued the far west of Hsi-Hsia; the Khaghan himself was stationed in the mountains east of Chung-hsing, a vantage point from which he could overlook and contain the movements of the Sung and the Kin, should either wish to move against him, as well as any attempt by the Tangut to link with their Chinese neighbours. It was the end for Shidurgo; asking only for a month's grace 'to prepare the handing over and to lead away the people of the city', as the Arab historian Rashid ad-Din reports, he made his submission.

But another end was close. Genghis Khan himself, old now, still suffering from the after-effects of his recent wound and weary almost past endurance, realized that he was dying. What had preoccupied him for so many years had now become an urgent problem. He had to nominate, or at least suggest, one of his sons to succeed him. He had already divided his enormous empire among them. Chagatei would own the west – Kara-Khitai, the old Khwarismian empire south of the Aral Sea, the territory of the Uighur people; northwest ran the rule of Jochi's son, Batu; the east would be Ogadei's – Hsi-Hsia, the as yet unconquered lands of the Kin and all the other captured territories of eastern Asia. Tuli, as the youngest, by Mongol tradition succeeded to the home, the heartlands: he would be Khan of Mongolia, commander of its puissant army. Yet this partitioning was like deciding on a federation without determining its head, its unifying principle. To hold together, it would need a new Khaghan whom all would follow. Genghis underlined his anxiety with a parable, the story of two serpents, the first with many heads and one body, the other with one head and many bodies. When winter came, the serpent with the many heads could find no shelter on which all the heads could agree; they quarrelled, they snarled at one another, each head found its own crevice – left unheeded in the cold, the body froze to death. The other serpent pulled its several bodies under its one head, organized itself for winter and lived to see the spring. The moral was clear – there could be only one head if the empire was to survive. But who should it be?

All his sons had virtues, all had vices; none was a second Genghis. All were energetic, courageous, better than competent commanders. The weakest, the softest, was Ogadei, a self-indulgent man who drank too much, but a man of clear intelligence and conciliatory purpose, a man who listened, who charmed those about him, who could direct their virtues to the best advantage. He was, in short, a born chairman. In this convocation of magnates that Genghis Khan's sons and grandsons had become, it was a chairman that was needed, someone who knew how to bend when necessary, who could see the difference between the stone walls of pride and the open gates of compromise. It was Ogadei who, the dying Khaghan said, should follow him as the ruler of the conquered world. He knew, however, better than anyone, since the law was his own, that it was only the *kuriltai* that could pick the next Great Khan. Until that time arrived, Tuli should be regent.

Weakening, he kept the keenness of his brain. Once again he urged his family to agree, to act in concert. He made each break one arrow, then watched as one after the other they tried and failed to break a quiverful at once. 'You will be as firm as that if you all hold together. Believe nobody, never trust an enemy, help and support each other in life's dangers, obey my laws, my *Yasak*, and carry every

Genghis Khan died while leading his armies to the
conquest of Hsi-Hsia. When the Mongols carried his
bier back for burial in the mountains of their
homeland, every living thing which crossed their path
was killed. Here the court and family of the Khaghan
are shown in attitudes of mourning about his coffin.

action you begin to its conclusion.' He had summed up his life's experience; now he sent all but Tuli away for the last time – they still had armies in the field to command, duties that called them. To Tuli he outlined the strategy of the campaign that would, he was confident, destroy the Kin. It involved exploiting the enmity of the Sung against their northern neighbours; Kin determination to hold their new capital, Kai-feng fu, at all costs; and the use of interior lines of communication.

On 18 August 1227 – for the Mongols, the fifteenth day of autumn's Middle Month in the Year of the Pig – Genghis Khan, to quote Rashid al-Din, 'left the transient world and left throne, property and rule to his famous family'. He had given his last orders only a few hours before: 'Do not let my death be known, do not weep or lament in any way, so that the enemy shall know nothing about it. But, when the king of the Tanguts and the population leave the city at the appointed time, annihilate them!' Even after his death he would see to it that what he started would this time be brought to its proper, terrible conclusion. As when he was alive, his people obeyed his orders; when the population had followed Shidurgo out of the gates of Chung-hsing, the Mongols rode in on them from every side and killed and killed, their sword arms rising and falling as though in dreadful celebration of their departed Khan. Shidurgo himself was brought to the great pavilion of Genghis, no doubt expecting audience; there, he and all his ministers and servants were slain.

Homeward, then; the mourning army set out from Hsi-Hsia – and during that march, as dreadful tradition demanded, nothing that was living was spared. Man, bird or beast was hunted down as though its witness of the Mongols' desolation had marked it for death. The body of the Khaghan was laid in state near the source of the River Onon, the banks of which had seen so much of Genghis Khan's early struggle for survival, power, wealth and fame. Then it was carried up the steep, wooded slopes of Burkhan Khaldhun, the tall bulk of which had overlooked his birth and rise and triumph. Near its peak stood a solitary tree; out hunting one day, the Khaghan had rested under it, looked about him and remarked: 'This is a good place for me to be buried. Take note of it!' His grave was dug there, and he was laid in it with the wagon that had carried his body northwards. Eight white tents were set up, pavilions for prayer and meditation, shrines to his memory. Tuli would be buried there, and later the dead of another generation, Kubilai and Mangu.

Then the trees grew and multiplied, history at last lowered Mongol pride, the tents shredded in the bitter winds, the once-solitary tree stood, then fell, one in the multiplicity of a forest. Now the very place is lost. For us, Genghis Khan has vanished, leaving only the thunderous memory of his name.

Book Two
THE
IMPERIAL
DESTINY

# 4 THE GREAT KHANS

Two years of mourning, during which the Mongols had to come to terms with their loss; with this period over, however, the time had arrived to come to terms with their future. The Kin fought on in the east, the Muslims seethed in the west, the Tangut waited sullenly in the south. Also, to east and west, further horizons offered the chance of further conquest. The world remained untamed; the Mongols had the skill, the manpower and the ambition to tame it. It was necessary to put their affairs in order, elect their new Khaghan and reach for their further destiny.

The *kuriltai*, held for the first time at Karakorum, a place of buildings on the banks of the River Orkhon, the first true city of the Mongols, proved at first more difficult than Genghis Khan might have hoped. His sons were wilful and ambitious, rulers in their own right over lands he had given them, and they were by no means certain that they wanted Ogadei set above them. Feasting ended, discussion began; day succeeded day without resolution. Juvaini, in his *History of the World-Conqueror*, suggests that it was only tradition, Ogadei's formalized expressions of unfitness, that held up the decision, but it was all less polite than that. Finally, it was Yelui Ch'u ts'ai, still the chief minister and the living repository of Genghis Khan's intentions, who forced the issue. It was this day or never, he insisted, the moment was auspicious and would not return; it was time that Chagatei, as the eldest surviving son, prostrated himself and swore homage to the new Khaghan. 'This,' the old Khitan sage said firmly, 'was the command of Genghis Khan!' The potent name retained its force. Chagatei made his ceremonial submission and all the rest, brothers of Ogadei, nephews and *orloks*, followed his example.

Armies were sent westward, where Jelal ud-Din had reinvigorated the remnants of the Khwarismian empire; three *toumans* were set aside to contain him. Three more marched further, out of Asia altogether, into the lands that Subatei and Jebei had reconnoitred. The rest of Mongol strength turned south-eastward, to subjugate the Kin. By 1234, less than five years after he had become the Khaghan, Ogadei could announce the final capitulation of the Kin, the fall of their capital and the end of twenty-four years of war.

Later there would be other, equally successful campaigns, and these will be described in due course: it is war, after all, for which the Mongols are remembered. But with the conquests that had taken place and the new lands that were year by year added to the Mongol empire, the Khaghan was becoming a figure of immense power and almost unlimited wealth, with a prestige to which the whole world responded. It is hard now to peer past the curtain of centuries and the haze of imperial state to see the actual person who occupied this position. What he was obscures who he was. Yet we know a little about Ogadei from the accounts of historians and travellers, and the picture we have is a not unattractive one.

The one fact about which everyone agrees is that he drank very heavily. He said as much himself and contritely informed Yelui Ch'u ts'ai that he would in future drink only half as many goblets of wine as in the past. He then doubled the size of his goblets, a move that perhaps sums up his character as well as any single act can. In 1234 he called an enormous *kuriltai* to celebrate the victories that his forces were winning; Rashid ad-Din tells us that Mangu, who would in time become Khaghan himself, recognizing the faults of Ogadei's character, dissuaded him from leading more military expeditions in order to free himself for 'spectacles and pleasure and amusement'. The young man went on: 'Otherwise what use are kinsmen and emirs and a countless army?' Accepting that 'emir' is the Arab version of *orlok*, it seems likely that Mangu had understood the limitations of the Khaghan's nature. He was of course a warrior, as they all were, but in this role he was not indispensable. Chagatei and Tuli were, and so increasingly were some of the younger men, the grandsons of Genghis, like Mangu himself; the *orloks*, and especially the mighty Subatei, had their warlike role to play. But there was a capital city now, Karakorum, and a throne, a centre to the Mongol world, and it was right that someone should occupy it. So when, in 1236, a huge Mongol force set off westward for the subjugation of Europe, Ogadei remained behind.

He busied himself with the conquests of peace. He began to build a palace worthy of the Mongols' altered condition. For his father, the felt tents of the nomadic past had always been good enough; now, with merchants and emissaries coming from the wide and unknown corners of a surprising world, they would do no longer. He constructed a building tall enough to symbolize – at least in the flattering descriptions – the loftiness of imperial thoughts. Each wing was as long as one bow-shot, and the building was decorated with a great variety of paintings and designs. The Chinese name for it was Wan-an kung, or the Palace of a Myriad Tranquillities, but to the Mongolians it was simply Qarshi, the Palace. Ogadei ordered his brothers, sons and nephews to build pavilions of their own nearby, and these, clustered together, joined and enclosed by walls, soon gave the city some of the dignity he wanted for it.

With his palace established, Ogadei settled into the routine of what seems to have been a delightful existence. Far away his armies struggled from victory to victory, leaving everywhere behind them massacre as the Mongol message to the world. In Karakorum the Khaghan journeyed from delight to delight, moving on as the seasons demanded. In Rashid's words, he 'concerned himself with merry-making, travelling happily and joyously from summer to winter residences and from winter to summer residences, constantly employed in the gratification of all manner of pleasures in the company of beauteous ladies and moon-faced mistresses. . . .'

About a day's journey from his capital Ogadei ordered skilled Muslim craftsmen to build him a pavilion. The place stood among lakes and here Ogadei amused himself by riding out, a hawk on his wrist (or perhaps on that of a falconer), or by standing before his pleasant bungalow to watch the scream and stoop of his birds. In summer he moved to the south-east, not far from the River Orkhon; there his felt tent would be set up, a splendid portable palace in itself, flashing with gold studs on the outside, brilliant within under the shimmer of its brocade lining. At the end of August he would move further south, and from there after a month or so would move again, to his winter quarters on the River Ongin. Here, protected by the Khangai Mountains from the cold winds that keened southward from the Pole, he would pass the time in hunting. Then the season would relent and spring would call him, first back to Karakorum, then out to his spring pavilion among the lakes of Gengen-Chaghan.

There was, however, another side to Ogadei, an aspect of his character that made him, in Rashid's words, 'on all occasions turn his august mind to the diffusion of justice and beneficence, the removal of tyranny and oppression. . . .' He was, the historian tells us, 'imbued with the fairest of dispositions and the noblest of qualities . . . exercising the utmost generosity and liberality toward all classes of men'. Rashid, of course, was commissioned to write his history by the Ilkhan Ghazan, a later Mongol prince five generations removed from Genghis, and this will have influenced what he wrote, yet the stories that come down to us suggest that Ogadei was a ruler both subtle and magnanimous.

There was a time when a poor man, weighed down by poverty and perhaps incompetence, made a set of clumsy needles simply by sharpening a few unsuitable pieces of iron. He presented these to the Khaghan as the latter passed by. The attendant to whom he gave them thought the needles too unwieldy, too ill-made, to hand to the Ruler of the World. Ogadei, however, made him go back to fetch them. 'They will do very well for the herdsmen to mend the seams of their *koumiss* skins,' he said, and rewarded the man with a *balish*, a 'pillow' or ingot, of precious metal.

On another occasion a Turk followed a Muslim who had bought a sheep, climbing up on the roof and watching the Muslim, secure as he thought in his own house, kill the sheep by slitting its throat. This, the prescribed method of slaughter according to Islam, was forbidden by the *Yasak* of Genghis Khan. The Turk leaped down, smashed his way into the house and dragged the unfortunate Muslim off to the court. Ogadei did not like what he could understand of the story; he sent officers to investigate more closely. Finally he let the Muslim go; the Turk was executed for breaking the *Yasak* by clambering on another's roof.

Then there was the fanatical anti-Muslim, a man who had seceded from that religion, who came to Ogadei with a story of having seen Genghis Khan in a dream. The great father of the present Khaghan had told him, he said, to order his son to kill as many Muslims as possible, for they were evil people. Ogadei thought about this for a moment, then asked mildly whether in the dream Genghis Khan had spoken in his own voice or through another's. 'In his own voice!' the man affirmed, without hesitation. Ogadei had him executed. The man spoke no Mongol; Genghis Khan had spoken nothing else.

Ogadei seems to have had a kind of calculating generosity, which often reckoned up the advantages of kindness. When he supported over and over again a somewhat reckless merchant whose function, as *ortaq*, was to invest a prince's money in trade, his advisers suggested that he ought to stop the man's credit. The *balish* he received, they said, he spent on entertainment and on worthless acquaintances. Ogadei, however, pointed out the ingots were still in existence and, circulating in his realm, were still in effect in his hands. When the city of T'ai-yuan fu petitioned him to help with its debt of eight thousand ingots, he mused: 'To force the creditors to be easy with these people will cause them to suffer loss; to do nothing will be to cause the

A Mongol coin, struck in north-western Persia during the thirteenth century. For a while, paper money was to supplant the Persian coinage, with disastrous results.

people distress.' He ordered the amount to be paid out of his treasury – Rashid points out sourly: 'There were many who pretended to be debtor and creditor . . . and so they received double. . . .' Those distraught under a burden of debts seem always to have found Ogadei sympathetic, although it is likely that he sometimes looked closely at their claims. Yet it is reported on one occasion that he saw in his strong-rooms nearly twenty thousand ingots of precious metal: 'What profit do we derive from storing all this, since it has to be constantly guarded?' He ordered that whoever wanted some should simply come and get what they needed.

He understood very clearly the effect such generosity would have on the people as a whole, and often upbraided his court advisers when they tried to hold up or diminish gifts and payments on which he had decided. Once when drunk he wrote a draft for two hundred ingots to be given to a stranger who had presented him with a Persian cap. Officials held up payment; he increased the amount. Again they delayed and again he increased the sum. When it had reached three times the original number of *balish*, he called the officials and asked them: 'Is there anything in this world that endures for ever?' Piously they agreed that there was nothing. 'You are wrong,' he told them sternly. 'Good repute and fair fame will endure for ever.' He ordered one or two of them to be punished for their obtuseness. On another occasion, he handed one of his entourage a *balish* with which to buy sweets from a little stall they were passing. The man gave a quarter of the ingot in payment, itself double the usual price. The Khaghan was angry. 'When in all his life has that stall-keeper ever had a customer like us?' he asked, and ordered that the merchant should be given the rest of the *balish* – and ten more besides.

That he was taken advantage of must have been obvious to all his court. No doubt they took advantage of him themselves. But he knew very well what the situation was. He explained it once after a falconer had brought in a falcon which, he claimed, was sick and could be cured only by the flesh of birds that he himself could not afford to buy. Ogadei ordered that he be given a *balish*; his officials so organized the payment that it could be used only for the prescribed therapeutic poultry. The Khaghan was furious when he heard. 'That falconer did not want a fowl; he used that as an excuse to get something for himself. Everyone who comes to us . . . I know they have each of them made a net in order to catch something. But I want everyone to have comfort from us and to receive his share of our fortune.'

At the same time, although he was always careful to keep the law of his father, Genghis, he permitted some of his magnanimity to seep into his judgements. Indeed one of the most famous stories about him concerns his complicity in perverting justice altogether on an occasion when, with his brother Chagatei, he observed a man washing himself in a stream. The law forbade this (one imagines for hygienic reasons, but Juvaini and Rashid claim that the Mongols believed it caused thunderstorms) and Chagatei, something of a stickler, insisted that the man should be arrested and punished. Ogadei, however, said it was late to sit in judgement – the morning would be better. The offender was locked away; secretly, Ogadei suggested the story he should tell – that all he owned had accidentally fallen in the water and he had been looking for it when falsely arrested. At the same time, the Khaghan gave instructions for a silver ingot to be thrown into the water at that spot. The moment for pleading came; men were sent to verify the story and of course returned with the *balish*. 'So this poor man has sacrificed himself for a wretched amount like this,' declared the Khaghan, outraged, and not only set him free, but gave him ten ingots more to go with the one he had so miraculously acquired.

Naturally, all this time Yelui Ch'u ts'ai remained at Ogadei's side, dealing with the complexities of imperial administration, leavening Mongol greed and occasionally Mongol cruelty with his own urbane mixture of expediency and firmness. It was his preference for taxation rather than plunder that led to the empire's fiscal and bureaucratic structures. Once, however, after the *kuriltai* of 1234, his master's generosity nearly destroyed what he was constructing. Ogadei had almost handed over wholesale the territories of the Kin, his beneficiaries a horde of clamouring princes, when his Khitan adviser stopped him. Stemming imperial munificence was no easy task, but Yelui was firm; at last, ruler and minister reached compromise. The nobles were not to take out of the conquered territories they now ruled more than was gathered by the normal tax collections. It was Yelui Ch'u ts'ai who best understood the philosophy behind Genghis Khan's use of massacre, his wielding or sheathing of the sword according to circumstance. When Kai-feng fu surrendered and the two million within its walls were to be killed, it was he who persuaded Ogadei that for the most potent effect it would be better to spare them. The subsequent collapse of all other opposition showed how well-judged his advice was.

Throughout the period of Ogadei's open-handed rule, the period of his dalliance with the moon-faced in palace or pavilion, his sifting through the silks and artifacts which merchants came thousands of miles to bring him – he always paid much more than their worth, then gave them away – his hawking and hunting and drinking, the Mongol armies were thrusting outwards, carving their frightful path across eastern Europe, clutching at the Mediterranean, grappling covetously with the Sung. It was as though he had set a machine in motion and now sat back while it faithfully continued its relentless rhythm. But in 1241 it came to an abrupt halt. Its mainspring had given way – Ogadei had died.

With his death there returned to Mongol affairs something that the blazing power of Genghis had managed to blot out for two generations – the plotting and planning, the subversions and betrayals of those with great ambition, mediocre ability and no conscience. In the west Jochi's son, Batu, and Kuyuk, Ogadei's son, had already unravelled Mongol single-mindedness in the heat of their rivalry. Kuyuk, the Khaghan's son, could not bear Batu's position as commander; Ogadei had had to call him back since his attitude was threatening the whole campaign along the Volga. Once released from the exigencies of war, he must have seemed a true offspring of his father, spending month after month in the easy pleasures of the camp; only the news that Ogadei was dead finally brought him back to Karakorum.

That news he had received in a letter from his mother, Turakina, a determined and subtle woman whom Ogadei had made regent on his death-bed. Batu might be the son of Genghis Khan's firstborn, but Kuyuk, she determined, should follow his father as Khaghan.

Almost at once her influence began to alter and corrupt the court. A nominee of hers named Abd al-Rahman usurped more and more of the functions of Yelui Ch'u ts'ai; indeed it was only the Khitan sage himself, strong in having been chosen by Genghis and having served without blemish for twenty-five years, who refused point-blank to take Abd al-Rahman's orders. Though tempted, even Turakina did not dare to provoke the opposition that his arrest would have caused; however his death, timely for her, allowed her to suggest he had taken bribes. At her orders his apartments were searched. He had the final vindicating laugh – his musical instruments, his collection of paintings, his books and the essays he himself had written were hardly the treasures she had expected. Nothing else was found. With his passing, nevertheless, her last obstacle had disappeared; day by day she worked Kuyuk further into a position that soon became impregnable.

Batu, when he heard of this, knew that his chance to become Khaghan had been swept from him. Yet he would not help to elect his rival. He remained in the west as the months dragged by, became years and these, too, began slowly to pass. With a defiant swagger he marched his armies down the Danube valley, to and fro about the Russian plains, sending back to Karakorum excuses and explanations that became constantly weaker. At the centre Turakina handed out largesse and re-coiled from all the unpopular duties of the ruler – after all, she had the coming *kuriltai* to think of: not to make enemies was her first duty if she wished her son to be elected. The empire was in danger of disintegration. Thus coerced, Batu sent his brother to vote in his place. The *kuriltai* could do as it pleased.

Vast and colourful, Genghis Khan dominated the great meeting. Pictures of him and his colossal doings decorated the fence of the central compound. At one gate, guards checked everyone who passed, for only the two thousand or so descendants of the first Great Khan were allowed in to vote. The other gate stood unguarded – it was the route through which the new Khaghan would step out into the world. And it was indeed the world that waited now. The *kuriltai* had drawn to it repre-sentatives of monarchs, princes in their own right, ambassadors of a dozen shimmering and half-legendary realms. The Caliph's emissaries had come from Baghdad, the chief of the Ismaili Assassins had sent his representatives, brocaded princes from China and Korea strutted in their state, the arrogant Prince Yaroslav of Kiev brought with him the last pride of the Varengi, those Vikings who over two centuries before had established his East European principality. Over four thousand ambassadors waited for the decision of these wiry, round-faced, thin-bearded people with their long surcoats and their rough sense of humour, waited to see the man who would, perhaps, within a few years come whirling out of these bleak plains, strike down their houses, scatter their names and annex their lands. Yet they waited, as the knife-edged winds slashed down from the north, until the moment when Kuyuk at last entered into the inheritance his mother had manufactured for him.

If Abd al-Rahman thought that he was now set fair for riches, installed as he had been as governor of Khitai, arrest and execution would surprise him. Kuyuk turned out to be very little like his father, despite the slightly laboured generosity

Turakina, mother of Kuyuk Khan, was Regent when this coin was struck in Tiflis. Her ambitions for her son caused much disruption in the court and administration of the Khaghanate.

with which he continued the tradition of imperial munificence. He proved to be hard, harsh, unapproachable, unsmiling. He was, Rashid tells us approvingly, 'filled with the arrogance of greatness and the haughtiness of pride', and he speaks too of 'the severity and terror of his justice'. Almost at once he repudiated the schemes of his mother; her over-shrewd slave, Fatima, who had been Abd al-Rahman's mistress and Turakina's confidante, he had arrested as a witch. 'She confessed after being beaten and tortured', Rashid says, 'her lower and upper orifices were sewn up and she was thrown into the river.' He took from the greedy princes the lands with which Turakina had bribed them, and restored both the edicts of his father and the wise men who had helped draw them up.

It is clear that he wanted the Khaghan to become the central authority in a much more organized structure than had been the case hitherto. He set limits on the despotism of his magnificent cousins, suzerains though they were of vast territories; he insisted that from the booty of all conquests a regular proportion should be paid to the imperial treasury; he reiterated the power and relevance of Genghis Khan's *Yasak*. He also curbed the free-booting propensities of the *orloks* and generals, who had a habit of levying their own private taxes as a reward for war's labours.

The bright glitter of his pride shines over one meeting that took place in his day, a curious and tentative attempt at building an intercontinental connection, doomed from the beginning by prejudice, incomprehension and arrogance. For among those at Kuyuk's electoral *kuriltai* were two men, almost certainly made uneasy by the bright, festive robes that had been thrown over their normal brown habits. They were the Franciscans Giovanni Carpini, known too as John of Pian, and Benedict of Poland; they were there as the emissaries of Pope Innocent IV. With them they had brought two papal Bulls, one introducing Friar Giovanni as a missionary whom the Khaghan should listen to closely in order to be able to follow 'his salutary instructions' and so come to 'acknowledge Jesus Christ and worship His glorious Name'; the other somewhat brusquely demanding an end of Mongol devastation of Christian lands.

The two friars had set out in 1245, Carpini already in his middle sixties and rather stout; they had been passed from region to region, chief to chief, Batu himself sending them on to Karakorum. From the moment they entered those lands where the Mongols held sway, no danger threatened them, there were frequent stages at which they changed horses, they slept easily at night. The organized peace of the Mongols had similarities with that, long past, of Rome. In four months, the friars crossed three thousand miles of mountain, plain and desert.

Carpini has left some descriptions of Kuyuk's newly formed court (it was the recently elected ruler's first audience), writing of a chamberlain named Chingei (presumably Ogadei's great Mongol minister, dismissed by Turakina, reinstated by her son) who announced the Khaghan's visitors in a loud voice, after which 'each of us had to bend the left knee four times, and they cautioned us not to touch the threshold, and having searched us carefully for knives . . . we entered the door on the east side, for no one dare enter on the west side save the Emperor. . . . It was while here that on a hill some distance from the tent there were more than five hundred carts, all full of gold and silver and silken gowns, all of which was divided up between the Emperor and the chiefs; and the various chiefs divided their shares up among their men as they saw fit.' In another tent, 'all of red purple', Carpini saw the Khaghan's throne on a high wooden platform: '. . . and the throne was of ebony, wonderfully sculptured, and there were also gold and precious stones and, if I remember rightly, pearls; and one went up to it by steps. . . .' He says little of the morose man at the centre of this magnificence, telling us only: 'This Emperor may be forty or forty-five years or more old; he is of medium stature, very prudent and extremely shrewd, and serious and sedate in his manners; he has never been seen to laugh lightly or to show any levity. . . .'

The unsmiling Kuyuk was not the man, perhaps, to be handed the kind of haughty demand a pope usually sent to the world's rulers. He knew little of the Pope, almost certainly thought him yet another monarch who needed to be taught his place and replied in terms that underline what is known of his own character.

A museum in today's Mongolia, this building preserves
the shapes once dominant in ancient Karakorum.

He took the Bull to be an offer of submission, made by the Pope after consultation with his vassal kings. 'If you act according to your word,' Kuyuk advised him, 'then come, great Pope, in person . . . and pay homage to us. We shall then instruct you in the commandments of the *Yasak*.' He referred to the Pope's suggestion that he should accept baptism: 'This request we cannot understand,' he wrote, dismissively. Turning to the Pope's demand that the Mongols should cease their destruction of Christian lands, he said that he did not understand that, either. It was, after all, quite plain to him that it had to be done – heaven itself had commanded that the world should be subordinated to the Mongol will. If the world refused, it had only itself to blame when the Khaghan's hordes punished it for its recalcitrance. They, for their part, were doing no more than the stated will of God. The Pope had himself spoken of God, assuming himself by virtue of his position to be on terms of some intimacy with the deity. Kuyuk did not know what his position was and refused to be impressed. 'How do you know whom God will absolve and whom He will show mercy? How can you think you know, that you use such words?'

Kuyuk then affirmed his own claims as World-Conqueror. 'Through the power of Heaven, all lands from sunrise to sunset have been given to us. . . . Now, however, you must say from a sincere heart: "We shall become your subjects, we will place our power at your disposal." You, in person, at the head of the monarchs, all of you without exception shall come to pay homage to us and offer your service. Then, we shall take note of your submission. If you do not obey the command of Heaven and act contrary to our orders, we shall know that you are our enemy.'

Ominously, the message ended with a warning – if the Pope did not do as he was asked, who could know what might happen to him? 'Only Heaven knows,' Kuyuk dictated – having, however, a fairly good idea himself, one imagines. Back travelled the Franciscans, their message strained through Mongol and Persian into Latin, their heads and notebooks full of the wonders of Mongol organization, Mongol ferocity and Mongol power. Above all they had picked up rumours of the new campaigns planned in the west. Europe faced such a storm out of Asia as might sweep it away. Carpini, with considerable foresight, warned that no European country on its own would be able to withstand the hordes that were already preparing. Only an alliance, a unified command, could defend Christendom. Meanwhile, in fear of the worst, whatever was precious should be packed away and hidden at once.

Still in the mid-forties of the thirteenth century, other Christian missions brought back messages and information underlining Carpini's fears. Ezzelino of Lombardy and André de Longjumeau travelled eastwards, the first as far as the Mughan Steppe, where he stayed in the camp of the local Mongol governor, Baichu, the second to Tabriz. Ezzelino (also known as Ascelin) seems to have been something of a zealot; his Christian arrogance made enemies of the Mongols and turned him into a buffoon. Baichu and his entourage seriously considered killing him and sending back his body, stuffed with chaff, as an indication to the Pope of what their views were. Mongols, however, did not murder envoys except in extreme circumstances; in the end, almost off-handedly, a party returned with him as ambassadors to Rome. Despite the message from Baichu that Ezzelino brought with him – 'The unalterable will of Heaven and the *Yasak* of the Khan who rules the world decide what we do. . . . Whoever fails to obey the *Yasak* . . . will be eradicated and annihilated' – the Pope treated these strange envoys well, presented them with furs, gold and silver and, though keeping the meetings strictly secret, spent long periods in conversation with them.

As for André de Longjumeau, he would be one of the central figures in a curious muddle of diplomacy and proselytizing zeal, compounded by the unexpected death of Kuyuk. For that morose man – most unlike his father in that drink drove him even further into gloom – had set out westward, either to begin the new drive into Europe so long prepared for or, more plausibly, to put down his rival Batu once and for all. Batu had also gathered his forces and begun to move towards his advancing cousin, either to make his submission to the new Khaghan or, more plausibly, to assert himself once and for all on the battlefield. The war that might have split the half-formed empire was, however, made redundant by mortality; on the other hand, Kuyuk's illness and unexpected death brought out into the open all the dynastic stresses that attend the problems of succession.

While the Mongols awaited the decision of a new *kuriltai*, Ogul-Gaimish, the dead Khaghan's principal widow, took over the regency. It was she who was in charge when the mission led by André de Longjumeau arrived. In 1248 Ilchikadei, the Mongol governor of Persia and Armenia, had sent envoys to Louis ix of France, then preparing in Cyprus for a campaign against the Mamlukes of Egypt. Ilchikadei was contemplating an assault on Baghdad and a certain measure of collusion between his army and that of the Crusaders' would have clear strategic advantages. His message had spoken of the tolerance offered to all Christians in the Mongol realms; the Nestorian envoys carrying it had gone further and spoken of Mongol princes ready to accept baptism, given a little persuasion from the West. Delighted, Louis had sent off his interpreter, André, with a gift for Kuyuk – a portable chapel of gold-edged scarlet, embroidered with scenes from the life of Jesus, the ornate furniture to go with it and a casket containing a fragment of the True Cross. With this, and a letter of exultant joy at his forthcoming conversion, André had made the long journey to Karakorum, only to be received with the news of his prospective convert's death. And worse was to come: the new regent blithely accepted Louis's gifts as what, given their sumptuousness, they could only be – symbols of Frankish subjugation and homage. Graciously she put together a few gifts of her own (including a sheet of Chinese asbestos that was to cause astonishment in Europe and end up, presumably because of its miraculous properties, in the vaults of the Vatican). In her message to Louis she expressed her pleasure at his acceptance of Mongol overlordship, urged him to pay his tribute regularly and, if possible, to come in person to do so the following year. One might have thought that such an unexpected outcome would have cured Louis of any further Far Eastern ventures, but this blue-eyed monarch, brought up in monastic discipline and due to be canonized for his Christian zeal, was to send yet another missionary across the steppes to Karakorum.

The Mongols, however, were less concerned with approaches from the distant lords of Christendom than they were with the immediate business of choosing their new Khaghan. Batu might now have snapped up this position, but there was a trace of indolence in this son of Jochi. His father had had his notable sulks and now Batu himself lurked in his western fief, plainly sufficiently pleased with its enormous size and endless fertility. He had no need to add the older half of the empire to the lands he had already seized; enough of his old rivalry remained, however, for him to insist that no one of Ogadei's blood should inherit the throne. This *diktat* from

Lamas brought the iconography of Tibetan Buddhism to Mongolia and China.

the west opened the way for Tuli's line, thus laying the foundations for the two reigns, that of Mangu and of Kubilai, which were perhaps the most magnificent in the whole century of Mongol cohesion and success.

The immediate reason for Batu's support of Mangu seems to have been the latter's acceptance of an invitation to the great camp on the Volga when all his cousins had refused. It was there, at a clan gathering of his own, that Batu promised him support; at the *kuriltai* that followed, in the hallowed shade of Burkhan Khaldhun, all the princes were present – except Batu himself and some of the most powerful among Ogadei's and Chagatei's descendants. These, covering the avoidance of duty under a smokescreen of pretexts so thin as to be insults in themselves, remained absent. There was delay, impatience and finally, prompted by the distant but powerful Batu, ultimatum. If they did not arrive to vote, the vote would be taken without them. This left legal problems for the future, but at least it got the business done. It was a united, if incomplete, assembly that at last elevated Mangu to his new greatness. The universe smiled – clouds that had covered the sky for days parted and, to the delight of the astrologers, the sun came out.

The result of this *kuriltai*, predictably, was a convulsion in the Mongol leadership. The disgruntled princes of the elder lines, when they finally appeared, had settled for conspiracy. The drunkenness of the feast would be their opportunity for murder. By chance a falconer who had lost his camel stumbled on one of their wagon-trains full of arms; horrified, he 'travelled three days journey in one', as Rashid tells us, and warned the celebrating Khaghan. At first no one believed him, since the breach of the *Yasak* involved was too appalling to contemplate. The truth, however, could not be avoided once investigation started. Mangu faced the need to begin his reign with an unprecedented act of internecine justice. Perhaps he remembered Genghis Khan's injunction to bring every action to completion; in any case, once his instinct for clemency had been overcome by the logic of dynastic security, he extirpated almost all the princes of Ogadei's line, and all the *orloks* and khans who had supported the conspiracy. Throughout his realm his minions travelled on a wave of arrests, judgements and executions. In the few areas where his wrath either missed its mark or was held back, his descendants would have cause to regret his inefficiency or mercy. Just as those who died accepted that their fate was just, so those who survived never wavered, despite the passage of the generations, in their allegiance to their own blood-line. But now even Ogul-Gaimish, her regency misused in this welter of plotting, was dragged naked into court – 'How can others see a body which has been seen by none but a king?' she demanded – questioned, sentenced, wrapped in felt and thrown into the river. The mother of Shiramun, once Ogadei's preferred heir, was dealt with in a similar way. The world had been cleared for Mangu to rule it.

Mangu was a conservative; Genghis Khan would have approved of him. Like his grandfather, he delighted in war and in that training-ground of war, the hunting field; little else really interested him, since he considered the culture of the city-bred a danger to rather than an enhancement of the Mongol traditions. State-craft, however, captured his full attention, nor did his personal puritanism much modify his magnanimity as a monarch. He prevented dignitaries, even in the service of great magnates, from making themselves an unnecessary burden on the people among whom they travelled; he limited or countermanded the many decrees lesser khans had issued since Kuyuk's death; he introduced graduated taxes which varied with the means of those who paid them, at the same time requesting the various grades of collector to 'tread the path of leniency and compassion'; he reaffirmed his detestation of bribery or partiality in those who administered the empire; he lifted from the peasantry the burden of arrears of taxes. Finally he paid in full merchants who had delivered goods not only to Kuyuk Khan, but also to his servants, sons and nephews, the total amount, we are told, being more than half a million ingots of gold and silver. As both Juvaini and Rashid ask, rather breathlessly: 'In what work of history is it told that one king paid the debt of another?' In the meantime Mongol armies pressed on westward under Hulagu, Mangu's brother. At the same time Kubilai, appointed governor of northern China and discovering an unexpected affinity with what were in effect his subjects, first consolidated Mongol rule about Kai-feng and then began the reduction of the Sung realms across the River Yangtze. From Syria to the China Sea, therefore, the word of Mangu ordered all men's affairs; from the foothills of the Himalayas to the frozen tundra of the Arctic his dictates settled human destiny. The weight of his authority pressed peace out of the disparate peoples and contradictory religions he controlled; there was a saying that a young woman with a pot of gold on her head could walk unharmed from one end of the lands he dominated to the other. Where the Mongols had conquered, where the blood of their victims had blackened soil and leaf, there now flourished a respect for law, a concern for individual security. As a result caravans made their laborious and profitable way across the steppes, linking, with the network of routes they established, the civilizations of East and West. Europe grew more and more aware of the power and age of Asiatic cultures; Asia became increasingly conscious of the wealth and mercantile skill of Europe. In particular, the eager and energetic city-states of Italy, their trading posts already established on the edges of Asia, looked eastward for a lucrative increase in their trade. And from time to time, trade paying its dues to eternity, a caravan would carry into the heart of Mongol territory the disapproving glare and threatening book of some Christian missionary.

One of these was William of Rubruck (or, more accurately, de Rubruquis), sent to spread the word by the diligent and saintly Louis. Although this Franciscan friar had already travelled widely in the Middle East, he had by no means made his internal peace with infidels. He detested them, in the most Christian manner, thought of them with an indiscriminate contempt and met their own pride with a sometimes sanctimonious disdain. The naïve voracity of Mongol ambition moved him to an alarmed indignation. He was, however, a precise observer and a copious note-taker.

He described Mangu's palace in Karakorum as:

> . . . like a church, with a middle nave and two sides beyond two rows of pillars, and with three doors to the south . . . and the Khan sits in a high place to the north, so that he can be seen by all; and two rows of steps go up to him – by one his cup-bearer goes up and by the other he comes down. . . . On his right side, that is, to the west, are the men, to the left the women. . . . To the south, beside the pillars on the right side, are rows of seats raised like a platform on which his son and brothers sit. On the left side it is arranged in like fashion, and there sit his wives and daughters. Only one woman sits up there beside him, though not as high as he.

Excavation has given us more information about this palace, which stood within triple walls perhaps twenty feet high on a mound nearly a hundred yards long. Many of the roofs were of glazed tiles, their colours red, blue and yellow, set sometimes in several tiers and supported by great wooden beams. The remains of pottery and of cast-iron cauldrons have been found scattered under the floor area, and with them animal bones, presumably discarded after meals. Three gates guarded the entrance hall, which must have been impressive with its great width of some fifty feet. Its roof writhed with green and yellow paintings of winged dragons and the gates themselves were decorated, figures in high relief standing beside representations of lions and bears, glittering with gilt. About the palace, which stood to the north of and higher than this gate-house, other buildings stretched and twined, store-houses and pavilions, some of which attracted the finicky curiosity of Friar William and are mentioned in his report.

About the palace stretched the town itself, and it is a measure of Mongol power that its defences were little more than token – a moat less than six feet deep, a wall some six or eight feet high, topped by a wattle fence. The walls ran north and south for just over one and a half miles and east to west, at the widest point, for about a mile. As was common with a busy city, however, people had spilled beyond these limits in haphazard suburbs that followed the line of the principal roads. When the eastern gate-house was excavated, a brick stove was discovered from which hot air had been carried by stone flues to other parts of the building. There was a long, narrow building that could be barred at will, a sort of passport control for arriving travellers; when none appeared, the guards gambled away their boredom, and left behind them their bone pieces when they passed on.

There was evidence in the town of industrial activity as well. Cauldrons found there had been cast in metal that could not have been heated by hand-bellows; water-wheels must have produced the power to create the necessary blast. And there, still to be found, is the canal that brought the water from the River Orkhon. The products made in these smithies included arrowheads, swords and gigantic axle-

The Bactrian camel was as indispensable to the merchants
of Central Asia as the horse was to the region's warriors.
Some remain in use today, wandering past the Mongol *yurts*
as they did in the days of Genghis Khan.

boxes, clearly intended for no ordinary wagons, but rather for those bearing the great, constantly spread tents of princes or the engines of some *orlok*'s siege-train. Wooden dies nearby still bear the word *idzhi*; this is the sign of royal command and ownership – it means 'decreed'. Signs of other crafts were found – kilns, some with pottery still in them, the glazes delicate, the colours pale brown, blues both dark and light, drab olive-green or grey. Pick-heads, plough-shares, mattocks and sickles proclaim the agriculture practised on the nearby plain; bone-yards tell of butchery and, at one remove, of the richness of flock and herd.

Near the centre of Karakorum stood a house, twice burned down and twice rebuilt, named by the excavators 'The House at the Crossroads'. Its roofs were brightly tiled, the dragons guarding its doorways were here modelled in clay, flowers brightened the plastered walls, painted there beside curious pictographs; the house's inhabitants could face the winter, like the guards in the city's gate-house, comforted by central heating. Perhaps it was in a house like this that William of Rubruck first met Mangu, writing down afterwards that it was 'all covered inside with cloth of gold, and there was a fire of briars and wormwood roots . . . and of cattle dung in a grate in the centre of the dwelling. He was seated on a couch, dressed in a skin spotted and glossy, like a sealskin.' And he described Mangu, a little man, flat-nosed, of medium height and aged about forty-five (the year was 1254).

At this first meeting the missionary friar asked permission to remain in Mangu's territories and teach the Christian religion, or at least 'to remain here till this cold has passed away, for my companion is so feeble he cannot with safety to his life stand any more the fatigue of travelling on horseback'. Although in the end they were to stay for over half a year, Mangu at that first audience permitted them to stay for two months. Afterwards some of the Khaghan's court began to question the good friar about his native France, 'whether there were many sheep and cattle and horses there, and whether they had not better go there at once and take it all. And I had to use all my strength to conceal my indignation and anger. . . .'

William of Rubruck kept his head, however, avoided controversy and looked clear-sightedly about him. He was intrigued by the position of his rivals, the *shamans*, and mentioned their astrological skills; they predicted which days would be lucky and which not, when it was auspicious to begin a campaign and when it was not – he wrote that Hungary would have been attacked again long before, had it not been for the diviners' prohibition – and when sun or moon would go into eclipse. During an eclipse there seems to have been a ritual terror in the Mongol camps, for everyone would store up food, shut the door of his tent or hut and not stir outside until the darkness had passed. Thus hidden from heaven, he would play instruments, beat drums and yell defiance until, sun or moon restored to him, he would come out to a feast of celebration. Rubruck mentions witchcraft too, and a woman accused and tortured who after seven days had still not confessed. Mangu ordered that she should be released – the old law held good and without confession there could be no conviction. The accusation concerned a lady suddenly stricken with an inexplicable pain. The diviners ordered one of the maids of that household 'to put her hand on the painful spot and pull out whatever she should find. So she arose and did this, and she found in her hand a piece of felt. . . . They told her to put it on the ground; when it was put there it began to wriggle like some wild animal. Then it was put in water, and it became like a leech. . . .' No wonder the

This pavilion at Karakorum displays the luxury which, from
the time of Ogadei, was to be found in the Khaghan's capital.
Yet all the Mongol rulers continued to move with the seasons, travelling
attended by great retinues to their summer or winter quarters.

zealous Franciscan mourned his failure to convert Mangu with the words: 'Had I
had the power of Moses to work miracles, perhaps I could have convinced him.'

Eventually Friar William rode back to the uneasy West, his route through
central Asia to the banks of the Volga, along the shores of the Caspian Sea and the
southern slopes of the Caucasus Mountains to the Mediterranean coast of Asia
Minor, by ship from there to Cyprus and from there again to Acre, where he at last
settled down to write his account. With him he brought a message from Mangu to
Louis, demanding of the French monarch that he should come and abase himself
before the Khaghan. If the king refused, trusting to distance and his own army to
protect him, 'we shall remember what we have commanded'. So ominous a phrase
may be permitted a ruler with three generations of victory behind him and an
army of more than a million trained men to turn his every threat into a reality of
devastation.

In China his brother Kubilai followed conquest with magnanimity. Broken, the
country was worthless; restored, its wealth and harvests could be taxed. From
Karakorum, however, matters looked different. To Mangu's advisers it was as
though the Khaghan's brother had begun to prefer the people of his eastern fief to
his own and to put his duty to them higher than his duty to the Mongol ruler. He
had Chinese governors and bureaucrats administering the territories he had
conquered, while his closest adviser was his old tutor, the Chinese sage Yao-shi.
It was Yao-shi, however, who through his advice restored Kubilai to favour. When
Mangu ordered him home and appointed a new viceroy over China, Kubilai
wanted to resist with force of arms; Yao-shi pointed out the folly of this and advised
him to make a full and most humble submission.

Mollified, Mangu not only restored Kubilai to his command but set out himself
at the head of an army to help in pincering the southern Sung once and for all, thus
sweeping forward the borders of Mongol territory far beyond the Yangtze. After
sacrifice and dedication within sight of Genghis Khan's uplands tomb, Mangu
moved with a huge force south-eastward to Hochow. Besieging the fortress, his
army tumbled into sickness. Cholera attacked his men; dysentery first weakened,
then killed them. Did it kill Mangu? Juvaini and Rashid thought so; other reports
tell of an arrow wound. It is of no importance. In the eighth year of his reign, aged a
little over fifty, Mangu died. As with his grandfather, they brought his body back to
the banks of those rivers from which the Mongols had first set out to take the world,
and they mourned him there, clan by clan, before carrying him high above the
river valleys to where in Burkhan Khaldhun Genghis and his youngest son Tuli
already lay, and they buried him there beside his peers, in the holy solitude of that
most revered mountain.

The memory of Genghis Khan was fading, the force of his commandments had
been eroded by time, distance and success. Until now everything the Mongol
leaders had decided had been within the general rules laid down by their forceful
ancestor. Mention of his name had been sufficient to discipline the recalcitrant or
instruct the forgetful. With the death of Mangu, however, a period began that
Genghis had foreseen and tried to guard against – a period of dynastic war.
Established in Karakorum was Arik-Buka, younger brother of Mangu and Kubilai,
left there as governor when the Khaghan had marched against the Sung. Round
him were the same advisers who had for so long mistrusted Kubilai, men who
regarded the wealth of China with an ancient suspicion and, sharing the conserva-

tism of Mangu himself, despised the softness of its city-based civilization. Their nostalgia for the ancient tents of their people made Kubilai's acceptance of Chinese ways a threat. Now their worst suspicions were confirmed. Not bothering with a *kuriltai* in the Mongol heartlands, nor with Genghis Khan's absolute commandment that all his descendants should choose the new Khaghan together, Kubilai, at a gathering of his generals and governors, the men who ran his Chinese territories for him, had himself proclaimed Khaghan.

At an equally partial *kuriltai* in Karakorum, the conservative faction chose as their Khaghan the younger Arik-Buka. The surviving older brother, Hulagu, might still have prevented the struggle for which all were now preparing. Baghdad and Damascus had fallen to his troops, Egypt lay open before him. Leaving a holding force under his best general, Ked-Buka, he turned eastward either to keep a watchful eye on events or to try to restore balance to the rulership. But he had left behind him insufficient force. Ambushed, surrounded, the Mongol army was destroyed by a huge Egyptian array, called out in determined counter-attack. Ked-Buka was captured and beheaded. Hulagu marched back again, not yet aware that war and circumstance had for the first time turned against him, nor that his inability to reach Karakorum would let the mercury of power trickle eastwards towards China as though down a tilted plane. For Kubilai was not satisfied to be only the Mongol Khaghan, although the spuriousness of the *kuriltai* that had chosen him was more than matched by the genuineness of the army which could reinforce that choice. He gathered together the Chinese princes, the governors and generals he had appointed, the senior bureaucrats who ran these lands he had conquered and which he loved so much; and with their acclamations ringing about his head, he had himself crowned Emperor of China, Son of Heaven, successor to the dynasties of three millennia.

At a stroke, he had undone all the efforts of his family, all the achievements and expectations of Genghis Khan. He had snatched power from the steppes and placed it once more where it had been before the Mongol breakout – in Pekin. From being the capital of the master of half the world, Karakorum became the ramshackle centre of a peripheral state. If there were doubts on that score, the swift and repetitive campaigns that followed soon dispelled them. Arik-Buka fought again and again, and each time the Chinese armies, led by Kubilai's Mongol commanders and stiffened by his Mongol troops, defeated him. The taxes and tributes that had flowed from the eastern territories, enriching the central and ancestral lands of the Mongol khans, came to an abrupt end. Mongolia became impoverished, too impoverished to sustain a war. Arik-Buka submitted, broke his word, submitted again, broke his word a second time and, only after repeated defeats and the defection of some of his own supporters, finally surrendered unconditionally.

Thereafter, opposition to Kubilai was led by Kaidu, the grandson of Ogadei; he took up the traditions of the Mongol chief as against Kubilai's role of Chinese emperor. He raided China; Kubilai squeezed him into the steppelands. If he broke into the wide plains, Kubilai nipped off his columns, surrounded him, broke him in battle, drove him back. The Mongols remained Mongols, but the Chinese had learned new tricks from their change of masters. Now their numbers were supplemented by Mongol tactics – and tactics that had been developed over the years. They had a mobility unknown to them before; in addition, they brought to battle not only cavalry, on the Mongol pattern, but infantry, men with stabbing spears

A decoration, dating from the earlier Han period, which captures
all the speed and ferocity of a Mongol mounted archer.

or short swords who rode into action behind the horsemen, dismounted and
savaged not the men who faced them, but their horses. Dismounted, the Mongol
raiders were cut down by Chinese swords. Once established in Pekin, therefore,
the attacks of his cousins worried Kubilai no more than the raids of the Mongols
had worried the Kin emperors in the days before Genghis Khan.

But Kubilai was far greater than the Kin had been, far greater than any ruler of
China had ever been, perhaps. The Sung at last gave way before him, so that all
the territories traditionally belonging to the Son of Heaven became his. But as
Mongol Khaghan, now without real rival, his writ ran not only in China, but far
to the west. He sent armies south-westward, into Yunan, east to Japan, south to
Java. His levies were raised on the slopes of the Caucasus as well as on those of the
Altai, on the banks of the Dnieper as well as those of the Yangtze, on the borders
of Byzantium as well as the shores of Korea, in the streets of Kiev and Moscow, of
Tabriz and Isfahan, of Pekin and Han-chou. One could ride for five thousand miles
almost due west from the mouth of the Yangtze and not come to the end of those
realms that called him overlord.

Kubilai proclaimed his rule in 1260. At once he organized reforms Genghis would
have recognized. Post stations were set up, and two hundred thousand fast horses
were put at their disposal. He began the repair of the Chinese waterways, damaged

in the incessant wars of the previous decades. Two hundred years earlier the states-
man and reformer Wang An-shih had outlined policies for the control of famine;
Kubilai ordered the building of the granaries he had proposed, and the state
purchases through which those granaries would be stocked against times of bad
harvest. He established a system of charitable relief for the poor, including in that
category not only the orphaned and the sick, but also aged scholars no longer able
to command income and respect. He ordered the construction of hospitals. Above
all, so far as his reputation in the world and in popular memory is concerned, he
began almost at once the reconstruction of Pekin, his winter capital, a marvellous
and dazzling efflorescence of domes and pavilions, of great halls and widespread
parks, of paved courts and rolling lawns, of man-made lakes and man-made hills,
of cunningly planted shrubberies, coppices, orchards, of paths and arcades and
avenues, through which wandered or paraded, like the brilliant toys of monarchy,
the ambassadors, princes and great merchants of the earth.

Meanwhile his wars continued, his armies spreading further and further south.
When, during the second decade of his rule, the whole Sung kingdom lay under his
domination and the young child who had been that dynasty's final heir had been
sent to a Buddhist monastery for his education, the last resistance disappeared. For
a while the baby brother of that final Sung emperor was carried, zig-zag and willy-
nilly, about the islands and inlets of the southern China coast, his junk the evasive
quarry of a fleet of Kubilai's ships. Cornered at last, pursuers poised for boarding,
the imperial ship, the last piece of the world still under Sung rule, shuddered,
settled in the water. One attendant, an officer or courtier, picked up the child and
jumped with him into the sea. 'Death before dishonour' – the final defiant slogan
of every idealism, every party, every aristocracy; with that arrogant drowning, the
ambition of Genghis had been fulfilled and the campaigns that had begun with his
training forays into Hsi-Hsia had ended with his grandson triumphant. He had,
however, never reckoned on the cost – the long fall back into obscurity of the very
lands from which he had sprung.

In a sense, because of that collapse and even more because of Kubilai's character,
this seventy-year-long invasion ended in the invader's defeat. For if the Mongol
Kubilai held China, so did China hold him. So completely did he succumb to its
culture that even its own surviving aristocracy did not think of him, as they had of
his predecessors, the Jurchens and the Khitans, as a barbarian. The arts and literature basked in the wealth his peace encouraged. Trade ranged from Italy and
Russia to his eastern shores. Silks travelled across the steppes, their value returning
in the form of furs. At the great entrepôt cities of Persia, fur and silk were transformed into the ceramics and metal-ware of Islamic craftsmen. The routes by
which these goods travelled were both policed and well-maintained. Bridges speeded
the caravans on their way, artificially smoothed gradients eased the labours of their
animals. Along these roads the messengers of the Khaghan, the 'arrow riders',
swept on their urgent way, covering three hundred miles a day, day after day if
necessary. The empire thrived, it knew itself to be homogeneous, it remained peaceful; yet it was changed at its heart with the change worked in the heart of its ruler.

Not that he was unrecognizable as the grandson of the first Khaghan. Genghis
had summoned wise men to him; now Kubilai invited artists and philosophers,
scholars and engineers from every corner of his domains, and from the wide world
beyond. He decreed the creation of a new scheme of writing, an order resulting in a

Kubilai Khan, who in the thirteenth century united China
once and for all. Founding the Yuan dynasty, he succumbed
to the beguiling culture of his subjects and even when
Khan of the whole Mongol empire remained in Pekin.
This emphasis on the role of China certainly contributed
to the collapse of Mongol unity.

complicated and short-lived script devised by a Tibetan lama named Phagspa; this interest in literacy was not unlike Genghis Khan's adoption of the Uighur alphabet. Like Genghis, Kubilai was tolerant of other religions, and within his borders Buddhists, Taoists, Muslims, Christians, Confucians and Jews worshipped untroubled in their several ways and, in some cases, even enjoyed especial protection. Of these, it was the Buddhists who made the greatest impression on Kubilai himself and Phagspa was named Teacher of the Realm, an archiepiscopal position that he used to whittle away the privileges of his major rivals, the Taoists. Missionaries came in the footsteps of the earlier friars, Odoric of Pordenone and John of Montecorvino; his own Nestorian Christians sent missions to the West, Rabban Sauma travelling to several of the city-states of Italy and being received at the courts both of Philip the Fair of France and of England's king, Edward I.

Kubilai would also have pleased Genghis with the delight he took in hunting; the old nomad might have been less pleased with the howdah Kubilai rode in, high above discomfort and danger on the back of his elephant, and with the trained cheetahs that did much of his stalking for him. His hunting tent appeared like that of Genghis when one approached, its walls and roof of the brindled skins of leopards. Inside, however, luxury had decreed trimmings of ermine and sable. Like his grandfather, again, he had a voracious appetite for women, but these were no longer brought to him as the booty of war or the prizes of diplomacy. Now there was a twice-yearly gathering of beauty, a judging, a selection; thirty or so were picked out, to be watched for defects of body, mind or manner. Those whom the women of the court approved were divided into batches of five; each of these little groups was then at Kubilai's disposal for three days and nights. His *koumiss* was made of the milk of snow-white mares, and brought to him by servants wearing gauze before their mouths, so that their menial breath should not contaminate the imperial potions. His 'arrow riders' telescoped ten days' journey into two to bring him the fruits of the far south, the bells they wore jangling a warning to each post station, the fresh horse ready, the rider in a whirl of coat and boot out of one saddle and into another, the soft hammer of the hooves already receding, the groom perhaps for a moment staring after the disappearing figure, one hand restraining the steaming and discarded horse, his eyes on the road north, his mind on that fabled capital where the alien emperor held unimaginable court.

In all this the lineaments are clear of that coruscating Kubilai Khan whose Xanadu lit up the opium dreams of Coleridge. One can see the true grandeur of the great Emperor of Cathay, the most famous description of whom, and of his realms, made 'a Marco Polo' during five centuries the Italian synonym for a fantasist, an exaggerator, a hopeless liar. For there was of course a Xanadu – Shang-tu, on a southern spur of the Khitan Mountains, where Kubilai's marble palace stood, surrounded by the slow paths and padding beasts of his parklands, and where with an architectural obeisance to his nomad past he had erected a vast tent, its roof and uprights gilded and its hundred supporting ropes of glittering silk, a structure mobile in theory, but in practice never taken down. Friar Odoric of Pordenone saw his stately progression back to his capital when summer was over, and speaks of the four armies of horsemen who went fore and aft and on each side, a personal guard covering a day's march in every direction. He wrote of Kubilai's two-wheeled carriage, 'covered over with great and fine skins, and set with many precious stones', which was drawn by one team of four elephants and another of four horses.

Four great lords travelled in close attendance, and Kubilai carried with him 'twelve gerfalcons, so that if he sees any birds pass he lets fly his hawks at them'.

And equally, Marco Polo saw true and described coolly, mistaken only when he relied on hearsay and story instead of on his own experience. For seventeen years he criss-crossed Kubilai's domains as a roaming emissary, a peripatetic ambassador, an imperial representative with no standing except that given him by the trust of the Khaghan. He and his father and uncle worked for this alien monarch, earning his respect and their own millions, leaving at last in their patron's old age, despite his imperial and imperious opposition, to return to the ridicule and disbelief of their native Genoa. Ridicule they buried under a cascade of precious stones, the kind of affirmation that can always win the respect of men; disbelief dogged them all the years of their lives. Yet by the middle of the fourteenth century Pekin would have become a Catholic diocese, the trade routes between Europe and the ends of Asia would be charted, well known and well trodden, and guidebooks would offer the adventurous traveller such information as he needed to prepare him for his place in yet another caravan bound for the riches of Cathay.

By that time Kubilai was dead. During his reign, Mongol armies, in Syria, in Java, off the coast of Japan and elsewhere, learned to bear the traumata of defeat. After he was gone the great empire, which Genghis had envisaged and which had for a while seemed not impossible of achievement, succumbed to the burdens of distance and the stresses of dynastic rivalry. But by that time Mongol success had reached its crescendo. One by one the descendants of Genghis Khan had taken on the burden of continental rulership, the ambition of world conquest. For all their qualities, each had seemed out of place, diminished by the power he wielded, pitting cruelty or a traditional simplicity against the awestruck expectations of the world. For a glittering moment, however, a handful of years, a man had matched the grandeur of his role. In Kubilai, with his humanity, his administrative skill, his quickness to seize on the best of advice, his delight in his adopted civilization, his ability to pick strong-minded and supremely competent ministers, his ambition to translate the Mongol triumph into cultural and artistic terms, so that at every human level his rule should be pre-eminent, in Kubilai, for those brief years, there appeared a true world-monarch. Pride and hastiness were his flaws, and his armies suffered for them, flung into battle to avenge tiny or non-existent slights. But he was, after Genghis himself, the greatest of the Khaghans, and certainly the most civilized. It was right that he should be the last of them, but more than fitting that he should be the first of a new dynasty in China.

# 5 WESTWARDS FROM THE VOLGA

**W**hatever the magnanimity or tyranny, the simplicity or magnificence at its centre, the Mongol Empire, perhaps more than any other in history, retained its equilibrium through the dynamism of conquest. When its borders ceased to expand, it was as though it had lost its *raison d'être*. Genghis Khan had charged his successors with the task of annexing the whole world. His example had shown them how and his precepts had governed them. It was at the points where their ferocity met the astonished defences of their neighbours that the Mongols established the reputation that they hold in history. Did Genghis really say: 'The joy of man lies in treading down the enemy, tearing him up by the root, taking from him everything he has . . . in making one's bed upon the belly and navel of his wives.'? It was what the world heard him say when it watched the blood-spattered, unrelenting advance of his hordes. 'Courageous, bloody and cruel,' Juvaini called him. 'A just, resolute butcher.' Throughout central Asia, jackal and raven grew fat on his butchery, the air stirred with the wails of the bereaved, the screams of the dying. Whole populations disappeared, cities slipped broken out of human memory, bones in white heaps stood as the sepulchres of the defeated.

At Nissa seventy thousand of the captured, having tied themselves together at Mongol command, were slaughtered where they stood screaming in their bonds. At Merv the invaders, with steel, fire and water, killed over a million. At Nishapur, Genghis Khan's daughter watched unmoved as every living creature, down to the infants, down to the very rats, was butchered, watched as each body was beheaded and the head flung on a growing pile which, rotting under the Persian sun, would stand at last as a gaunt tower of white skulls. Then she drove away, satisfied: her husband had been killed outside those walls. So the heart was carved out of Persia and its wealth, dragged off for Mongol use, made way for desolation. Half a dozen centuries would not bring back the prosperity and happiness that had existed there before the hordes' arrival.

Even enriched, however, the Mongols did not, could not, stop. They had drawn to themselves the luxury of China, the cunning craftsmanship of Islam. Their two major wars had brought them plunder, enough to make them great, and had opened to them the revenues of enormous territories. But they knew, or their leaders knew, that to stand still would be to fall apart. They were nomads, steppe fighters, raiders; they understood the dynamics of robbery, they feared the dangers of stillness. Men followed their khan as long as he fed, protected and enriched them. He could do that only by taking from others. A khan remained of consequence only as long as men followed him. It was his duty, therefore, his obligation to

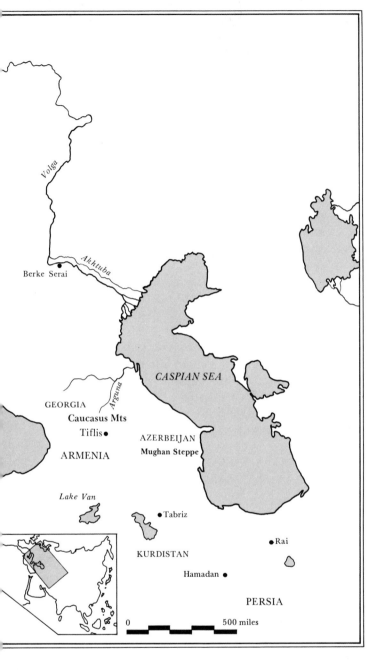

Berke Serai

*Volga*

*Akhtuba*

CASPIAN SEA

*Arguna*

GEORGIA

Caucasus Mts

Tiflis•

AZERBEIJAN

ARMENIA

Mughan Steppe

*Lake Van*

•Tabriz

•Rai

KURDISTAN

Hamadan •

PERSIA

0                    500 miles

*Russia and
Eastern Europe
during the
Mongol era*

himself and those about him, to lead the way to plunder and yet more plunder: if he would be the conqueror of the world, to ceaseless plunder. When expansion halted and other men's riches no longer flowed into Mongol hands, what would be the purpose of the chieftain's life? Genghis Khan knew the answer to that question – there would be no purpose. The Mongols would grow fat, they would become lazy, they would forget their heritage of movement, toughness, simplicity. When that happened, they would be the rich, and elsewhere, beyond their borders, some leaner, sparer race would take up the torch of their ancient greed. They would quarrel for what they already owned, rather than take more, enough for everyone, from the wealth of the world outside. They would fall victims to enemies, exterior and interior, and their empire would collapse upon itself. For that reason, therefore, neither the rich acres of northern China nor the great trading cities of Persia could satisfy him. He himself looked to the east, to the subjugation of the Tangut and the destruction of the Kin. But beyond the Caspian a new continent beckoned, and he had no intention of ignoring it.

Subatei and Jebei, great *orloks*, had stepped energetically to the very edge of Asia while in pursuit of the Khwarismian Shah, Muhammad. He had died of pleurisy in 1220 and left the Mongol armies free to continue, out of north-western Iran and into Azerbeijan. Subatei, after his ride across Persia to confer with Genghis Khan, had brought with him the commands he needed to exploit this freedom. Raiding across Azerbeijan, Kurdistan and Georgia the Mongols had already seen that here were new lands, rich plunder, defenders whom it would be worthwhile and possible to overcome. In 1221 they set out in earnest, for the first time to assault the chivalry of Christendom.

Thirty thousand men under Subatei appeared in the kingdom of Georgia. The state was small, yet had earned its reputation for military enterprise and courage. Its knights were already gathering to go on crusade when, abruptly, the infidel appeared on their own doorstep. Not that they were sure of the invaders' religion – indeed they thought them to be Christians because of what they took to be a white cross on their emblems – but were soon convinced of their unfriendly intentions. Swiftly the Georgians gathered, their battle lines formed, their spears and lances bristled as, in a glitter of metal, they began their advance. The Mongols fought, wheeling, galloping in and out, their arrows loud as hornets. Then, suddenly, they were fleeing and, arrogance confirmed, the Christian knights were after them. For a moment it seemed as though Christian valour had broken Mongol temerity. Subatei, leading the retreat, perhaps in his great battle-wagon, more probably himself on horseback like the rest, his bulk concealing his shrewdness, calm among the dust and the hoof-drum, his eyes preoccupied, calculating, led the Georgians that long-established dance of death, beckoning them with visions of victory into the swift horrors of ambush. From nowhere Jebei rose. His column swept into the Georgian flank, cut like some great spear into those unprepared ranks. And Subatei wheeled at last; his men flung their ponies about, began to retrace the line of their contrived retreat. Struck from two sides the Georgians wavered, broke, attempted flight, then died.

Their ruler, Queen Russudan, wrote to the Pope, describing the invaders of her realm – 'A savage people, hellish of aspect, as voracious as wolves and as brave as lions' – but claimed a victory. Certainly the Mongols had passed on, but they had been driven by curiosity, not defeat; there were other lands to see, and Genghis

Khan had given them only three years to see them and return. They left behind
a shattered land, its fighting force destroyed: 'Alas,' wrote the queen, 'we are no
longer able to take up the Cross as we had promised Your Holiness we would do.'

Now the Mongols clambered over the Caucasus range, a journey almost as
difficult as their crossing of the Pamirs a few years earlier. They abandoned their
siege-engines, animals died, they themselves struggled over high, precipitous
passes and some of them perished. When they came down at last, their route the
long river of a glacier, they saw before them familiar terrain – steppeland, the
enormous plains that carry one north of the Black Sea and deep into the heartlands
of Russia. Barring their way, an ominous but hastily assembled alliance, the centre
of its resistance the nomadic Kipchak warriors, braced itself to give battle. But the
Kipchaks were Turks and thus cousins of the Mongols; their way of life was
similar, they were perhaps predisposed to friendship and even alliance. There was a
day of battle, followed by a Mongol assault of a different kind, the diplomatic
assault of gifts. Subtlety serving where force had not, Subatei separated his enemies.

The Kipchak Turks had allied themselves with the people of the Caucasus
regions, the Alans, the Circassians; these, abandoned, went to their inevitable
defeat. Subatei turned on the now friendless Kipchaks. Believing liberty and
grazing rights to be at stake, the Kipchaks fought hard, but in a piecemeal fashion.
Tribe by tribe, the Mongols searched them out, broke them, destroyed their pride

A Mongol warrior grooms his horse, plaiting its tail. Their steeds were
the Mongol armies' first concern. The speed of their advance, sometimes almost
two hundred miles a day, depended on their horses – and their horsemanship.

On the Kipchak steppe, Genghis Khan
prays to Bai Ülgän, the sky god.
These plains were the furthest west that
the founder Khaghan ever penetrated,
but from his headquarters in Persia
he sent out the galloping columns
which first tore at the security of
eastern Europe.

and their effectiveness. Slowly at first, then more swiftly, the dust-clouds of battle, the hungry stretch and thrust of Mongol hooves, the dancing threat of the *orloks'* yak-tail banners, moved westward. When the Kipchaks complained of treachery, Subatei charged them with treason. These steppes, he said, were the lands of Jochi, given them by the Ruler of the World – why had they not made their proper submission to Jochi's emissaries? Thus, in righteous belligerence, the Mongols – something under thirty thousand of them – rounded the Sea of Azov, crossed the Dnieper, then the Dniester.

The world shuddered. Sudak, a Genoese outpost in the Crimea, had tried to withstand a Mongol siege. Weight of numbers, endless aggression, finally fire, had reduced it. The survivors, the oars of their galleys flashing desperately, had made off across the Black Sea, to come home at last with their tales of devastation and cruelty. In Byzantium, the news of Georgia's defeat was followed by a clamouring influx of Kipchak refugees. The Emperor resettled them in Asia Minor, then turned with desperate energy to his defences. At the edges of Asia men awaited the next onslaught of these mysterious invaders and, while they waited, compounded their ignorance of them with speculation, rumour and fantasy.

The reality, however, was overwhelming enough. Kotyan, a Khan of the Kipchaks, still wealthy despite flight, brought to his son-in-law a train of gifts and begged for help. His son-in-law was a prince of Russia, Mstislav of Halicz; understanding the danger that faced Russia itself, he summoned his peers and all their forces. Over eighty thousand men gathered, an assembly intended to destroy once and for all the Mongol threat. The Mongols tried a second time the diplomacy of division; they sent envoys to the Russians to explain that their quarrel was not with them, but with the Kipchaks, those disobedient vassals of Jochi and the distant Khan. The Russians killed the ambassadors; this gave the Mongols no alternative to war. When the Russians advanced to fight, their troops supported by war-flotillas on the Dnieper, Subatei and Jebei turned again to one of the oldest of Mongol tactics, but on a scale almost unprecedented. They retreated, travelling eastward day after day, stretching behind them the exultant columns of their pursuers.

On the ninth day, the land at last in their favour, they turned. Raging against them came the advance guard, composed largely of Kipchaks intent on revenge and confident after this long witness of their flight. As the glittering waters of the River Kalka flowed silently past in the background, the Mongols unleashed their ferocity again. The Kipchaks reeled; their ranks tore apart and the tatters recoiled; disorganized, in hapless rout, they crashed back into the main body of the advancing army. This had become separated into its constituent detachments during the rush across the steppes. One by one these now fell to the Mongol *toumans*; their superiority of numbers was nullified by the speed of the Mongol attacks, the precision of the Mongol manoeuvres. Disorder foundered into indiscipline, indiscipline into panic. In flight Russian vulnerability became complete. Under the Prince of Kiev some ten thousand men dug themselves in, high on the river bluffs. The rest of the army fled; Mstislav of Halicz took to water, commandeering one galley and burning the rest. It trapped his comrades, but prevented Mongol pursuit. The small Kiev army held for three days; its prince had been responsible for the death of the Mongol envoys and had nothing to hope for from his enemies. When his forces had finally been flung backwards to the Dnieper, soldiers hanging bloodless in the

Although this picture, found in a Sofia manuscript, dates from the fifteenth century, the desperate confrontations between Mongol invaders and Russian defenders two centuries before must have been almost identical.

river's slack backwaters or gathered limp and white into its steady flood, he learned he had been right to give up hope: the Mongols laid him, as was proper with a nobleman of royal blood, in a great carpet, so stifling and pressing him to death. Five other princes died, and seventy great lords of Russia. Not eight thousand men lived to return to their homes; of the army of Kiev, hardly any. In one swift campaign, the whole of southern Russia had been rendered defenceless.

North, then east; the Mongols were on their way home. The thirty thousand men they had started with were fewer now and had never been enough to conquer Russia. But they felt they had Europe's measure and they knew they would be back. In the meantime, war had almost ended for them. An army of Great Bulgary, the state which lay in the fertile crook of lake and marsh where the Kama and the Volga meet, had to be brushed aside, but from then on the easy stages of their journey were interrupted only by their acceptance of a sequence of submissions from the tribes of the Volga valley. Here and there a town had to be stormed, a skirmish fought, but the major business of their campaign was over. Only one loss marred it. As they neared Turkestan on the last stage of their journey, already safe within the lands of which Jochi was suzerain, Jebei died – 'The Arrow', the straightforward, the swift-moving, the man whose honesty so long ago had won him his place in the history of Mongol domination. Genghis Khan, who had been so quick to recognize his worth, was now anguished by his loss.

But he had Subatei, and Subatei had his tales of victory. For weeks the smiling genius of the battlefield, the great commander, overweight, subtle, totally devoted to his master, repeated again and again the stories of the campaign, described the countries seen, the riches gained, the victories won – and the conquests waiting to be made. It would be more than a decade, however, before those conquests would be attempted. By then Jochi, the lord of the west, was dead, as was his father, Genghis Khan himself. Ogadei had become Khaghan of the Mongols. But just as he retained Yelui Ch'u ts'ai as his chief minister, so he made Subatei his principal general in the west. As titular head of the new expedition, however, he set Jochi's son, Batu, who had hereditary claim to the territories into which they were once more to venture. This was because, as Rashid recounts, it had already been decreed that 'Jochi should proceed with an army and seize and take possession of all the northern countries . . . as far as the Iron Gate on the Caspian. Jochi neglected this command, and when Ogadei acceded to the Khanate, he charged Batu with the same undertaking. . . .' Europe would have been pleased if the Mongols had in truth conquered no further than the Iron Gate, that rugged defile in the Transyl-vanian Alps, through which the Danube tumbles out of the lush plains of Hungary and on to its multiple mouth on the Black Sea.

Ogadei's mistake was to add to the complement of leaders his son Kuyuk and others of the new aristocracy; Genghis Khan's descendants were already falling into that bickering, that rivalry, upon which their empire would founder. It was from this expedition that Ogadei recalled his son, leaving Kuyuk in a limbo between obedience and disobedience, neither fighting in the west nor paying a vassal's homage and a son's respect in Karakorum. This was a minor matter of internecine politics, however, made important only by the quarrels over the succession that were so soon to begin; when the first exploratory columns reached out towards the Volga late in the year 1236, they began a campaign which, certainly for Batu, Subatei and others like them, would finally outweigh in importance any merely dynastic matters taking place in Karakorum. For they knew they were not engaged in any light enterprise – Subatei's estimate of the period of warfare stretching between them and victory was eighteen years. It would be the year 1255, he calculated, before Europe had been drained of its riches, its armies broken, its cities destroyed. But by then it would have become the third great source of wealth, after China and Persia, contributing yet another flood of gold and furs and slaves, yet another endless river of taxes, to the insatiable coffers of Mongolia.

Those first *toumans*, therefore, rode, brandishing terror, across the plains east of the Volga. The people here, Turkish in origin, were cousins of the Mongols; defeated, they were prepared to transfer their allegiance. Thousands of them turned about, committed to service in Batu's cause. Once again the swift Mongol ponies hammered out their terrifying rhythms across the broad lands of Great Bulgary, sweeping over that right-angle made by the Kama and the Volga. The Bulgar capital fell, the state collapsed. With their enforced allies drilled to follow Mongol tactics, with Subatei and the main body of his armies impatient to move forward, the hordes stepped out across the ice of the winter-silenced Volga. It was December 1237.

The scene stands etched against history, black on white, the tiny ponies trotting on silent hooves across the long, white horizontals of the Russian winter. Steam rises from their nostrils, and from the nostrils of their riders. A corona of fur glitters about each warrior's head, he sits hunched against the cold, his long coat hanging in dark folds down his horse's flanks. Arrows stand from the quiver on his back, his sabre dances at his side, his spear challenges the horizon. Voices call, standards swing and flutter in the hard wind, there is the sudden ring of metal. Perhaps snow tumbles in cruel flurries from a sky of steel. Wagon wheels scream, wooden frames creak in the cold, drivers drag their coats closer, yell encouragement to beasts. The eye moves left and right, far left, far right – everywhere the dark shapes move, a whole continent in motion, a world seeking its obscure vengeance, column after column winding westward, rank after rank, a group now trotting swiftly on, another dallying, a man turning, laughing suddenly, his round face creased with the happiness of action, his eyes narrowed, almost invisible, his sparse beard beaded with ice; for a moment his face remains like that, light striking its cheek-bones, his breath white about him, the smile dying, the lines of his face hardening now, the planes altering, the mouth settling into a line of determination, his eyes cooling to cruelty; then he has turned, become anonymous again, one of the tens of thousands streaming almost silently, utterly relentlessly, across these steppes to where, their gates thundering shut, the great princes of Russia prepare to give them battle.

For Batu had demanded the obeisance of these princes, demanded a tenth of their property, a tenth of their subjects. The princes knew their own strength and the weakness of the nomads – while the people of the steppes had mobility, the princes had walls. They had not heard of the campaigns of Genghis Khan nor realized how much the Mongols had learned from them. When the great siege-trains arrived outside their city gates, it was too late. The aristocratic arrogance with which they had killed the Mongol envoys was punished by a force at which they had not been able even to guess. In their pride, too, they had refused to band

Russian men-at-arms ride out to do battle.

themselves together; Prince Yuri of Vladimir, the Russian chronicles tell us, had rejected an appeal to come to the aid of Riazan 'as he wanted to fight the Tartars alone. . . '. One by one, and swiftly, their cities fell. 'On 21 December,' the chroniclers record, 'the Tartars took the city of Riazan, burned it completely, killed Prince Yuri Igorevich and his wife, slaughtered other princes and of the captured men, women and children, some they killed with their swords, others they killed with their arrows and threw them into the fire, while some of the captured they bound, cut and disembowelled.'

The horde moved on. 'They took Moscow . . . they slaughtered people, old and young alike. Some they took with them into captivity. They departed with a great amount of wealth.' Neither wealth nor captives slowed or halted them.

On Tuesday, 3 February [1238] the Tartars approached Vladimir. . . . After they made camp . . . from early morning till evening they built scaffolds and set up rams, and during the night they surrounded the entire city with a fence. . . . On Sunday, 8 February, early in the morning, the Tartars approached the city from all sides and began to hit the city walls with rams and to pour great stones into the centre from far away, as if by God's will, so that it seemed like rain within the city. Many people inside the city were killed and all trembled with fear. The Tartars broke through the wall at the Golden Gates, also . . . at the Oriniy and Copper Gates, and at the Volga Gates and in other places. They destroyed the whole city, threw stones inside and . . . entered it from all sides like demons. Before dinner they took the new city, which they set on fire. . . .

Death followed, by metal and flame; then the Mongol columns swept on. From here the Tartars advanced . . . some went towards Rostov, while others went towards Yaroslav, which they took; some went along the Volga and towards Gorodets and burned everything along the Volga as far as Merski Golich. Some went towards Pereyalslav and took that city and slaughtered the people. And from there they set the entire countryside and many cities on fire. . . . In February, in the Rostov and Susdal principalities alone, they took fourteen cities in addition to villages and churchyards.

In three months the principalities of northern Russia, created two and three hundred years before by the action of Viking Swede on patient Slav, had crumbled away. Riazan was in Batu's hands, and Susdal, Moscow and Vladimir, Yaroslav and Tver; Novgorod, where the Scandinavian Varengians had established their first stronghold, the early capital of the Rus, who gave the whole country their name, lay only some hundred miles beyond the thrusting Mongol patrols.

But the expected advance did not come. Was it, as has been suggested, because Subatei knew what the melting snows of spring would do to the plains of northern Russia? With mobility gone, his forces would lose their advantage. They had spread terror and contrived victory by the ferocious speed of their advance, the suddenness with which they could change direction. Driving day and night without cease, eating and sleeping in the saddle, changing horses whenever necessary, they had confused Europe over their very numbers; each man was multiplied into a squadron, each squadron into a regiment. At fortress after unprepared fortress, their abrupt descent, unexpected and incomprehensible, brought discomfort and dismay to their enemies. It seemed to the Russians as though there were a million Mongols loose in their domains. But mud would slow them, delay their communications, give European garrisons time to prepare, render their tactics clumsy. It was necessary, too, to rest a little, recover after these swift campaigns, regroup, and to train the new levies conquest had attached to them. (Inaction, however, would bring its own problems – it was now that the Mongol leadership foundered on its rock-like pride and Ogadei was forced to recall his son.)

There was, however, another reason for Subatei's switch southward. Kotyan, that leader of the Kipchaks who, using his marriage connections, had alerted the unfortunate Mstislav of Halicz and persuaded him into battle during Subatei's first campaign, had reacted to the Mongols' second appearance by fleeing nearly a thousand miles westwards, bringing his flocks, his tents and some two hundred thousand of his nomad subjects under the protection of King Béla IV of Hungary. For Batu, as for his father, Kipchak herdsmen and warriors owed their obedience to Mongol rule and their khans were his vassals. That, at least, was the rationale that had lent the Mongol invasion its only fragile basis of legality, and consistent with it Batu now sent an ambassador to King Béla. He demanded the Hungarian's recognition of the Khaghan as overlord. Béla reacted with contempt – like the Russian princes, he knew the nomads and their ineradicable inferiority. Hungary was no small principality, but a great kingdom. With arrogant fury, he refused the Mongol request, the envoy – as it happens, an Englishman, precursor perhaps of many such later to grace the Foreign Office – having to use all his diplomacy to avoid the unpleasant fate earlier messengers had suffered at Hungarian hands.

It was now the winter of 1240. The ground had hardened under the long northern frosts. The rivers were frozen again. Subatei was on the move, his *toumans* crossing the Dnieper, their faces towards Kiev. Since the time of the first Prince Yaroslav some two centuries before, this had been one of the cultural centres of eastern Europe. Its church of St Sophia was the greatest of the five vast buildings he had commanded for his capital. Its thirteen cupolas, its Byzantine mosaics, its coruscating frescoes all made it one of the most famous churches of eastern Christendom. The city round about conformed to it; it was gracious, proud, a centre of trade, of art and of literature. When the Mongol envoys arrived and demanded its surrender, Michael of Chernigov, its princely commander, threw them from his white city walls. Even as he made this act of defiance, his own city was falling; soon the swift-riding hordes were almost within sight of Kiev. Michael took to his heels, becoming one of that flood of aristocratic refugees who, crowding into his court, might have made Béla IV wonder if his rejection of Mongol terms had been over-hasty.

Under a *boyar* named Dmitri, the Kiev garrison prepared to fight. But contemporary accounts describe the army that now surrounded them:

[The Mongols were] like dense clouds. The rattling of wagons, the bellowing of camels and cattle, the sound of trumpets, the neighing of horses and the cries of a vast multitude made it impossible for people to hear one another inside the city. . . . Batu ordered that rams be . . . placed near the Polish Gate, because that part of the wall was wooden. Many rams hammered the walls ceaselessly, day and night; the inhabitants were frightened and many were killed, the blood flowing like water. . . . And thus, with the aid of many rams, they broke through the city walls and entered the city, and the inhabitants ran to meet them. One could see and hear a great clash of lances and clatter of shields; the arrows obscured the light, so that it became impossible to see the sky; there was darkness because of the multitude of Tartar arrows, and there were dead everywhere. . . . During the night the people built new fortifications around the Church of the Virgin Mary. When morning came, the Tartars attacked them and there was a bitter slaughter. . . . The Tartars took the city of Kiev on St. Nicholas Day, 6 December. They brought the wounded leader, Dmitri, before Batu and Batu ordered that he should be spared because of his bravery.

ABOVE Kiev is one of the most ancient cities of Russia, founded in the ninth century by the Viking creators of the state and their Slav companions. One of its greatest princes was Yaroslav the Wise, whose sarcophagus is pictured here. In 1240 the Mongol onslaught smashed through the Kiev defences. The town was destroyed and almost all its inhabitants massacred.

Kiev's icons were especially awe-inspiring. This, known as the Orant Virgin of the Great Panagia and dating from 1114, is among the few artifacts to survive.

For a long time Kiev would have no more than a notional existence; of the Kiev that had been, only a handful of walls and towers remained to indicate a vanished beauty. Among these, some might think miraculously, stood the cathedral of St Sophia. But excavation by archaeologists has shown what Mongol victory meant to the people living in the cities they took. In the mud of Kiev their skeletons still stretch where Mongol swords cut short their resistance or their flight. The bones of two little girls lie curled in the oven where they attempted, vainly, to hide. Under what had been the Desyatinnaya Church lie the skeletons of those who had sought refuge there, in a cellar storeroom. They had tried to tunnel their way out to a nearby hillside, but before they had dug more than a yard or so – their spades were found where they had dropped, with the iron hoops from buckets meant to carry off the earth – Mongol siege-engines had brought the church down above them, the enormous stones crashing through masonry, beams splintering under the sudden stress, the walls falling inwards, the floor collapsing then on the doomed and cowering refugees. Among the dead was a craftsman who had run from a nearby workshop carrying with him what he valued most in the world – his moulds. On one of them there remains as a symbol of transient ownership his name: Maxim.

On the site of the Mikhailovsky Zlatoverkhy Monastery storerooms and work-shops have been found, including one, now called the 'House of the Artist', where catastrophe halted time so completely, so abruptly, that a cooking-pot still stood on a hearth, a wooden spoon in the gruel it contained. Six hundred pieces of amber lay ready for working, some already rough-cut; fourteen pots containing paints of different colours were ranged ready to take a brush that would never dip for them again. In another house not far away a broken amphora and a trail of beads, with blackened walls and timbers all about, tell of another moment – the fire hurling upwards, the panic-stricken craftsman rushing for the open, his cut-glass and cornelian beads in the pot he carried, clambering up the steps towards his doorway, then . . . what? Tripping, perhaps, falling there, the amphora crashing to the ground, the beads spilling? Or seen, picked out, a rider swinging in his saddle, sword already biting, the beads now scattering beyond the reach of death? In any case, flight ended there, in that semi-basement entry, its traces to be uncovered seven centuries later, the mark and signature of Mongol savagery.

Other towns vanished during this onslaught – Vshchizh, Vyshgorod, Belgorod, all with their walls, their citadels and cathedrals smashed, burned down; all of these, and many more, depopulated. In 1245, Giovanni Pian de Carpini, the papal legate, wrote of seeing only two hundred houses left standing in Kiev, while the plains round about were still whitened by the bones of the slain, their cleaned and petrifying skulls their only memorial. Kiev would revive in time – even for Carpini it was an important staging-post on his journey east to Karakorum. Elsewhere, however, what had been great cities continued their existence as small villages; other again remained broken and desolate for ever. So perished southern Russia, in a victory that built for Subatei the base for his assault on Hungary.

Now the Mongols could reap the benefit of all the contacts they had had over the previous two or three decades with the West. Their questioning of merchants and missionaries had not, after all, been haphazard, nor had their own rare envoys kept their eyes and ears serenely closed. Genghis Khan had always emphasized the value of information, had even developed a system for gathering it, and his de-scendants had not forgotten what he had taught them. Thus while for Europe the Mongols were almost wholly mysterious and had therefore become surrounded by the swift superstitions of the fearful, the Mongols had a great deal of sophisticated knowledge about Europe, its politics, its military methods, its alliances and rivalries and the complex intertwining of its dynasties.

They knew very well that the main attention of the whole continent was focused on the rivalry between the papacy and the Holy Roman Empire, the latter's ramshackle institutions stiffened by the ambition of its ruler, that Frederick of Hohenstaufen whose Sicilian arrogance and amazing erudition had caused the abbot of St Gall to dub him, for all time, *Stupor Mundi*, the 'Wonder of the World'.

To the Mongols, of course, it did not matter in the least where supremacy would eventually come to rest in this European struggle, since they knew themselves to be the God-ordained conquerors of the world; what did matter was that the two greatest powers of the West, either or both of whom might have organized an alliance of defence against them, were too busy establishing their own authority to make more than token gestures of aid to the distraught nobility of eastern Europe.

That nobility, however, as the Mongols realized very well, would not willingly allow itself to be destroyed piecemeal; through it ran skeins of marriage and alliance, of blood-relationship and interdependence that would, given time, produce a protective cohesion even the Mongols might find it hard to break down. Nobles of various countries – Poles, Bohemians, Germans – were all related to Béla IV of Hungary and would certainly come to his aid. It was necessary, therefore, to attack Béla not only directly, but also by destroying all possibility of a supporting alliance. Ogadei's grandson, Kaidu, was therefore sent on a wide sweep westward to smash the armies of the Polish Dukes Boleslav of Sandomir and Konrad of Masovia, of the German Duke Heinrich von Schlesien and, if necessary, the Bohemian ruler, Wenceslas.

An army under Kuyuk's brother Kadan was dispatched to attack the southern provinces. Subatei, meanwhile, flung himself upon central Hungary. His columns had the capital, Gran, as their target, a city where Béla IV awaited them with a hundred thousand men. If Béla waited, however, he was nevertheless not ready when they arrived. He had done everything orthodoxy demanded – he had blocked the Carpathian passes, he had sent reinforcements to their commander and he had summoned a parliament to discuss what should be done. Had he been facing the kind of army he was used to, he might have saved his kingdom. The Mongols, however, were something quite new. They brushed aside the frontier forces, smashed their way through the easy passes into the spreading plains beyond, then advanced at forty, fifty, even sixty miles a day, too swift for the Hungarians to rally, too swift for parliamentary discussion. Two days to cross the mountains, three days to reach the capital – events had already outpaced the speed of Béla's reactions. The northern half of his country was split, the south was being ravaged by another force, his capital was under pressure, though not yet under siege. Predictably, perhaps, the people turned on the Kipchak refugees, who, they said, had brought this scourge upon them. Civil war distracted them, when only determined defence or whole-hearted surrender might have given them some hope.

The Kipchaks, reviled and reviling, struggled southwards into Bulgaria – they were nomads, after all, and owed no further allegiance to Hungary. Béla rallied, his army grew, he rode out to give battle. Batu and Subatei gave ground, one whole day, then another, then two more. When the Mongols halted, their position flanked by two rivers, Béla paused. He set up camp, surrounding himself with a bulwark of wagons. The Hungarians had not long to wait for action. The Mongols crossed the River Sajo, were repulsed, attacked again – it may be that this time they used cannon. The weight of descending stones and the noise of explosions, never heard before, disconcerted the Hungarians. Fatally they withdrew; when they returned to the attack, it was to find the Mongols too well established to be pushed back across the river. When they fell back a second time, perhaps in the hope of drawing the counter-attacking Mongols on to prepared positions, they found themselves the victims of a double-pronged assault.

ИЗОБРАЖЕНІЕ ДРЕВНАГО НОВГОРОДА СЪ ИКО

Novgorod, the first city to be settled by the Northmen, the Rus, was probably saved from Mongol attack by the spring thaw of 1240, which immobilized the Mongols by turning the steppelands to mud. A contemporary picture shows how it looked in the thirteenth century.

rent en latre ceturquie
+ la cōquiſtrēt en lan m̄e
ſeignoꝛ·ꝏ·cc·ꬶ iiij.

paꝛ mer laguꝰ ti tu tieẏ
ſont mlt cngꝛgnoꝛs m̄a
erēt lomes qui ſauoiēt
noer ⁊ ceaur entrerent

This version of a battle between Mongols and Hungarians is from a decorated manuscript, the *Floire des Estoires*. The scene shows a disputed bridge across the Danube, and the Mongols, here called Turks have been given knightly helmets and an anachronistic Crescent symbol. The date, visible in the text above the Hungarians, is 1244.

During the night, while the Hungarian army had been attempting to contain one bridgehead, the Mongols had established another downstream, feverishly throwing together a bridge of their own, leading their horses across this or taking to the water, man and beast together, Subatei their leader, finally to whirl through the morning along the river bank and take their enemies in the flank. Ringed now, besieged within their wagons, Béla's troops fought with the ferocity of the doomed. They sallied, but were driven back. At last the Mongols used against them the tactic they had perfected far to the east, in their wars against the Tangut, the Khwarismians and the Kin. They gave way at one point, offered the simulacrum of sanctuary, let the desperate stream through, the line of their flight marked by the helmets, the shields, the swords and armour that they flung from them in their desire for greater speed, more distance. But neither speed nor distance would ever be enough; the Mongols followed, as always; their contempt for those who ran was sufficient reason for murder. They fanned out, their neat ponies stretched into the gallop, then swung and veered and turned like sheep-dogs rounding up recalcitrant members of a herd. Where Hungarian soldiers moved, they were hunted into death; where they took refuge, they were flushed out, by arrow-shot or fire, then cut down. For three days the running slaughter continued, and at the end of it, seventy thousand men had died on those blood-blackened marshes, plains and river banks. 'Their bodies lay everywhere, like stones in a quarry,' wrote someone who had witnessed it. In a few short weeks the Christian kingdom of Hungary had been shorn of all protection; now it lay ready for plunder. There was no force left to defend it.

To the west, Hungary's allies, who might have stemmed this torrent of destruction, had suffered the assaults of Kaidu's *toumans*; now, bleeding, they could come to no one's aid. The invasion had started at Przemyśl, where today the border runs between Poland and the Soviet Union, with Kaidu's advance columns crossing the Vistula in February 1241. Sandomir burned, doubtless to the chagrin of its duke; a fortnight later the whole of the Mongols' western army was slashing across the central Polish plains, their faces towards Germany. By 24 March Cracow had fallen, its ruins marked by an unfurling column of smoke; a few days later the Mongol riders were in sight of Breslau, Silesia's capital; on 8 April they came to halt near Liegnitz. At last the opposition had rallied, had ridden out against them. Heinrich von Schlesien, known to history as Henry the Bearded, had expressed the royal ambitions he held for his son by summoning every soldier and knight he could, whether from his own dukedom of Silesia or from the nobility of Poland. The Templars had rallied to him, the Hospitallers, the Teutonic Knights – the very core of northern European chivalry had assembled under his banner. When Henry's brother-in-law, Wenceslas of Bohemia, arrived at the head of his fifty thousand-strong army, Christendom might face even the Mongols with confidence. But if the northern knights knew this, so did the Mongols.

Mobility was the basis of Mongol tactics, swift communications the method that brought it into action, a disciplined unity its means of expression. The European knights, on the other hand, relied on strength, on weight, on mass. Their armour not only protected them, it made them inert forces moving forward rather like the tanks of later wars. They drove ahead, crashing through the ranks of their enemies like battering rams. Lance and sword gave them their cutting edge; their following foot-soldiers, often villeins and serfs brought reluctantly from feudal fiefs, dispatched those that their advancing lords had crushed, unhorsed or brushed aside. Barons, dukes and princes, each a landowner, each absolute lord in his own domains, resented rather than welcomed cooperation. They stood for an extreme and aristocratic individualism, each bringing the pickings of his own courage to the collective pile of victory.

They trained for war, by practising the individual skills of horsemanship, sword-play, dexterity with lance or axe. Their men were comparatively untrained, pressed levies brought from sheep-fold or rye-harvest, woodmen, drovers, plough-boys or, in the case of Silesia, miners (though these, it is true, were free men, come to battle willingly – but no better trained for that). The armies that such warriors formed were *ad hoc* collections, their skills uneven, their experience varied and their attitude towards one another one of a limited and easily disrupted trust. Brought together by temporary expediency, they sometimes included dynastic rivals or men divided by family feud; they were driven by jealousy and often foundered on the treachery of those who composed them. At this moment, on this particular April day in 1241, they might acknowledge that Henry of Silesia commanded them, but such acknowledgement was far short of absolute obedience. The Mongols, led by the fluttering signals of their officers, moved as one; when the European armies moved as one, it was usually briefly, until in the stress of battle their lines broke and each man chose his own fight and struggled for his own prize.

Henry, uncertain of where exactly Wenceslas was, decided to march southwards to meet him. Determined to prevent the meeting, Kaidu struck at him, early on 9 April. The place where he did so is now called Wahlstadt, a plain of no great distinction overlooked by low hills. Almost noiselessly for once, the Mongol horsemen swung across the grasslands; arrows, as always, arched across the sky like some rainbow draped in mourning. As Henry's advance column half broke up in confusion, the Mongols turned. Suddenly, they seemed to be in disorder. A brave counter-attack scattered them further. They fled, though keeping up a still-accurate stream of arrows as they turned in their saddles and tugged their short bows to the usual devastating effect. Seeing them in such haste to retreat, the knights set their horses to the gallop. They had never doubted that their collective might, once mobilized, would turn aside this nomad threat from the east.

Their pursuing column, as had so many others before, stretched eagerly across the plain like the long neck of some unfortunate bird brought by instinct and stupidity to run over and over again into the same trap. For once more, out of hollows or from behind the sparse bushes – perhaps even, as some reported at the time, from behind their own smoke screen – the hidden Mongols came careering, their war cry now on their lips, their arrows once more in unerring flight, their horses driving in, wheeling, retreating, leaving behind a horse or slow, mailed rider struggling in a welter of pulsating blood. Riven, the northern chivalry foundered there on that Wahlstadt plain. Henry the Bearded died, and with him thirty thousand others, or perhaps forty thousand – no one was certain. Kaidu's men cut the ears off the dead and sent them in nine sacks as a message of victory to Batu.

A detached Mongol force had meanwhile smashed the army hastily raised to defend Lithuania, then travelled parallel with the Baltic coast towards Germany. It swung through Pomerania before joining Kaidu outside the ruined walls of still-smouldering Liegnitz. In the meantime Kaidu had received messages telling him of Batu's victory in Hungary. He considered his position. Wenceslas was falling back; he had reached Königsberg, near Dresden, in an attempt to join the marshalled forces of Saxony, and of Thüringia further west, which were barring the advance of the Mongols. Kaidu seemed about to move against them, then suddenly swung south; while an agonized Wenceslas – who seems to have had a genius for being in the wrong place – hurried to try and cut him off, he savaged the peaceful towns of Moravia. As these Germano-Slavic centres one by one collapsed into smoking and blood-stained rubble, as the dying stared without comprehension at the dead and the raped dazedly regarded the ruined, the unhappy ruler of Bohemia floundered after the swift-moving Mongol *toumans*. Before he could intercept them, Kaidu had joined Subatei and Batu, and Kuyuk's brother, Kadan. The latter had spent these weeks in bringing fire and the indiscriminate sword to the southern provinces, Moldavia, Bukovina, Transylvania, winning three pitched battles, and, on the same day as Batu had so savagely defeated Béla IV, had taken the heavily fortified and bravely defended centre of Hermannstadt.

Béla had fled his kingdom. Kadan was sent to hunt him down, as earlier Subatei, with Jebei beside him, had hunted down the Khwarismian Shah Muhammad. The Hungarian king, landless and with neither friends nor subjects, stumbled into the prisons of Duke Frederick of Austria, his imprisonment the price of an old debt. All his cash and valuables paid for his release; he appealed to the rest of Europe for help, but papal piety and imperial promises wielded no swords. While in his own kingdom the siege-engines of the Mongols tumbled the walls of his great cities, Béla travelled despondently into what is now Yugoslavia. From Croatia he moved to the Adriatic coast. Kadan, relentlessly on his trail, followed him into Dalmatia. Across the mountains, another Mongol column was making for Udine and perhaps for Venice, some sixty miles beyond; a third was destructively active on the outskirts of Vienna. Béla left the mainland, settled on an island, as Muhammad had so fatally done before him. Kadan also took to the sea; the Hungarian king's small fleet was humiliatingly scattered. Béla fled down the coast, Kadan still vengefully behind him. He hesitated in Spalato, today's Split, where the ruins of Diocletian's palace may have hinted at the fragility of grandeur; soon, he had taken refuge again on the islands. Kadan prepared to follow once more.

At this moment it was as if Europe faced imminent destruction. What had happened in the north and the east could happen in the south and west. Northern Italy stood threatened, as did Germany from two directions. Monstrous tales of terror, as the Mongols had intended, magnified the power and ferocity of the invaders. The very name men used for them, 'Tartars', had altered the original word to one deriving from *Tartarus*, the ancient world's Hell. Mongols, then, were more devils than humans. They had risen from the Pit itself to overthrow Christian serenity. That Pope and Emperor had already made a mockery of Christian solidarity was overlooked; the devils from the east, these dreadful Tartars, would destroy both faith and hope. They were, it was said, cannibals, eating those they captured, especially the women; the breasts of virgins were a delicacy reserved for officers. Breathlessly, their next move was awaited.

When it came, it was the only one nobody had expected. Everywhere the *toumans* packed away their booty, chained up their captives and, laden with the wealth of half a continent, rode quietly away. Word had come from Karakorum, brought halfway across the world by a bandaged 'arrow rider': Ogadei was dead. For a moment Batu hesitated, Europe in his grasp. Then Subatei, the living incarnation of the traditions of Genghis Khan, reminded him of the *Yasak*. The descendants of the first Great Khan had the absolute duty when one ruler died to gather together for the election of the next. It was time to return to the heartlands.

Europe shuddered its relief. Mystery succeeded surprise – the peoples of the West could understand the retreat as little as they had been prepared for the advance. Then, as the reality of the Mongols receded, diminishing slowly into one of those potent myths of terror that lurk in the collective unconscious of the continent, they turned again to their own disruptive affairs. Nervously they sent missionaries to Karakorum – Carpini, William of Rubruck and the rest – in the hope of changing the Khaghan's misunderstood religious tolerance into a Christian conviction. Perhaps they hoped to turn their expectations of a distant Prester John into a practical truth; or possibly they were displaying only one more facet of that proselytizing dynamism which, while spreading the Cross throughout the world, would in the end discredit it by associating it with the military and commercial rigours of empire. In any case, the missionaries were to find little success among the tents and in the unlovely settlements of the Mongols, nor would the zealous potentates of Europe often find here the allies they hoped for in their crusades against Islam.

Batu, in the meantime, realized, as we have seen, that he had been out-

manoeuvred by fortune and Kuyuk's mother, Turakina. So well established was
Kuyuk's faction in Karakorum that he had no hope of being chosen Khaghan.
Moodily he wandered with his army along the line of the Danube, watching the
smoke rising as though to symbolize the death of his own hopes above whole series
of cities, towns and villages. Kadan, during the same period, devastated the
Dalmatian coast (though King Béla had returned to Hungary and, his depopulated
acres repeopled with disliked German immigrants, would continue to reign until
1270), then swung inland after destroying Ragusa and Cattaro (Dubrovnik and
Kotor today). Defeating the Bulgarians, he took the submission and tribute of their
ruler.

When Batu and Kadan met near the mouth of the Danube, in what is now
Rumania, they settled the new frontiers of this western wing of the Mongol Empire.
Batu, as Jochi's son, would be its overlord and one can believe that its vastness and
wealth compensated him to a great extent for his disappointment over the imperial
succession. Near where the border between Mongols and Europeans had once
been, along the line of the Volga, Batu now set his capital. Sarai, on the River
Akhtuba, one of the tributaries of the Volga's lower reaches, standing some sixty-
five miles north of Astrakhan and the delta on the Caspian Sea, soon became a
place of swift construction. This may perhaps be taken as the manifestation of an
ambition as pronounced as had been that which Ogadei had displayed in his plans
for Karakorum.

Yet, like all the Khaghans before Kubilai, Batu led the restless, peripatetic life
of a nomad prince, ranging his territories far to the north, hunting, living for the
most part under the felt roofs his fathers had preferred and retaining, for all the
magnificence of his dress and accoutrements, the rough, ancestral simplicities of his
people. His western boundaries were the mountain ranges – the Carpathians in the
north, the Transylvanian Alps in the centre, the Balkans in the south. Beyond them
lay the lands he had already plundered, lands that, weakened after their defeats
and irresolute as a consequence, he need no longer fear. North of the Carpathians
lay the rich territories of what had been the Russian principalities of Kiev-
Novgorod. Like the Bulgarians in the south, these now paid tribute to him. They
were his own domains, their princes were his vassals, their lands and cities his to
cherish or destroy. It would be more than two centuries before his descendants
would see these provinces slip from their grasp.

The *kuriltai*, as we know, was held without Batu. He settled into his western
rulership, an independent monarch in everything but name. That sharp-eyed
voyager, William of Rubruck, visited him in 1253: 'He was seated on a long seat as
broad as a couch, all gilded, with three steps leading up to it, and a lady was beside
him. Men were seated on his right, and ladies on his left; but where the room on the
women's side was not taken up – for only Batu's wives were present – men occupied
it. . . . His face was all covered at the time with reddish spots.' Friar William compared Batu's height with that of 'my lord John de Beaumont, may his soul rest in
peace' – not the most accurate description for a posterity with little idea of this
nobleman's dimensions. But he tells us of the court, where 'they had spread a great
awning, for the dwelling could not hold all the men and women who had come

A Persian view of Mongols striking camp and preparing to move on.

there', and of its etiquette: nothing was to be said 'until Batu bid us speak, and then to speak briefly'. Led forward, he noticed the 'profound silence' that gripped everyone; to speak to Batu he went down on one knee, but was asked to bend the other and did so, 'not wishing to dispute over it. Then he bid me speak and I, imagining that I was praying to God, since I had both knees bent, began my speech. . . .'

Not more than two years later Batu was dead. His son, and after him his grandson, ruled so briefly that finally the fief came to his younger brother Berke. But the cement that held Batu's conquests together did not give way. Sarai became a centre for travellers, missionaries, craftsmen and merchants. A new city was built and became the first staging post for the overland journey to the Far East, a journey more and more people were making, bringing back tales of wealth and wonder for the gawping stay-at-homes. And when the empire broke up, and this huge western area at last became autonomous, its endless plains and distant vassals continued to support the Golden Horde and its successors until, time having done its eroding work, it dwindled into impotence some four centuries later.

# 6  THE RESILIENCE OF ISLAM

In the west the armies of the Mongol succession had struggled with some success to fulfil what Genghis Khan had considered to be his due – the domination of the world. But before his death he had specified both China and western Asia as areas that were swiftly to be brought within the empire. Once elected Khaghan in 1229, Ogadei not only sent Subatei and Batu across the Volga, he sent armies thrusting towards Mesopotamia, and others to range beyond the walls that had for so long now failed to protect the Kin. Despite his own apparently limited capacity as a warrior, the new Great Khan had the armies and the generals to take that curious Mongol revenge on the world for its refusal to do him instant obeisance. From his father he seems to have inherited the illogical certainty that the whole earth was already under his rule and only obstinacy, pride and an inhuman ignorance prevented those who governed its peoples from acknowledging the fact: in the eyes of the Mongols, their swift, cruel columns had been dispatched not so much for conquest as for punishment, not to redraw the world map but rather to restore it to its proper, predestined order.

While Genghis had been active far to the east, Jelal ud-Din had been reviving and extending the remains of his power. In Kirman and Shiraz he had raised a large and dangerous following; many of the other cities of what had been the Khwarismian empire looked to him for deliverance and a renewal of collective power; he himself loomed for a moment like the champion come to restore Islam to its rightful place along the Amu Darya. Jelal himself seems to have discounted any further Mongol assault and as a result felt himself free to struggle for personal supremacy. He had conquered in northern India; now he would tackle the Caliph in Baghdad, the Seljuq Sultans in Anatolia. Where he might have made sensible alliances and led an eastward-facing Islamic front against the Mongols, he wasted time and substance in what were no more than wars of aimless ambition, fighting for glory rather than from a shrewd assessment of necessity.

In 1225 Jelal, leaving his brother to govern his regained lands in western Persia (or Iraq Ajami), marched north against the Christians of Georgia. At Tiflis he massacred thousands of those who followed this rival religion, a course of conduct that might have commended him to other Muslim leaders had he not already incurred their suspicions by his attempt to dominate Caliph Nasir in Baghdad. Now, on the shores of Lake Van, he turned on the forces of that declining Syrian dynasty, the Ayyubids; these managed what he himself had tentatively attempted, an alliance with the Seljuqs. A warlike people once as capable as Jelal himself, the latter had stood as the western defenders of the Samanids in Persia, and eventually

ufage quilt nolet eftul.
te teur fergnoz. Je apefte
·ij·fops a leducmon telem

quites nont volu anguer
tenr pmer ufage· A pres
ce q chagnifchi fnfnit·x

Again from the *Floire des Estoires*, this scene is said to show a battle between Mongols and 'an oriental army'. The Mongols bear the Crescent of Islam, which makes it hard to be certain from which part of the Orient their opponents come.

defeated Masud, king of Ghazna, to found an empire of their own. This, by the end of the eleventh century, stretched through Iran, Mesopotamia, Syria and Palestine, and included in its battle honours victory against Byzantium and the capture of one of that ramshackle anachronism's emperors. Religious dissension, nepotism, dynastic rivalry and the sinister pressures of the Assassin sect weakened them; Jelal's father in carving out his Khwarismian empire brought their power in Persia to an end. Now, in 1230, the Seljuq strength that still remained, well entrenched in Turkish Anatolia, saw its chance for revenge. Kaikubad, Sultan of Rum, marching with the Syrians, trapped Jelal at Arzinjan, high on the western arm of the Euphrates. Jelal, recoiling, discovered an even greater menace to the east: Ogadei had sent thirty thousand men pushing towards Asia Minor and the Mediterranean seaboard under the *orlok* Chormagan and his son Baichu. Turning again, beset and bewildered, Jelal fled westward; support that might still have been his had he agreed to lead Islam against the new Mongol assault fell away as his indecision and weakness persisted. In August 1231, in the Turkish district of Diyarbakir, he died, without sense or profit, after a dispute with a Kurdish tribesman.

The Mongol armies halted on the plains of Azerbeijan, where there was grazing for their horses and from which Baghdad, the Seljuqs and the Christians of the Caucasus could be equally threatened. It was against Georgia, however, that they turned first, perhaps to weaken the Christian flank before Subatei's drive westwards after 1236. By 1238, certainly, Georgia, once a united kingdom, had become a scene of bloodshed, turmoil and confusion, its nobles turned against the throne and the throne itself claimed by two princes, confounding easy slogans by being both named David. To the south, a confederation of Iraqui notables had been defeated. In 1239 the ancient capital of Armenia, Ani, was taken and razed and all its population except the craftsmen and the children killed. It seemed as though the Mongols were determined to take notable revenge upon all Christians for some unknown and unknowable insult. With Subatei and Batu ravening across the steppes and the Russian Grand Duke Yuri swept aside, with Novgorod threatened and Béla of Hungary under pressure, it took an objective vision to realize that to the Mongols Christianity and Islam were beliefs equally plausible, equally irrelevant.

That this was the case, however, became evident when in 1241, now under the sole command of Baichu, the Mongol armies turned to attack the Seljuq Sultanate of Rum. Ogadei, with Nestorians in his following and a church in Karakorum, was not a man with a religious grudge. Indeed, appealed to by the Christians of Georgia, who used the principles of the *Yasak* itself to underline their plea for religious tolerance, he sent a Nestorian bishop to the Mongol commanders in that field, a man named Simeon whose task it became to warn them in the name of the Khaghan that churches were sacred and not places to plunder. Thus there was reason in the hopes of King Hayton, ruler of the small Asia Minor kingdom, Little Armenia, which lay between the Taurus Mountains and the sea. He felt that if the eastern Christians allied themselves with the Mongols, they could between them destroy Islam's hold on Mesopotamia, Iraq and, above all, Palestine. He had therefore no difficulty in subjecting himself to the distant presence, but very visible power, of the Great Khan, this acceptance of vassalage, as such bowing to the wind had done since the first wars of Genghis, ensuring his own safety and that of his people. The proud princes of Russia, however, the lords of Poland, the King of Hungary and all his retainers, were being driven like dead leaves before this wind, were being hurried into a graceless oblivion. All thoughts of alliance had to be put in abeyance while, from the Volga to the Danube, from the Black Sea to the Baltic, Christendom's eastern defences were being torn to shreds by this storm.

By the end of 1241 that storm was abating – Ogadei's death brought Batu growling down the Danube, taking with him the motive power behind the western conquests. Ten years of struggle for the succession now followed in Karakorum, interrupted only by the brief stability of Kuyuk's reign, before there emerged, in 1251, the dedicated figure of Mangu, a Khaghan harder in character than Ogadei, as fierce in his ambition as Genghis himself. Looking directly west from his new throne, he saw only chaos. The ravaged provinces left without centre by the collapse of Khwarismian power, the Iraqui Muslims torn between their fear of the Mongols and their respect for the Baghdad Caliphate, the Seljuqs broken after Baichu's defeat of Sultan Kilij Arslan at Köse-Dagh in 1243, the petty kings and princes who, constantly threatened by the Mongol armies still based on Azerbeijan, were united only in their sullen vassalage to the Great Khan – all this added up to a confused and general weakness open to exploitation by any new hero prepared to challenge the expansion of Mongol power. The fact that successive governors of Khorasan had been enlightened, incorruptible and far-sighted was admirable, but the increasingly high standards of culture, commerce and administration in the territories under their stewardship only emphasized the ramshackle disharmony of the region as a whole.

Mangu decided that it was time the Mongols imposed a decisive control over

Masyaf, one of the strongholds of the Assassin sect. For two centuries these dedicated terrorists brought fear to the hearts of Muslim and even Crusader notables. Then, in a single relentless campaign, Hulagu and his general Ked-Buka destroyed them for ever.

Asia Minor and the eastern seaboard of the Mediterranean, as well as establishing a new and stricter rule over Persia and Persian Iraq. All the lands that had for six centuries lain firmly in Muslim hands were to be taken over. In order to achieve this, it was necessary to destroy such centres of alternative power as existed – in effect, this meant the extirpation of the Ismaili Assassins and the enforced collapse of the Caliphate. What seemed to watching and over-hopeful Christians as a war against Islam was in fact a cold-blooded political conflict intended to remove all challengers for the power that the Mongols coveted. In 1255 Hulagu, Mangu's brother, with an enormous army – two in every ten soldiers in the Mongol forces were assigned to him, as well as a thousand Chinese engineers to man his siege-trains and flaming engines of destruction – settled himself in a camp near Samarkand, crouched and tensed like a beast preparing its devouring leap, then on the last day of the year crossed the Oxus, the Levant and Asia Minor his immediate prey.

Founded in 1090 by Hassan ben Sabbah, the sect of the Assassin had in two centuries become a powerful political weapon, a force altering and often distorting the flow of administrative logic and religious development. Enthused by reinforced convictions of paradise, the single-minded murderers in the service of the Old Man of the Mountains brought uncertainty at best, and at worst abject terror, into the minds of rulers who felt themselves to be under threat. Prepared by any conciliation or surrender to ward off attacks that legend increasingly advertised as both ruthless and infallible, these rulers obeyed every command given them by the sect; those with enemies or rivals, however, paid vast sums in order to be certain of their destruction. Thus, from his stronghold in Alamut, high in the mountains of Kuhistan, the Sheikh-al-Jabal, the Old Man of the Mountains, through successive generations was able to control or influence a vast area of western Asia and at times to strike well beyond its frontiers. As a result, by the time Hulagu marched, this Ismaili sect was said to hold 360 mountain fortresses and strongholds, from which, at the behest of their sheikh, its devotees, the *fedayin*, could set out on their implacable missions.

Now, however, a greater power, as implacable and cruel as they, had come out against them. In their own ranks there was dissension. The old Sheikh, Ala ad-Din Muhammad, might have been strong enough to resist for a long time, but he was succeeded and probably murdered by his son, Rukn ad-Din, a much weaker man. Hulagu ordered him to dismantle his mountain castles, his 'eagles' eyries'; he agreed, then prevaricated, finally did nothing. The Mongol leader sent three columns against his vast fortress, Maimundiz, under General Ked-Buka (a Naiman and, as a Christian, probably relishing this task); the young Sheikh was besieged and finally, late in 1256, starved out. Its central figure thus made captive, the sect elsewhere lost certainty and, one by one, the fastnesses on cliff-top and escarpment ridge surrendered or were taken – Alamut itself only after a three-year investment. The latest successor to the Old Man of the Mountains – paradoxically young, robbed of all power, even of dignity – was marched away to Karakorum where Mangu refused to see him; still aimlessly on the road, he was killed by his guards.

So Muslim heresy was punished, even if at the hand of pagans, and there must have been some rejoicing, one fancies, among those Iraqui princes whom Hulagu had forced into alliance with him against the terrifying Assassins. But Hulagu's next move was against one of the central pillars of Muslim ascendancy, the Caliphate itself. It was in the eighth century that Abul Abbas, exploiting a tenuous relationship to the Prophet, established himself with the help of largely Persian followers as Islam's ruler and pontiff. He massacred almost all those connected with the previous dynasty, the Umayyads, and set up in its place his own, the Abbasids. The great Haroun al Rashid was of this line and it had now stretched unbroken for five centuries, always powerful although often restricted by counterbalancing power and at intervals threatened by uprising or heresy. One need not, therefore, be surprised that when Hulagu demanded that the present Caliph, Mustassem, should abase himself before the Great Khan and demolish his protective fortifications in order to demonstrate his surrender, the answer he received from Baghdad was arrogantly uncompromising: 'Young man, misled by a time of good fortune you have become in your own eyes Lord of the Universe and think

your commands the decisions of fate.' The Caliphate was eternal, Baghdad had resisted all past attacks, 'from West to East all who follow the True Faith are my servants' – Hulagu would do best to return peacefully to Khorasan.

Alas, Mustassem was neither as powerful as his rhetoric nor clever enough to turn rhetoric into action. He gathered an enormous army, then neglected to keep them contented by regular payment. With a somewhat illogical confidence he awaited attack, while Hulagu brought Baichu from Turkey, pushed forward Ked-Buka after his successes against the Assassins, sent on from Kurdistan a great

A Persian painting depicting the advance of Hulagu –
attended by his yak-tail banners and shaded by a
canopy – against the Assassins.

column of reinforcements led by three of Batu's nephews, then advanced himself in
command of his main force. The Caliphate army marched forward to meet Baichu,
crossing the Tigris to face their enemies on the west bank. Alas for them, however,
the Mongols had forgotten nothing of the duplicity of war. By smashing a vital dam
they let loose a sudden flood on that riparian plain; trapped, the Caliph's forces
could neither advance nor retreat. Over a hundred thousand of them are said to
have died; only a few struggled through mud and yellow-brown shallows to the
safety of the beleaguered city. By the beginning of 1258 Baghdad had been encircled.

A drawing of Hulagu in the field, resting during a campaign.
When his fighting days were over and his ferocity spent,
he passed his days and nights in drunken carousing.

Now began a ferocious siege. In his history the Persian chronicler Wassaf writes,
with a typical flurry of similes:

The arrows and bolts, the lances and spears, the stones from the slings and catapults of
both sides shot swiftly up to heaven, like the messengers of the prayers of the just, then fell
as swiftly, like the judgements of fate. . . . In this way Baghdad was besieged and terrorized
for fifty days. But since the city still held out the order was given for baked bricks lying outside the walls to be collected, and with them high towers were built in every direction,
overlooking the streets and alleys of Baghdad. On top of these they set up the catapults.
Now the city was filled with the thunder and lightning of striking stones and flaring naphtha
pots. A dew of arrows rained from a cloud of bows and the population was trampled
underfoot by the forces of weakness and humiliation. The cry went up, 'Today we have no
strength against Goliath and his army!' The River Tigris, which flows through the centre
of Baghdad as the Milky Way flows through the centre of Heaven, was blocked in both
directions and all possibility of flight was barred.

The eastern wall gave way first, its strength breached by Chinese siege-craft.
The Persian Tower, commanding that length of the defences, collapsed. The
Mongols came screaming down the lanes of the city's eastern section in appalling
glee. The terrified inhabitants ran for boats, for rafts, for the treacherous security
of their river. Mongols followed; the pale water darkened with the blood of the
trapped. Confronted by these ferocious facts of his defeat, the Caliph surrendered.
Eight hundred thousand people came out of his great city, were counted by the
Mongols, and were then systematically killed.

The massacre was so great that the blood of the slain flowed in a river like the Nile. . . .
The broom of looting swept out the treasures of the harems of Baghdad and the hammer
of fury smashed down the battlements head-first, as though they were disgraced. Palaces
whose canopies had because of their rich design made the seats of Paradise hide in shame
and cover their shortcomings were destroyed. . . . Golden couches and cushions, encrusted
with jewels, were slashed to pieces, torn to shreds; those hidden behind the veils of the
Great Harem were dragged . . . through the streets and alleys, each of them to become a
plaything in the hands of a Tatar monster, and for these virtuous mothers the brightness
of day became darkened.

Thus Wassaf, of the aftermath of defeat.

For six days and nights this destruction continued, an act of terrorism so thorough
and so appalling that its memory has never left the Arab world. For a while Baghdad
ceased in any real sense to exist. As for the Caliph, he was shackled, insulted,
starved. When he was brought before Hulagu, the Mongol prince, it is said, offered
him some of his own gold to eat. 'How can one eat it? No one can eat gold,' Mustassem replied. Hulagu nodded. 'If you knew that, why didn't you send it to me?
If you had, you'd still be in your palace, eating and drinking without a care.' The
Caliph was mocked, too, for not having used all his riches – the accumulated
wealth of five centuries of Abbasid rule – to defend himself more effectively.
Finally, he was taken to a nearby village, rolled in a carpet, then trampled to death
by galloping horses. The date was 20 February 1258; Hulagu and his victorious
forces, their strength established in Persia and Turkey, with Batu's near-autono-
mous rule to the north and north-west securing their rear, and with Baghdad now
collapsed before them, were poised to strike at an Egypt apparently ready for the
taking.

To the Christians of the eastern churches Hulagu at this moment was, whether
by his own wish or not, an ally. He had crushed the very centre of Islam and was
now about to exploit the consequences of the Caliph's downfall. Not only that, he
himself was believed to be on the verge of turning Christian – an optimistic view
of a pagan with Buddhist leanings, but one encouraged by the fact that his chief wife,
Doquz Khatun, was a Christian herself. She was a Kereit and the grand-daughter
of that dubious friend and patron of Genghis Khan's early years, Toghrul; she was,
moreover, the widow of Hulagu's father, Tuli, and as such entitled to special
respect Rashid ad-Din tells us that she gave the Christians strong support and that,
to please her, Hulagu too protected them. Near her tent, it seems, she always had a
chapel, a portable building 'where bells were rung', a fact notable to Rashid
because bells were specifically forbidden in Muslim lands. To this formidable
lady's pressures was added the influence of Ked-Buka, the Naiman general whose
successes had helped gain him his commander's deep confidence. It is no wonder
that the Christian communities, crushed by Muslim intolerance for so many
years, should now have begun to arise again, like grasses lifting after the weight of a
footfall. It was no mere vegetable passion that animated them, however – their
theme was revenge. The fact that the Nestorian community of Baghdad had been
spared while elsewhere the slide of blood had darkened every path and narrow
lane only encouraged the Christians to extend that example of murder.

Hulagu carried his booty back to the security and pasture-land of Azerbeijan.
He had the gold melted down into ingots, which he stored in a fortress he had
specially built on the shores of Lake Urmia. Meanwhile he rested and reinforced

his army. As its numbers climbed towards half a million men, he received – one does not know with what sardonic reaction – Bohemund IV of Antioch, who brought into the Mongol camp the only detachment of western fighting-men ever to take their place there. Bohemund's father-in-law was Hayton of Lesser Armenia, still pursuing his dream of a Mongol–Christian alliance against Islam; he too joined Hulagu with sixteen thousand Armenian followers.

Now Mesopotamia and Syria discovered the bitter logic of Mongol conquest that earlier Persia, Asia Minor and the Russian steppes had been made to learn. Whoever fought died; whoever surrendered was spared to live in vassalage. It was 1259 when Hulagu came marching refreshed out of Azerbeijan, to sweep across Jazirah, the northern province of Iraq. The Emir Kamil Muhammad died by having pieces hacked from his living body and stuffed into his mouth. Syria, made witness to his dreadful death by his paraded head, shuddered and gave way. Hulagu crossed the Tigris, built a bridge of boats at Manbij and crossed the Euphrates on it, then moved on Aleppo. Here he enacted once again the bloody drama of Baghdad; resisting, the city was besieged, its walls breached by the hammering of twenty catapults, its defences overrun. Sultan Nasir Yusuf, heir of the Ayyubid line of the great Saladin, fled just in time and made for Damascus. That city, terrorized by the example of Aleppo and Baghdad, prepared to surrender without dispute; Nasir fled south, while behind him Bohemund, Hayton and Ked-Buka in Christian amity took triumphant possession of the city.

With a Damascus mosque already altered by decree into a church and Muslims in the street bowing to the Cross, Ked-Buka took up the pursuit of the Sultan. It was never Mongol policy to leave at liberty anyone capable of rallying loyalty or drawing allegiance away from the Great Khan to whom it rightfully belonged. Nasir fled from Damascus to Gaza, but there treachery tripped him. Captive, he was sent to Hulagu, suffering and death. For the Mongol leader he had already become irrelevant – his attention was now on Egypt itself.

Egypt at this time was ruled by the Mamluks, a word which, literally translated, means 'owned men'. It was a ninth-century Caliph who first employed slaves in large numbers to defend his interests and his possessions; soon every Muslim ruler had enormous slave armies. It was thought that by creating an army actually owned by its commander, disloyalty and faction could be avoided; this was a theory which, perhaps because of the nature of the word 'slave', overlooked the possibility that such an army might develop a loyalty to itself and its immediate generals. Thus by the thirteenth century slaves in many states held and maintained the balance of internal power. In Egypt, after the death in 1249 of its Ayyubid ruler, Al-Malik as-Salih, the weapon he himself had created to defend his country against the Crusaders and his throne against rivals became the means of ending his dynasty. It was a Mamluk general who followed him as ruler, and for well over two centuries it was Mamluks who were to govern beside the Nile. As it happened, this may have done Egypt very little harm, for they were ambitious, clever, unscrupulous and devoted to reviving the importance and a little of the imperial grandeur of ancient Egypt.

Such men were not liable to take kindly to the grandiloquence of a Mongol surrender demand. 'You have heard how we have conquered a vast empire and purified the earth of the disorders tainting it.' Thus Hulagu, setting forth his credentials. 'It is for you to fly and for us to pursue – and whither will you fly and by

The citadel of Aleppo, a town which
for all its formidable defences was captured
by Mongol armies on more than one occasion.

what road escape us? Our horses are swift, our arrows sharp, our swords like
thunderbolts, our hearts as hard as mountains, our soldiers numerous as the sands.'
And Hulagu added a sentence that summed up Mongol successes in the west:
'You are now the only enemy against whom we have to march.'

By an irony there was one enemy Hulagu cannot have considered, but whose
existence now drew his attention after all from Egypt. The year was 1259; far away
to the east, Mangu failed and died. When Ogadei died, Europe had watched
Batu's mysterious withdrawal in amazement; now the Egyptian leaders, one may
imagine, regarded with equal astonishment, and equal relief, the abrupt departure
of Hulagu and his threatening forces. It was not that he himself had dynastic
ambitions; it was rather that in the Mongol heartlands fraternal conflict had
broken out, with Kubilai Khaghan in China and his (and Hulagu's) brother
Arik-Buka Khaghan in Karakorum. With such a struggle in his rear Hulagu dared
not keep his communications extended down the Mediterranean seaboard and
across the Sinai desert. Instead, watchfully, he withdrew to Azerbeijan; he must

certainly have felt that his Egyptian campaign had only been postponed. To maintain his presence he kept Ked-Buka and a depleted army as a screening force in Syria.

Thus the Mamluks were spared their decision between resistance and surrender – though it is unlikely that they would have mildly given up what they had so recently won. Now came one of those almost forgotten moments upon which history sometimes turns. The Mamluks under their Sultan, Kutuz – who had taken the throne under cover of the Mongol crisis – executed the envoys who had brought Hulagu's letter, each one in a different quarter of Cairo. Then, conscious that it was with them that the responsibility for defending Islam lay, they gathered an army of well over a hundred thousand men, a heterogeneous collection of Syrians, Turks, Arabs, Persians and Egyptians, of volunteers, the conscripted and the forcibly pressed, and, placing it under the command of the Kuman Turk, Baibars, ordered it off to the north.

In order to attack the Mongols in Syria, the Egyptian army had to march across Palestine. There, however, along the coastal strip, the Crusader nobles kept desperate state; their permission had to be sought. In high perplexity, they met under the tall walls of Acre. Should they allow the Mamluk request and let the Egyptian army through, or should they place their trust in the Mongol–Christian alliance, that chimera which had led King Hethum and Bohemund into the Mongol camp? But the crusaders of the Palestine coast were Catholics; they owed no allegiance to the eastern churches. The Pope was their spiritual master, and the Pope had excommunicated Bohemund for placing his banner among the yak-tails of the Mongols. In Poland fellow-Catholics were once again struggling against Mongol invasion – it was surely the Mongols who were the greater immediate danger? In any case both they and the Mamluks were now, or would be in the future, enemies of Christendom – let them fight each other: whoever won, surely the Crusaders could not lose? They gave Baibars permission to make his advance.

This general, Baibars, was a man who had quite probably learned his warrior skills fighting for the Mongols, the cousins of his own people. He had later been bought as a slave in the markets of Damascus by a Mamluk emir, had fought with such bravery and cunning that he now stood as the most powerful man in the Egyptian Mamluk army. His determination was the stiffening in Mamluk resistance that had enabled it to stand firm even against the menace of Hulagu. He had trained his forces in techniques borrowed from the Mongols themselves and, confident in success, had suggested attack as the profitable policy as soon as he discovered Hulagu's preoccupation with the Karakorum *kuriltai*.

Ked-Buka commanded a much smaller army than the Egyptian – the greatest number conflicting accounts credit him with is thirty thousand men, a quarter of the force available to Baibars. Given these circumstances, Ked-Buka may have thought it a good augury that, when the armies met on 3 September 1260, it should have been at the spot near Nazareth where David was said to have killed Goliath. Over what really happened at this place, Ain Jalut, some argument continues. Baibars seems to have held his own highly trained force back, while pushing forward the bulk of his multinational army to face the Mongols. Ked-Buka attacked; at the fierce advance the Mamluk ranks gave way. Was this perforce, or had it been planned? Was this Mongol cunning learned and turned against its originators? The Mongols pressed forward, clawing as fiercely as ever for the victory they now

A sixteenth-century painting of a captured Mongol warrior. By then the Mongol fury had largely spent itself – its memory, however, remained potent.

looked on as theirs by right. They struck aside units from Syria, detachments from Turkey, the refugee remnants of those in the Islamic world who had already fled before them once. But, as their opponents seemed on the point of disintegration, as they advanced towards yet another beckoning triumph, Baibars rose from nowhere. As meticulously ruthless as any Mongol khan, he took the astonished Ked-Buka in the flanks, pressed on him unexpectedly through the breaking ranks he had been pursuing, slashed him down and scattered his men, drove him into captivity and death, his men into defeat and the invincibility of the Mongols back on to the shelves of legend.

Thus, by admitting Kutuz and Baibars through their territories, the Crusader lords had created the condition for the Mongol setback; in time Islam's victory would prove their own defeat, but the moment for the last Christian baron to relinquish his hold on the Holy Land had not yet arrived. What did for a while seem possible was that the Mamluk advance would push the Mongols to unprecedented retreat; Kutuz and Baibars were already thinking of restoring the Caliph to Baghdad. In anticipation of some final victory Muslims in Syria began to massacre the Christians, who so short a while before had been basking in the approval and protection of Mongol overlords.

The Mongols, however, stopped at the defensible line of the Euphrates. Aleppo and Damascus were in Muslim hands; Baghdad remained as yet beyond recovery. In Syria a triumphant Kutuz handed out emirates, reward for service. Pettiness betrayed him, however; jealous and afraid of Baibars, he gave that commander nothing, thus making an enemy of the only man he should have placated. Home-ward-bound, Baibars almost contemptuously turned his power on his master. Kutuz died and, as it proved, was little mourned. The crowds come out to acclaim him in the streets of Cairo were as happy to welcome Baibars – happier, since they knew that it was Baibars who had won the war.

Only the new Sultan himself realized that what he had won was little more than a skirmish; the Mongols had suffered a slight setback. A column prancing once more, and as destructively as before, into Aleppo, showed in the ruin they left behind them what power remained to Hulagu. Yet it was a column finally forced to retreat as, near Hims, Mamluk forces drove them back. In a sense Hulagu was trapped. Before him, Baibars, energizing his minions and allies, burned the Mesopotamian plains, destroying the fodder that might have maintained Mongol horses. Behind him the struggle for the succession continued unresolved, leaving him, a declared ally of Kubilai's, too vulnerable to attack Egypt again. All the while Baibars was consolidating his position, setting up a Caliphate in Cairo, having himself then proclaimed by this vassal pontiff the commander of all Islam. His ambitions might be too clear to be attractive, but the Muslim world had need of him, and knew its need, and knew he answered it.

Hulagu, on the other hand, found himself unpleasantly hemmed in and circum-scribed. It was not until 1262 that Kubilai was confirmed as Great Khan and he knew that he was supported by the Mongols' central authority. The new Khaghan, however, had his headquarters in China; his main concern was with his own vast and many-cultured fief, and western Asia was a long way from Pekin. Much nearer, across the Oxus, stood an old supporter of Arik-Buka, Alghui, the grandson of Chagatei; by the time he had broken with his dangerous patron and allied himself with Kubilai, a more important internecine conflict threatened.

Batu had died in 1255. His successor was his brother, Berke. Originally the overlord, under his brother – and he under the Great Khan – of territories on the western shores of the Caspian, Berke had commanded one of the main trade routes connecting Persia and the Middle East with eastern Russia. Being a Mongol, it was probably expediency rather than conviction that persuaded him to accept Islam – most of the merchants controlling this trade were Muslim and the thought of a coreligionist as their protector would draw them to the routes he guarded. His diplomatic conversion proved successful, so much so that it undermined his posi-tion; a jealous Batu moved him to an area where his influence was less and the pickings thinner. Now, he himself had become Khan of the Golden Horde. When he glanced again over the lands he controlled, however, he discovered that Hulagu, too, was active in the Caucasus. It was Hulagu's forces that had brought the power of the Seljuqs to an end, Hulagu who, apparently in the forefront of the fight against Islam, had drawn to him the support of the Georgian princes and such Christian monarchs as remained in Asia Minor. Between Berke and the rich lands of Syria and the valleys of the Tigris and Euphrates, therefore, lands with which he would dearly have liked to have a direct connection, lay the cordon of Hulagu's pagan rule, tolerant of all religions save the Muslim.

Berke's ambition to bring religious conviction and commercial interest into profitable union once again was delicately supported by the alert Baibars. The death of Mangu was the solvent that disbanded the long-standing alliance between Hulagu and the Golden Horde. Berke was the grandson of Jochi, Genghis Khan's

Hulagu on the eve of one of his most decisive campaigns
presides over a feast of farewell and anticipation.

eldest son, and perhaps felt his seniority meant that he could now disregard the
authority of the distant Khaghan. In any case he withdrew his forces from Hulagu's
army; those in Syria simply went over to the Mamluks. (Hulagu's treatment of
them may have contributed to their discontent.) Baibars received them with
honours and gifts; many of the leaders discovered that their short, treacherous
journey had led them directly to an emirate. The Mamluk Sultan sent an embassy
laden with gifts to Berke himself. Thus when, with the succession dispute almost
resolved, Hulagu prepared to revenge himself for Baibars's victories, he discovered
Berke threateningly on his flank. Religion and self-interest had outweighed mere
blood connection. For the first time two of the great khanates confronted one
another in a conflict over their own local interests.

In the winter of 1262 conflict came to its peak of battle. Then, as the partisan Wassaf put it: 'An army of Mongols under the command of Berke Khan, filthy as demons, devils of savagery and numerous as the falling raindrops, rolled across the frozen river in waves as swift as wind or fire.' Elsewhere the conflict between Arik-Buka and Kubilai was coming to its resolution of surrender and triumph; here, a long struggle seemed only just to have begun. One may imagine the glee with which Baibars, firmly entrenched in Cairo, regarded this prospect. Hulagu was forced back from the River Terek and it seemed as if Muslim Berke might after all be able to join hands with Muslim Mamluks in Syria. Despite Berke's victories, however, Hulagu stood firm in the Caucasus. When Al-Malik as-Salih of Mosul rebelled, when David v of Georgia attempted to wrest his independence from the Mongols, Hulagu crushed them. Byzantium, its emperor Michael viii happy to sign a treaty with him, supported his flank. Kubilai, his own struggles over, sent him another thirty thousand men. Berke, sullen but intelligent, halted his offensive, Derbend his most southerly garrison. What he had gained in Persia, Iraq, Asia Minor and the Caucasus, Hulagu held. But by the time this situation had clarified, all question of a renewed thrust to the south had ended. The existence of a hostile Berke taut and watchful on the Caucasus made any move by Hulagu against the Mamluks impossibly dangerous.

In this way the west Asian conquests of the Mongols were stabilized. Hulagu built himself a capital, Maragha, near the eastern shores of Lake Urmia. As before, it was the well-watered plains of Azerbeijan that remained the centre of his power. From this area between Lake Urmia and the Caspian he administered, or took tribute from, lands that stretched from the Oxus to the borders of Byzantium, from the Caucasus to the Euphrates. He ruled in the name of the Great Khan, but in fact he ruled without trammel or interference. His view of religion, welcoming to Buddhism, protective to Christianity, hostile to Islam, determined the levels of tolerance in his realms. His name had become a synonym for the terrible in Muslim lands, but he seems finally to have quietened into an acceptable despotism, no more idiosyncratic, demanding or tyrannous than was common in those lands and at that time. When he died, in 1265, he was only forty-eight years old; like many another monarch before and since, having survived the exigencies of the battlefield he seems to have succumbed to the excesses of the banqueting hall. Mourned perhaps above all by the Christians of eastern Europe, he was buried in a vast tomb on the island of Sahi, near the north-eastern shores of Lake Urmia. He left behind him a reputation for systematic, cold-blooded destructiveness, the territories he had won and welded into an empire within an empire, and the dynasty that in the generations to come would govern it.

# 7 THE FALL OF THE CELESTIAL KINGDOM

**W**hile Ogadei was being elected by the 1229 *kuriltai*, those much-battered but resilient enemies of the Mongols, the Kin emperors, took the opportunity to strengthen their position. In Shensi Province, and Honan, they took back territories from the invaders. At the same time, seeking diplomatic victories, they sent an embassy to Ogadei; their envoy received the shortest possible shrift from the new Khaghan. He refused to hear his congratulations, refused to accept his gifts: 'My father grew old and died in war against the Kin,' he said. In response the Kin leaders, still trusting to walls, built a line of fortresses along the Huang-Ho; a hundred thousand men were placed in these defences, while behind them twice that number awaited the Mongol onslaught.

Tuli, with Subatei at his right hand, commanded the Mongol columns that in 1230 began to make their way into China. In eastern Kansu, they found they could make no headway against determined defence. Held up, they remembered Genghis Khan's final instructions; they asked the Sung Emperor in the south for permission to pass through his lands. Such was their dislike of the northern dynasty, whom they still thought of as barbarian usurpers, that the Sung allowed themselves to be persuaded. In this way, with what westerners might think an uncharacteristic lack of subtlety, they allowed the buffer between themselves and their dangerous new allies to be destroyed.

There now followed a three-pronged invasion of the Kin lands. Tuli came east into the Wei valley and the plains of Sezchuan, Ogadei struck south into Sanshi. At Kun-chou a huge Kin army was destroyed; the remaining forces drew back defensively upon the famous 'southern capital', Kai-feng. It was in the summer of 1232 that the siege of that enormous city began, the Mongols investing walls and fortresses protecting a population that has been estimated at two million. Bewildered by the complexity and technical novelty of the Chinese defences, they trusted nevertheless to their own tenacious ambition, their deeply rooted patience. Ogadei himself turned for home but was, in Rashid's phrase, 'overtaken with an illness'. Tuli, the story goes, picked up a glass of water over which the Mongol *shamans* had murmured their spells and in which their healing amulets had been washed; praying that he should be taken, rather than the Khaghan, if death was God's intention, he drank it down. 'By divine providence, the Khaghan recovered and Tuli Khan, having taken leave, set out earlier to join his heavy baggage. On the way, he fell ill and died. . . .' Thus the superbly competent Subatei was left in charge of the campaign and the unrelenting siege.

Fearing that, with sickness and natural wastage, his army was becoming too small to keep its grip on the city, he asked the Sung emperors for reinforcements. Those rulers, as innocently obliging as before, sent him twenty thousand men under one of their chief commanders, Meng Hung. Now, as so often, famine and disease proved the besiegers' most powerful allies. With so many within the walls, provisions were an enormous and, in the end, an insoluble problem. Hundreds, then thousands, fell ill; many of them died. Early in 1233 there began the kind of internecine plotting that had so often undermined the determination of Kin resistance. While the general Tsui Lui took over, the emperor, Ai-tsung, fled further east, to Kuei-te. Tsui Lui took the imperial family prisoner and handed them to the Mongols. It was, in effect, a gesture of surrender; Subatei sent a message to the Khaghan – he was ready to massacre the city's entire population, the traditional punishment for those stubborn in their resistance to the Mongols. For days the far-sighted Yelui Ch'u ts'ai worked to persuade Ogadei of the folly of such an outcome. The city was too rich to be destroyed, too valuable, it contained too many essential craftsmen: it should be spared, its inhabitants allowed to continue there unharmed, though under Ogadei's beneficent rule.

The orders sped to the eastern commander – the people were to be spared; only those who belonged to the imperial family, the Wan-yen clan, should be killed. Meanwhile, as always, a Mongol column was deputed to hunt down that potential future threat, the Kin emperor. Ai-tsung took once more to desperate flight. Tenaciously the Mongols followed; in the city of Ts'ai-chou the fugitive took his final plunge into the only security that still remained to him: he committed suicide. It was the spring of 1234 and after nearly a quarter-century of warfare, the Kin dynasty had come to an end and all their realms, the whole of northern China, lay in Mongol hands.

Sometimes a chess-player is so intent on his intended move that he cannot see the threatening configuration of his opponent's pieces. This was now the psychological condition of the Sung emperors. Despite everything they had seen of the Mongols, everything they had learned from the stories of conquest and massacre that had filtered across Asia, they still apparently discounted these new neighbours. As far as they were concerned, the Kin had been swept away in order to allow the Sung to take their place. In such a prediction there was no place for the Mongols; the corollary was that the Mongols could not really exist. With suicidal nonchalance, Emperor Li-tsung moved his forces into the cities of Kai-feng and Lo-yang, an act of justice as far as he and his advisers were concerned, but for the Mongols an act of war.

At a *kuriltai* in 1235, Ogadei decided that the Sung should be made to understand their presumption. Other matters diverted his attention, and before he could focus it again to the south-east, death turned his plans into inheritance. It was Mangu to whom that inheritance finally fell. He took over a situation that had fallen into desolate stalemate: Sung advances had been countered by Mongol raids, and the whole area between the embattled states had been scarred and scoured by a thousand skirmishes. It was, perhaps, Kubilai, now the commander in the Chinese wars, who saw that if direct assault showed small likelihood of succeeding, an outflanking movement, as so often in Mongol history, might prove the straightest path to victory. With a hundred thousand men he marched over what is in effect the eastern end of the Himalayan range. Setting off from the capital of Hsi-Hsia, once itself the scene of desperate Mongol attacks, he clambered over the high passes, among the

An early Sung emperor. It was rulers like this
who, refusing to accept the Mongol threat as real,
finally paid the price of their complacency.

مد و اانزل گرد و درین مدت مجاصره لیه ناره رسول لود

Kubilai Khan,
crossing a bridge of
boats during one of his
Chinese campaigns.
Under him, all
Chinese opposition to
Mongol rule was
finally crushed.

winds that walk and mutter between those peaks and call through those narrow valleys. As he went he beat off the ceaseless attacks of the mountain people, sinewy warriors who scrambled across their dangerous domains with a swiftness that confounded the plainsmen. He advanced a thousand miles over terrain no orthodox strategist would consider for manoeuvre, until he came, despite the bitter defence of its people, down into what is now the province of Yunnan. In fifteen months he had secured an outflanking base for Mongol invasions of Sung territory.

It was Uriangkatai, Subatei's son, who led a further assault south to the state of Annam; it has a capital, Hanoi, whose name war has made familiar to our ears, too. With the forests of South-East Asia to supply them, the king of Annam was able to use trained elephants in support of his fighting men. It was almost certainly the first time Mongols had been called upon to face such creatures; it was their horses that, on the only occasion in history, turned from their task. But fire redressed the balance – flaming Mongol arrows turned the elephants into terrified earth-crushers, all training lost. Whirling about, they trampled upon the astonished ranks of their masters and when the Mongols at last charged into that turmoil, the day, and the country, were already theirs.

Having thus hemmed in the still-oblivious Sung, Kubilai travelled north again, out of the unappetizing sub-tropical heat of Vietnam, back to the lands that the Mongols had wrested from the Kin. He had spent almost the whole of his life in China. He liked the Chinese, he trusted them and he used them as his administrators. He had learned from them, enough to understand the value of their culture and wish himself to be a participant, a patron. He understood, too, that a weakened China would become a liability to the Mongol empire; its people would be turned into sullen recalcitrants, desperate to unhook their conquerors' yoke, while its economy would provide nothing for the Karakorum exchequer. Like Yelui Ch'u ts'ai in the previous generation, he realized that over-burdensome taxation would in the end dry up the tribute it was intended to increase. But round the Great Khan there were people whose avarice was simpler, whose foresight was less or whose ambition felt threatened by Kubilai's existence. They persuaded Mangu that his brother had become more Chinese than Mongol, that his main concern was for his new subjects, rather than for the Khaghan. Disturbed, Mangu summoned his brother to Karakorum.

Kubilai's first instinct was to fight, to march north with an army. But he had a mentor, the wise Yao-shi, who counselled absolute submission. To know sound advice is the gift of monarchs who survive; Kubilai abased himself before his brother, offered him everyone and everything he held dear. Convinced by this humility, Mangu restored him to his Chinese satrapy. Moreover it was determined at their meeting that the war against the Sung should be pursued to the last bitterness of victory; Mangu himself would take the field against Chinese insolence. With the youngest brother, Arik-Buka, left in charge in Karakorum – a regency that would later hamper the easy succession of the khaghanate – he marched down into Sezchuan. Kubilai meanwhile, in a double-pronged attack from Honan in the north, drew the Sung reserves to the defence of Kin-shan and of the capital, Lin-an, in the Yangtze valley. At the same time, from far in the south-west, Uriangkatai came hurrying north to add his forces to the Mongol onslaught.

Through the second half of 1257, into the spring and summer of the following year, the long-prepared defences on the Lunk-kiang resisted the Mongol advance.

Mangu, however, besieged the key fortress-town of Ho-chou, the fall of which would open the way from the west. In the south Uriangkatai struck at Kwei-lin, captured it, then moved further north towards the Yangtze. With Kubilai already busy on that great river, a junction between the two Mongol armies now seemed likely. It would have cut the Sung kingdom in two. Kia-se-tao, the Sung emperor's chief minister, decided that it was time to let diplomacy win the battles that had proved beyond the soldiers. He offered withdrawal, a new, more flattering frontier for the Mongol holdings, an annual tribute, a recognition by the Sung of Mongol supremacy. His initiative was better-timed than he could have known; outside Ho-chou dysentery was cutting down the Mongol armies. Mangu himself, trapped by disease, fled to the mountains. The death he had contracted travelled with him however; on 11 August 1259 he succumbed. Accepting Kia-se-tao's terms Kubilai withdrew, to take up a watching brief in the north over affairs in Karakorum and his own destiny.

It was another five years before Kubilai had reduced Arik-Buka from serious rival to intermittent nuisance; pardoning him in 1264 for his attempts to oust Kubilai by violence, the Khaghan proclaimed himself in fact the new ruler of the Mongol world. But it was in China and not on the bleak plains and craggy valleys of the Mongol heartlands that he felt at home; Pekin and not Karakorum was to be his capital. If he saw himself more as the Emperor of China than as the Great Khan of the Mongols, however, he, less than any other descendant of Genghis, could tolerate the continued, if diminished, independence of the Sung. Since the fall of the T'ang dynasty at the end of the ninth century China had been divided. Not even the founder of the Sung dynasty, Chao K'uang-yin, grasping power in 960, had been able to oust the Khitans who had taken over the north-east of his country. Ever since, the two halves of China – the north now much extended by Mongol successes – had faced one another with mistrust and contempt. 'Northern idiots', the southerners called the people from beyond the Yangtze; northerners responded with man-tse – 'barbarian'. Such detestation meant that Kubilai could rely on the enthusiastic support of his northern subjects, where, as an alien ruler, he might have expected a sullen reluctance, sabotage, even rebellion. His own attitude had been determined not only by his long-term ambition to unify China, but also by the short-term desire for revenge – when his envoys met Kia-se-tao in order to discuss and ratify the treaty between them, the Sung minister, perhaps thinking himself safe because of the Mongols' dynastic war, had them arrested. (He had his own inter-necine problems, mainly caused by his desire to keep the emperor ignorant of the true situation.)

In 1261, therefore, Kubilai proclaimed a new dynasty for the whole of China. It would be called the Yuan, and its capital would be Pekin (confusingly then called Chung-tu and about to be renamed Ta-tu). The slow, laborious reduction of Sung power now began. Great fortresses and fortified cities had one by one to be besieged and taken. Siang-yan, on the River Han, was invested for five years of stalemate; the Yuan forces under their Chinese commanders, A-shu Liu-cheng and Shi Tien-tse, sat grimly under the walls while, from time to time, Sung convoys forced the blockade and revictualled the garrison by the river. The fortress of Fan-cheng, on the north bank, protected the passage of these supply boats and its fall in 1272 at last meant that the city could be wholly besieged. When it finally fell, contrary to Mongol practice in the past, Kubilai rewarded its stubborn

Mongol horsemen, weapons at the ready, whirl across country under the shadow of a defended wall. Where the Chinese trusted to their stone bulwarks, the Mongols as always depended on their mobility, supplemented by acquired skills in siege-craft.

commander, Lu Wan-huan, not with torture and death but by allowing him to continue as its governor.

By now a new generation of commanders had appeared among the Mongols, men who knew all the skills that had belonged to their fathers (literally their fathers in some cases – Uriangkatai was the son and Achu the grandson of Subatei). The greatest of these had learned his craft under Hulagu – Bayan, the man Kubilai now put in charge of the advance on the Sung capital, Lin-an, modern Hangchow. There a new emperor ruled, a young man named Tu-tsung who had just succeeded his uncle; the true ruler, however, was still that over-devious manipulator, Kia-se-tao. In 1274 it seemed as though his hold over the country had become even tighter when Tu-tsung died and his four-year-old son was proclaimed emperor, with his young mother as regent. But whoever was in charge could not alter the fact that the Sung position was increasingly precarious.

Four Mongol columns were now thrusting towards Lin-an. If the Sung army remained inactive they would simply be surrounded, bottled-up, eventually destroyed. Desperately, Kia-se-tao marched westward to face the Mongols and their Chinese allies. At Ting-kia-chou all his scheming came to an end; battle cut short his ambitions and, his forces broken, he fled. Thus defeated, his usefulness was undermined, his enemies free to join against him. He was put on trial, found guilty of treachery, misrepresentation, abuse of office – but above all of defeat – and thrown from power. Ostensibly sent into banishment, he was set on by his guards during the journey and murdered.

Lin-an contemplated the cost of resistance. It was a vast city, a place of wide streets and an infinity of canals crossed by more than ten thousand bridges. Its

A nineteenth-century version of a Chinese plan, dated 1270, of King-sze, the Sung capital, also known as Lin-an. In 1274 it fell to the Mongols; a few years later the Sung dynasty had vanished.

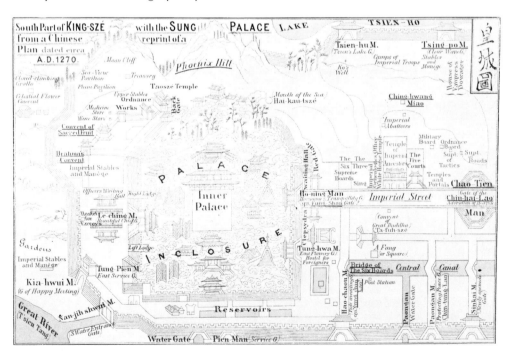

people had parks, public baths, a complex and highly efficient drainage system, a police force several thousand strong, a wide, palace-fringed lake for their recreation, an abundance of inns and hostelries for their visitors, the whole made wealthy by the crowded trade of its seaport and the rich variety of its markets. Its population ran into the millions – some four million men, women and children at least. For generations they had been secure, well-off, placid. Now they looked out from the city walls into the menacing dust of Kubilai's advance.

Convinced that victory was out of reach, that acceptance of defeat might avoid destruction, the Dowager Empress sent Bayan the imperial seal as a token of her surrender. In the days of Genghis Khan, one may imagine what uncountable booty would now have been dragged through Lin-an's gates. But two generations had passed and Kubilai, in any case, wanted his beloved China intact, with the continuity of its culture and commerce guaranteed. When the Mongol armies made their triumphal entry it was art treasures they sought, and the imperial treasury, and the seals of office that would give credence to their own decrees. For the ordinary people, life was to continue as before; neither their women, nor their possessions, nor their livelihoods, were to be touched. Even the great houses, even the temples and academies, remained unrifled. Nor was the young emperor taken prisoner, nor his mother placed in chains. Bayan, indeed, refused to meet her, not out of arrogance but because, like a bumpkin, he was shy, nervous of not knowing the proper behaviour, the rituals of etiquette. Kubilai sent for mother and son, and they travelled north to his capital. There they remained in wealth and security for another decade, the ex-emperor proclaimed a Prince of the Third Rank, before both followed the call of religion and humility, living out the rest of their lives in the circumscribed tranquillity of a Buddhist enclosed order.

Yet the war was not over. In Fo-kien, in the south-east, ministers loyal to the Sung dynasty and generals prepared to work with them carried on their resistance. They had two boys of the imperial family as figureheads behind which they could rally opposition. In Kiang-si, in Kuang-tung, as well as in Fo-kien, their forces held fast behind barricades. When dislodged, they retreated to fight again as stubbornly elsewhere. Forced to carry on this protracted, and finally illogical, contest, Kubilai ran short of soldiers. He emptied the prisons, thus making the recruitment of a further twenty thousand men the price of their liberty. Oddly, several of them were to have distinguished careers in his armies.

Under constant Mongol pressure, the Sung remnants drained and dribbled southwards; at last they found themselves hemmed in on the sea, Canton their final stronghold. Relentlessly the forces of the new dynasty, Kubilai's Yuan, advanced on it, surrounded it, pressed for its submission. Its defences crumbled, sagged. The stubborn defenders of Sung fortunes, still perhaps hoping for some miraculous alteration in their fate, took their young emperor, Shi, and fled to the offshore islands. In 1278, on one of these, Kiang-chou, the Emperor Shi died – of weariness perhaps, of the weight of broken promises and hopes. Under his cousin, the Emperor Ping, however, this futile struggle for a lost realm still went on. The Mongol forces took to the sea and with two pincering fleets attacked the islands. All land gone, the Sung Empire at last became entirely sea-borne. There was a day-long battle; by nightfall, hundreds of Sung ships had been captured or destroyed. In the darkness the few that remained scattered and fled. The largest, however, was the flagship, on which that bewildered imperial child had been placed in the last tatters of his irrelevant state. Too cumbersome to escape, it was brought to bay by a Mongol squadron. Its commander flung his own wife and children to their death, gathered up his emperor, last symbol of an eternal resistance. Lit by rocket-trail and naphtha flare, one sees him on the great junk's gunwale, the struggling figure in his arms. He yells an archetypal defiance at his closing pursuers: 'A Sung Emperor chooses death before captivity!' Then he has vanished, leaping across the yellow light into the darkness, the sea, the long oblivion of history. Kubilai had become the first emperor for many centuries of an undivided China. From his enforced healing of ancient rifts stems the single China of today: after him it was always a unity.

The art and culture of China exerted an overwhelming
influence on all the country's conquerors.
One can see why from the power and delicacy of this
Sung dynasty painting, now in Shanghai Museum.

For China there now began a period of prosperity, of an imperial concern so obvious that for a while it endeared Kubilai to the whole population. War had reduced that population by a third; the consequently plentiful land enriched the peasantry. The Mongol connection stretched westward into Europe; the consequently augmented trade enriched the merchants. The emperor had long been entranced by Chinese culture; the consequently patronized arts enriched the painters, writers, actors and scholars upon whom they depended. When poverty did strike, supportive provisions were ready; when these failed, imperial soup kitchens made good some of the deficiency. Trading junks probed the sea-routes to India, Ceylon, the Persian Gulf, perhaps even to Mombasa and Zanzibar. In order to make sure that wealth should not be too unevenly distributed, the empire's administration not only supervised the apportionment of land, it made sure that commodity prices had a ceiling that no one was allowed to exceed. Rich trade, enough land and maximum prices, the sick, the old and the poor provided for – after forty years of war, the people must have felt that their new ruler had brought them paradise.

Yet Kubilai was a Mongol, Genghis Khan's grandson. He was the Khaghan, inheritor of the conviction that the whole earth belonged to him and his people. The realization of that conviction in the detail of world-conquest meant that he could not allow himself to be halted by the incidental difficulties of an ocean crossing. He learned of the wealth of Japan and in 1267 sent a message to its emperor, demanding that he should accept the overlordship of the Mongols. Proclaimed a god, descended from the sun itself, the Japanese emperor did not even bother to reply. Kubilai asked the vassal King of Korea to intercede, to convey his demand to the Japanese. The Korean emissaries who were sent were forbidden even to travel to the capital, Kyoto. It was time for more decisive action.

At first, Kubilai sent an army not of conquest but of intimidation, a force intended to cow the Japanese into acquiescence. In 1274 its ten thousand soldiers, mainly Korean and Chinese, captured Tsushima, halfway to Japan, then went on to establish a far from deeply rooted bridgehead on the most southerly of Japan's main islands, Kyushu. Bitterly the Japanese counter-attacked; thus assailed, the invaders, never very enthusiastic, lost the initiative. Supplies were almost exhausted, they began to run out of arrows, finally a sudden storm turned even the ocean into an enemy. Afraid of being marooned and massacred, they made their way back to the mainland.

Again Kubilai sent envoys; encouraged by their recent successful defence of their coastline, the Japanese executed them. Ordering an invasion fleet of six hundred ships to be built at Yang-chou, Ch'uan-chou and other ports, Kubilai gathered an enormous army, some say of a hundred and fifty thousand men (only forty thousand of them Mongols) and in 1281 they embarked in as many of the ships as were ready. The enterprise, like the Spanish Armada three centuries later, was perhaps too large for success, too cumbersome, too riven by jealousy and faction. One fleet set out from the mouth of the Yangtze, another sailed from the ports of Korea. Their

In the second half of the thirteenth century, Kubilai Khan made several attempts to conquer Japan, but was always beaten back. This Japanese print shows Mongol troops on the attack.

intended rendezvous was Hakozaki Bay; the Chinese fleet arrived much later than the Korean, but after indecision and argument troops were finally landed on the Japanese coast. For a while they appeared to be successful; ominously, while they could raze villages and destroy crops, win skirmishes in the open and plunder isolated farms, the desperately defended fortresses and walled towns managed almost always to beat them off. Their situation became increasingly difficult – their very successes diminished the food and fodder available to them, while their failures, by leaving a line of strongholds between them and the coast, prevented them from marching away into the unravaged pastures of the interior.

Their lines of communication across the Tsushima Straits were precarious. As had threatened to happen the first time, apparent safety turned into a trap. Their fleet was struck, abruptly, by the indifferent savagery of a typhoon. Gripped by these winds, helpless before such waves, the vast fleet was flung about the waters, scattered, its very size rendered absurd. Alone, their timbers broached, many ships sank; others, by the hundred, were flung against cliff-face and rock as though an impatient universe had had enough of Mongol presumption. Tens of thousands drowned; commanders tend to have the best ships, and it was the commanders who returned to China. His grandfather might have felt differently, but Kubilai pardoned them. Meanwhile, the army still trapped in Japan fought on, surrounded and without hope. Daily its numbers dwindled and in the end less than a third of those who had set off on this adventure were able to surrender, marching off to slavery, imprisonment or execution. Twenty years earlier the Mamluks had defeated the Mongols at Ain Jalut and brought Hulagu's Middle Eastern expansion to an end; in eastern Europe, the Golden Horde and its khans of Batu's line were content to administer the territories their progenitor had gained; now here, along the eastern coastlines of Asia, Mongol power too had reached the limits of expansion.

Not that Kubilai recognized this; all his life it remained his intention to return to Japan and teach its rulers the impropriety of defeating Mongol armies. And far to the south-west his forces still struggled to extend the frontiers of Mongol rule. His forward base was Tali, in Tonkin, and from it he threatened the kingdoms of Annam, Champa and Mien. These all had relations with his court of a greater or lesser submissiveness, but Kubilai wanted his pre-eminence accepted without cavil or hesitation. Thus when the aged Indravarman v of Champa felt too infirm in 1280 to make his act of homage to the Khaghan in person, it was a portent of trouble. This was compounded by his son's seizing Mongol emissaries as they crossed the Gulf of Tonkin on their way west to southern India to make demands of tribute there. Tran Thanh-tong of Annam would not let Mongol troops pass through his domains; soon the whole of Indo–China became a Mongol battlefield.

Conditions here, however, were unlike any they or their Chinese allies had ever encountered. As later armies have discovered, the jungles of the Indo–Chinese peninsula, hot, humid and corrosive, make war a matter of slow movement and swift ambush. Nevertheless Kubilai's forces smashed their way into the Champa fortress of Mu Cheng, held it for a while, then were forced to retreat by the fevers endemic in these countries and by starvation. Again they advanced, led this time by Kubilai's son, Togan, and again disease and lack of food drove them back. As they retreated through Annam they were attacked again and again by the armies of Tran Thanh-tong; half their soldiers perished, their general Sugetu among them. A hundred thousand men marched south again in 1287, but though they fought

　　いとせめてゝねたければ。や
　　ゝもすれば恋しき人を。立
　　ながら。ねにも見えばや
　　松のした臥。

Japanese warrior knights like this helped
to repulse the Mongol-led invasions which
Kubilai Khan mounted from the mainland.

their way to the coast and captured Hanoi, they too were defeated by terrain, climate and Annamite courage. They had planned to be supplied from the sea, but the ships sent for that purpose, probably from Canton, were waylaid by an Annamite fleet and almost totally destroyed. Again the Mongols had to retreat, and again their march back to Sezchuan was harried by a series of destructive assaults.

In 1283 a large army, under the *noyan* Singtaur, was sent westward from Tali into the forests of northern Burma. Some ten years earlier another Mongol force had beaten a much larger Burmese army, once again terrorizing its uncomprehending elephants. Now the Mongols did not stop until they stood on the banks of the

For five centuries the kings of Burma ruled from among these elaborate
facades. Then one of them foolishly refused to send tribute to
Kubilai Khan. In punishment, the troops of Mongol China rendered
the royal city uninhabitable. It has stood empty ever since.

Irrawaddy. The King, Narasihapati, who had brought this trouble upon his people
by not only refusing to do homage to Kubilai Khan but also imprisoning his envoy,
was now poisoned by his son Sihasura; from 1293 this new and more pliable monarch began to send his tribute to the Great Khan of the Mongols.

In that same year a thousand ships left China to carry an army of twenty thousand
soldiers into the islands of what is now Indonesia. They landed on Java, where a
Mongol ambassador, come, as was usual, to demand tribute, had been sent branded
back to Pekin. One of the two main princes on the island, Tuan Vijaya, soon made
his submission; the other, Hadji Katang, fought stubbornly; his defeat was costly
to Mongol armies once more operating in unsuitable terrain. It was as a weakened
force, therefore, that they made their way back towards their ships; Vijaya, in an
act of Hindu–Muslim cooperation, ambushed them not far from the coast and it was
only with many losses that they were able to struggle to safety. Nevertheless, along
the curving skein of Malaya, in Ceylon, in the small kingdoms of southern India
(where once again the Mongol world came face to face with that of Islam as its
envoys mingled with dhow-borne traders from the Persian Gulf) there were rulers,
petty princes, kings, who were happy to pay tribute to Kubilai, the Great Khan, as
Master of the World.

In 1294, after a reign of thirty-four years, Kubilai died. With him the story of the Mongols had seen its greatest successes, its glittering stability and the beginning of its schismatic collapse. Settling in Pekin, he had dragged the balance of empire out of true. His magnificence in the east and the power of Hulagu and Berke in the west were too widely separated; the heartlands between were too poor in themselves to provide the necessary connection once the Khaghan had left them. At the same time, what Kubilai most wanted, an assured dynasty rooted deeply in the Chinese soil, was also denied him. Knowing himself popular, he was too prodigal of popularity: he might have altered China's social order, but to keep the support of the aristocracy he countenanced their avarice rather than responding to the peasants' need. At the same time, his swiftness to react by war to every real or imaginary diplomatic slight drained away wealth and wasted lives, just as the increase of the first seemed likely to make the second more worth while.

Thus by the time he died the acceptance his early successes had gained for him had already begun to erode. And, sadly, among the most educated, those whose approval he most desperately wanted, his foreignness, his clumsiness with their language, the necessary elevation of his own countrymen to positions of great power, aroused supercilious resistance no less determined for having to be covert. Not even his deep and genuine admiration for the culture of which they took themselves to be the guardians could alter that; in the southern provinces, conquered so late and after so much stubborn defiance, this continuing repugnance, this profound, unalterable, almost atavistic contempt, ran deepest and longest. This hostility was matched by that of a sizeable faction among the Mongols themselves who, like Genghis Khan before them, regarded the silks and literature and fine brushwork of this civilization with a puritanical horror. Real men lived in tents, rode hard and fought harder, killed their enemies and fathered their children; their recreation was hunting and *koumiss* and uncomplicated song. Everything on the Chinese side of the Great Wall was dangerous, corrupting, sapping of the nomad will. In the antipathy with which these two groups regarded one another, and the disillusionment of the peasantry, the beginnings of the Yuan dynasty's destruction could already be discerned before Kubilai's death.

But that was matter for the future. By then the Mongol Empire had begun, in fact at least, to break into its parts, those enormous fiefs held by the offspring of Genghis Khan. While Kubilai lived, however, he could stand as the magnificent apotheosis of two generations of ambition. From the eastern shores of the Baltic to the Gulf of Tonkin kings, princes, satraps and governors acknowledged the supremacy of the Great Khan, and of the family and people from whom he sprang. From Vietnam to Korea he had brought unity and peace to the lands he governed personally. Throughout the whole Eurasian landmass his name was spoken with awe, his possessions were described with reverence and envy. He was the greatest monarch of his age. When he died, he stepped, like his grandfather, gigantic into the world's legends. But while we see Genghis Khan through a haze of blood, it is the glow of gold that obscures the lineaments of Kubilai. Between the two stretches the thread of the Mongols' imperial destiny; with Kubilai's death, it snapped.

Book Three
# THE MANY-BRANCHED TREE

# 8 THE GOLDEN HORDE

In the north-west, the shores of the Gulf of Finland; in the south-east, the Aral Sea and the Upper Oxus; in the south, the Caspian, the Caucasus, the Black Sea; in the north, the edge of that even darker sea, the vast forest that reaches away eastwards into Siberia. These were the boundaries of the empire Batu bequeathed to his heirs. In his lifetime he administered it from his vast tent, gilded and encrusted with gold embroidery. The Mongol word for a camp is *ordu* and from that derives the English word horde. Thus one could speak of Batu's golden *ordu* – this is probably the origin of that exotic term, the Golden Horde, by which his followers were to be known to Europe throughout their powerful generations. Asia knew them as the Kipchaks. To the Russians who had been forced to submit to them, on the other hand, they were known more simply as the Tartars.

With those Russians in their principalities – Smolensk, Chernikov, Novgorod, Galicia, Kiev and the rest – the Mongol custom was watchfulness, diplomacy, a policy of rule by division. They kept the ancient rivalries of these dukes and princes usefully astir, and they made sure that, however much the aristocracy were divided among themselves, they were united with their masters against the people. In this way the rulers and the *boyars* of their courts acted as the Khan's policemen. They kept the people quiet, in their own interests and thus in the Mongols'; whether they wished it or not, therefore, they were their conquerors' allies, the collaborators of their age. To make sure they followed the path of cooperation there were Tartar officials at their courts, political advisers, diplomatic representatives, collectors of the specified tribute. And there was the title of Grand-Prince, marking out the chief of these ambitious rulers, a title which, in the gift of the Khan, could be used to encourage the most active. The one who had earned this bauble could conversely be kept in his place by the threat that he might lose it. As the different fiefs of the Mongol Empire began to draw apart and settle into independence, the symbiotic relationship between the Tartars and the princes became more important; eventually this close connection would be a factor in the Golden Horde's disintegration and collapse.

Beyond the principalities of Russia there were successive Grand Dukes of Lithuania with their eyes on eastern expansion, rivals of the collectivity of Russian rulers and in that wary relationship with their Tartar half-neighbours, half-masters that present-day Finland is with the Soviet Union. They, too, could therefore be used in the complex equations of Mongol domination. In a similar status stood the tsars of Bulgaria, neither truly mastered nor truly free, though always dominated; the more intractable kings of Hungary suffered the consequence of

The Grand Prince of Moscow sits in his fifteenth-century Kremlin,
administering justice to the Russian people. Moscow's pre-eminence
as the principal agent of the Mongol overlords helped to
establish the continuing tradition of Russian autocracy.

invasion and punishment on several occasions. On the Black Sea coast, settlements of Venetians and Genoese kept open the trade routes to the west, just as, across the plains, the Hansa merchants did who sent their goods into Russia through Novgorod and so down the Volga. In the east, the remains of what had been the Khwarismian empire provided not only the cunning crafts of Persia, but was also one end of the land-bridge to China across which poured the silks, jades and spices of the East.

In order to administer this enormous territory, Berke built a new capital, still named Sarai and still on the Volga, as Batu's had been, but now designated New Sarai or, more flatteringly, Berke Sarai. It stood without walls in the middle of a salt marsh, bright with water cooped up not only to drink but also, as at Karakorum, to provide power for the workshops of artisans. Because he was a Muslim – we know how much that contributed to his rivalry with Hulagu – the city was dominated by the domes and minarets of thirteen mosques. Elsewhere the white façades of palaces gleamed – his own dominated by a golden crescent – there were bathhouses for the people, five great bazaars, quarters for craftsmen. The city glittered with the brilliance of marble, porphyry, gold leaf, was lustrous with the genius of poets and painters drawn to it by the assiduous patronage of the Khans. Even the language of the Mongols altered, for although the courts and the officials still used the Mongolian brought from the eastern plains, throughout most of the area they dominated it was Turkish that they spoke. They had taken into their camps and armies so many of their western nomadic cousins – Kumans, Kipchaks – that these now predominated and it was theirs that became the *lingua franca* of the Tartars.

Yet despite this conscious act of urbanization, the resources of the steppes, the vast grasslands that stretched between the Aral Sea and the Carpathians, meant that they could continue their ancient nomadic way of life. There did not arise among the Golden Horde that polarization between adherents of the old culture and the new which was to help in undermining the Yuan dynasty in China. The problems of the western Khans would spring from simpler rivalries as the ambitious jostled for power and possessions and, to the south, the Ilkhans of Persia looked on with a watchful, jaundiced eye. And in these struggles, increasingly, the eager rulers of the Russian states would see their own opportunities for aggrandizement, subversion and, in the end, freedom.

In the meantime, however, the Khan of the Golden Horde, secure in his capital, himself distributed their coveted titles, a fact that brought a gaggle of competing claimants raucously to his court at every death. Since a title granted can be revoked by the same hand, the Mongol suzerainty meant a constant turmoil of intrigue, uprising, assassination and death among the Russian rulers, a turmoil augmented when the khanate itself threw up rivals eager to use these factions among their vassals as allies in their own cause. There was a constant buzz of legitimate heirs, rivals, hopefuls and discards about the great halls of the Khan, many of whom arrived with families and retinues for their support and safety. It was often the case that a princeling did not survive his journey to Sarai and it was not unusual that one faced with the necessity of going there drew up a will before he left.

Although it was Jochi who had first been granted these western lands and Batu who had conquered them, it was Berke who established the nature of Tartar rule. He was the first to be a Muslim and afterwards, although some of his immediate successors were pagan, it was on the whole Islam to which the Golden Horde

An impression painted by A. Maximov early this century of the Khan of
the Golden Horde sitting in state. Both the memory and the effects of Mongol
oppression have lingered on in the arts and the politics of Russia.

belonged. Berke's rivalry with Hulagu, the dispute between them over the Caucasus
and the treatment of the Caliph, originated the rivalry between these neighbouring
fiefs. It was the capital he built that stood as the abiding symbol of Mongol power
and, just as his name was added to his city's name, so the steppes that stretched
away to the east of it were called by the people 'Berke's meadows'.

When Baibars's ambassadors had their audience with him under the white felt
and pearl hangings of his ceremonial tent – continuing sign of Mongol heritage –
they found an overweight man in a silken tunic, on his feet boots of red felt, on his
head a round cap, his face large and round and sparsely bearded. Although at the
beginning of his reign his ambition and intransigence dictated his actions and
general mood, as time went on more and more of the actual power lay in the hands
of his nephew, Nogai. Thus it was Berke whom Baibars wooed and with whom the
Mamluks cemented an alliance, and he who led the advance against Hulagu in
1262. But in the Golden Horde's relations with Byzantium, it was Nogai, holding
lands north of the Black Sea, who was in the forefront.

The Emperor Michael Palaeologus in Constantinople had cause to be on good
terms with him; it was while Byzantine troops were harassing the Tsar of Bulgaria
that Nogai led twenty thousand troops to his rescue. His troops in flight, the
emperor was able to scramble to safety across the Black Sea only by the courtesy of
a Genoese skipper who took him aboard. The result of this was that, now aware

of who his friends should be, Michael Palaeologus gave Nogai his daughter in marriage.

In 1266 Berke died after a further bout of fighting with Hulagu's successor, and was followed by Mangu-Temor, his nephew and Batu's son. The new Khan seems to have developed the firm ambition to make the realm of the Golden Horde independent of the rest of the Mongol Empire. During his khanate the name and titles of the Great Khan disappear from his coinage and, to make the breach clearer, he became one of the strongest supporters of Kaidu, regarded by Kubilai and others as a renegade. Having set himself up as a ruler in his own right, he consolidated his position by diplomacy – he built a new toleration of the Ilkhans – and, upon that base, saw that civilization in all its aspects flourished in his capital. Architects travelled from his traditional allies, the Mamluks, to bring their Cairo sophistication to the banks of the Volga. Magnificent mosaics were designed by artists from the Middle East, making brilliant walls and floors, delights for their contemporaries, marvels for the archaeologists of a later era.

A result of this new upsurge in urbanization was to settle a little more the still-nomadic population. A city culture needs merchants, artisans, retailers and administrators, and these provided the basis of a new class. A settled state needs institutions less haphazard than those demanded by a nomad chiefdom, however vast. Land began to be owned, rather than merely grazed, and this in turn produced a class of landholders whose legitimacy derived from the patronage of the Khan. In return they promised to man his armies with tenants as beholden to them as they were to him; a rudimentary feudal system had come into being.

Mangu-Temor died, poisoned by the careless lancing of a boil. His younger brother Tode-Mangu succeeded him, a mystic, a follower of the Sufi way, a man with an eye on other dimensions than those inhabited by his subjects. He was more than happy that, on the mundane levels, so experienced a man as Nogai was able to assist him. With virtual autonomy, this great magnate, whose own lands rivalled those of any king – the Don, the Danube and the Carpathians were their boundaries – directed his attention to the west. Hungary seemed suddenly open and welcoming; its king, young and of Kuman blood, had turned his back on Christianity and was demonstrating his fascination with the gods of central Asia and their messengers, the *shamans*. Nogai moved into Transylvania; Tule-Buka, the Khan's nephew, marched on Poland. For a moment it seemed as though the fury Europe had known during the time of Batu was about to be unleashed a second time.

Certainly there was death again, and destruction, as before – the ancient cruelty, the lust for total domination, had not burned itself out. What was missing now was the ancient skill. Soon the part-Kuman king, Ladislas IV, found himself a fugitive; ironically, when he died in 1290 it was by the hand of a Kuman who had turned against him. The Pope had preached a crusade against him; now this Christian fervour re-established the Cross in a country that had already suffered much and often for it. In Poland, too, Catholicism, though it reeled at first, stood firm; the Mongol threat to Europe had finally been defeated.

Lost to the mundane, the Sufi ruler stepped from temporal power and Tule-Buka took his place. Having been halted in the west, he now struck in the east. Friendship once more forgotten, he thrust down through Azerbeijan at his Ilkhan rivals. These, however, proved at least as alert as the Poles and, repulsed, the new Khan saw his authority undermined by defeat. Nogai was now the most powerful man of the

Golden Horde. He had intervened personally to replace the Grand-Prince Dmitri on his throne of Vladimir, thus asserting his authority among the Russian rulers. This Dmitri was the son of a previous grand-prince; his enemy had been his brother Andrei, who had recruited Mongol help and with the consequent expected brutality driven Dmitri into exile. It was to Nogai and not to the Khan in his capital of Sarai that Dmitri went, it was Nogai who replaced him on his throne, it was Nogai who thus demonstrated his power to his peers in the Golden Horde.

Why did he not now become khan? Was it that he preferred the shadows, the private power of the king-maker, the certainty of royal gratitude? Was it that he was blemished and therefore not fit to rule – he had lost an eye in the wars against the Ilkhans? Whatever the reason, he now threw all his authority and power behind a new claimant, the young Toktu, a direct descendant of Batu. He must have thought that he could manage him – after all he had the Grand-Prince Dmitri in the hollow of his hand, the Tsar of Bulgaria had been his choice for the throne, the King of Serbia was his client, almost his vassal. Why should he not be able to manage a young man, one of little experience and unknown quality, one, moreover, who would be in debt to the great lord who had placed him in power?

The Venetians were the ostensible cause of disagreement between the two men. They asked Nogai to help them in their struggle to smash the Genoese grip on the Black Sea trade. The Genoese at once turned to Toktu to uphold their rights. Messages were sent, then armies marched; defeated beside the River Prut, today the border between Romania and the Ukraine, Toktu retreated. He might have been defeated now, but Nogai, in true Mongol fashion, turned aside to punish the Genoese, destroying two of their coastal settlements. By then the vigorous Toktu had been able to regroup his forces. This time it was near the Dnieper that the armies met. Perhaps the younger man had learned in the interval, perhaps the older thought he had nothing more to learn. Whatever the reason, Toktu broke the hardened forces of Nogai; that great lord was forced to flee and, in flight, was waylaid by a common soldier, a Russian, who killed and beheaded him and brought his head in triumph to Toktu. Alas, the reaction of a Mongol khan was always unpredictable; with the words, 'a commoner may not kill a king,' Toktu had the Russian executed.

There was opposition from Nogai's sons, soon crushed; then Toktu learned something from Nogai's example and married a daughter of Byzantium's Emperor Andronicus, though the girl this time was illegitimate. But the new Khan dismissed the religion of his predecessors, preferring that of his ancestors; perhaps it was this revival of the ancient gods that made him turn on the Genoese and somewhat foolishly ravage their Black Sea trade and the ports from which they carried it on. He picked up again the traditional rivalry with his neighbours, the Ilkhans, but was met by the firmness of an established and determined ruler, Ghazan. He swept away the remnants of the Seljuq dynasty (thus unwittingly leaving a vacuum in Asia Minor for the later Ottoman Turks to exploit), and resisted the attempts of Ghazan's successor, Uljaitu, to inavde his territories.

These external affairs were matched by a new restlessness among the Russians. They had observed, sharp-eyed as all reluctant vassals, that Mongols had turned on one another and reached the conclusion that, thus preoccupied, their masters might ignore their own activities. The Mongol officials who moved among them now found themselves in continuous danger, and several died. Tax-collection was made the business of the Russian princes themselves, so unsafe had it become for the Khan's underlings. Meanwhile the Metropolitan of the Orthodox Church had established himself in Vladimir, supporting with his spiritual authority the pre-eminence of the grand-prince in an effort to promote unity among the dukedoms and principalities. At the same time, the harassed rulers of western Russia, pre-occupied with the constant threat from Poland and Lithuania, and those of the south and east under the direct eye of their Mongol overlords, took less and less interest in the ancient rivalries of Russia itself. Their people moved to the safer territory of the central cities, thus helping to increase the importance of such principalities as Tver and Moscow at the expense of those from which they had emigrated. Now, during the khanate of Toktu, the Metropolitan as head of the Russian Church crowned Michael of Tver Grand-Prince of All Russia. A focus had been established for Russian nationalism, more natural and acceptable than the line of Mongols' men, supporters of the masters who sponsored them rather than upholders of their people's independence.

These developments, stirrings of a spirit that could only pose problems for Tartar rule in the future, began to preoccupy Toktu. He decided that he ought himself to speak with the princes, to move among them and emphasize his personal supremacy. He would have been the first khan since Batu to make that north-westerly journey; on its first stage, however, while still sailing up the Volga, he fell ill and died. The year was 1312 and within twelve months Toktu's nephew, Uzbeg, had become Khan in his uncle's place, bringing with his ascension thirty years of stability and magnificence to the Golden Horde and to many of its subjects. In the end, however, his rule, still remembered with affectionate awe by Muslim historians, was either to create or increase the flaws in the structure of Mongol suzerainty that eventually brought it down.

Among his earliest decisions was to remove the leadership of the Russian princes from Tver and give it to Moscow. Yuri of Muscovy had come to Sarai, married Uzbeg's sister and thus become the preferred candidate. Michael fought; in the struggle between the houses, Uzbeg's sister was captured and in this captivity she died. This not only sealed Yuri's victory, it also led to Michael's execution; there were slights the Khan could hardly overlook and the killing of his sister was clearly one of them. But with the Christians outside his realms, Uzbeg cemented a number of new ties. He allowed the Genoese to set themselves up again in Kaffa, razed by Toktu's men, though the Venetians were also given an official foothold at the mouth of the Don. At Kaffa, a Catholic bishop was established, while the Metropolitan of the Russian Church was made the Khan's representative in Constantinople. But when the emperor there, Andronicus III, agreed to let his daughter marry Uzbeg, the Khan stipulated that she had to accept Islam.

For Uzbeg was above all a Muslim and, unlike his predecessors, he was con-cerned that his religion should be the religion of his people. What Berke had begun out of little more, perhaps, than self-interest, had now, despite the continuance of Shamanism and the presence of Christian representatives at Sarai, become the central religious tradition of the Golden Horde and its rulers. It is hard to be clear why this should have occurred in the most westerly of the Mongol fiefs, the one most influenced by Christianity and its missionaries. It may be that the lack of agreement between these missionaries – Greek, Russian, Roman and Nestorian – undermined the certainties they sought to preach. More probably, there was a

An illustration, dating from the fifteenth century, of the battle of Kulikovo. Here, in 1380, Tatar autocracy was for the first time successfully challenged. The Mongols of the Golden Horde, although defeated, managed to reimpose their rule – but the memory of Russian victory gave a powerful impetus to the country's renascent nationalism.

certain fastidious reluctance on the part of the Khan to accept the religion of his subjects and vassals. From his vantage-point the followers of Christianity could point to few victories over those of other faiths. Less than a hundred years before his own ancestor had swept them before him like dust before the broom. In the Middle East the Crusaders presented a spectacle of greed, wrangling, stagnation, self-indulgence and defeat. Islam, on the other hand, glowed with the countless brilliances of a successful civilization. Its craftsmen, architects and artists seemed to be producing a thousand marvels every day. Its poets, philosophers and scientists made even the European elite appear by contrast crass, clumsy, under-educated. And the linguistic ties of the Golden Horde were not with the Latin of the Catholics or the Greek and Russian of the Orthodox Churches, just as their closest diplomatic ties were not with the countries that professed those faiths. For all the politic marriages into the Byzantine imperial house, it was with the Mamluks that Uzbeg's friendship lay (and to mark it Sultan Nasir of Egypt was given a princess of the Tartar house as his wife).

This raising of Islam into an official religion, however, was to lead to internal difficulties in Uzbeg's European fief. The vague nationalistic aspirations of the Russian dukes and princes were now sharpened by the difference in faith between ruler and ruled. The struggle for independence could now be given the fervour of a crusade. The natural fear of the people for the Tartars could be exaggerated into a terror of forced conversion. Thus in Tver, in the summer of 1327, the population became maddened by a persistent rumour that such conversions were about to begin. In fact it was no more than a Mongol tax commission visiting their city – it may be that there were those with good reason to spread disruptive rumours. On 15 August, Assumption Day, the people turned on their overlords and every Mongol within their walls was killed.

The act was suicidal. The Grand-Prince of Muscovy, Ivan Kalita, was given a Mongol army of fifty thousand men and with it he destroyed the power of his rivals. From this time on, the rulers of Moscow were the frightful henchmen of the Khans, their power, backed by that of the Golden Horde, making them supreme among the princely houses. Moscow stood in a magnificent natural position for establishing such a citadel, central in the territories covered by the principalities, able to watch in all directions while protected on every side, with both the Volga and the Oka to provide swift communications. Soon, having taken the burden of policing Russia from the shoulders of the Khan, its princes stood second only to him in the realm, just as Moscow itself stood second only to Sarai. If Sarai ever diminished in import- ance, if the Khan of the Golden Horde ever weakened, a city and a ruler had been established who could take their place.

Therefore when Uzbeg died, in 1341, he left behind him the appearance of peace and stability, but a reality of hidden decline. By then the victories won by Othman and his son Orkhan in Asia Minor had established the power base of the Ottoman Turks, the next century's vanguard in Islam's assault on Christianity. Uzbeg's elder son survived only a year or so before being assassinated by the younger, Janibeg. His was to be no greatly glorious reign, for during it his people were decimated by the Black Death and his only victorious campaign, for the capture of Tabriz, ended in his dying on the return journey.

There now followed a long decline, a slow chaos arrested only by the force and vigour of occasional atavistic figures imbued with the energy of the Mongol past. One such was Mamai, a manipulator of power, a king-maker, who entered his phase of significance when Batu's line at last came to an end in 1359. While Khans came and went, he remained, using his strength to distort the decisions and the succession of the rulers. Such games do not occur in isolation, however; in the west the Russian princes under the Grand-Prince of Muscovy, Dmitri Donskoi, thought they saw their long-awaited chance. In the face of their unrest, Mamai advertised the new weakness of the Tartars by seeking help from the Dukes of Lithuania. Such an alliance might have crushed the Russians: Dmitri marched preventatively against the Golden Horde.

The two armies met on 8 September 1380 at Kulikovo Pole, which translates as the 'Field of the Curlews'. Their melancholy piping may well have been heard keening for Mongol pride. The Russians placed their ranks between natural obstacles sufficient to force the Tartars to attack them head-on. For hours the ferocity of the battle offered no advantage to either side. Men toppled where they had been placed and as the day wore on, others and others again fell blood-striped on those early

Russian troops ride out from Moscow against the Mongol overlords.

corpses. Then, finally, there was movement. The Russian ranks began to weave; there were gaps, a staggering back. The Mongols pressed forward, thrusting for greater advantage, for final victory. As they forced their way forward, there came the sudden hammer-beat of hooves, a war-cry or two, a shrieked order. From behind a little wood where Dmitri had kept them hidden, a cavalry column poured, its ranks spreading, the spears level, the swords high. Taken in the flank, the Mongols could not turn. Cut down, they broke. Mamai and what remained of his men fled back to his ancestral plains beyond the Volga.

It seemed as though the Golden Horde had now come to an end. In the eastern part of its realms stood what is called the White Horde, commanding territories stretching to the Aral Sea. Here the local ruler, Urus Khan, descended from Ordu,

Jochi's eldest son, had been succeeded by the young and energetically ambitious Toktamish, his nephew. And in that succession lies the beginning of a new story, for Toktamish was under the protection of Timor, Khan of Samarkand: Tamurlaine the Great. Under that powerful patronage Toktamish had taken Astrakhan; by 1378 he had even captured the magnificence of Sarai itself. It now seemed as though a new sort of balance had been achieved – the Russians in the west, Mamai in the south, Toktamish in the east.

But already that balance was on the tilt. Victory had exhausted the Russians, wearied in any case by decades of war against the land-hungry dukes of Lithuania. Mamai, knowing this, was regrouping and almost ready to take his revenge. But Toktamish was the swiftest to move; by the banks of the River Kalka, not far from the Sea of Azov (and not far, either, from that battlefield where Subatei, defeating the forces of the Russians, first proclaimed the Mongol presence to the west), Mamai was forced into defeat, annihilation, flight. He sought sanctuary in Kaffa; the Genoese, by no means disposed to side with a loser, killed him.

For a while it seemed as though the spirit of Batu and of Subatei had once again been let loose in Europe. Denied the submission of the Russian principalities, Toktamish taught them with the bludgeonings of terror that the Mongols had forgotten little, that for the Russians the right hour had not yet come, that miscalculations of such a kind are punishable by death. As it had a century and a half earlier, smoke rose above the ruins of the Russian cities, a black twining of lamentation and despair. Not until all perceivable signs of resistance had been crushed did the new khan retire in contemptuous satisfaction.

Yet perhaps he should have learned some lessons from his victims' fate. Those who overmatch themselves in the game of conquest must suffer the consequences. Toktamish now revived one of the old ambitions of the Golden Horde by invading the Caucasus, rampaging across Transoxiana. Perhaps he had not understood the true significance of the change of rulership in these regions; perhaps he thought himself a match for Tamurlaine. Whatever the reason, in 1391 his mistake in angering his one-time patron caught up with him. Timor had marched north of the Caspian, crossed the Bulgar territories, then swung west of the Urals. Beside the River Kandurcha he savaged the army of Toktamish, captured his camp and his harem, and forced him to ignominious flight. Soon he had established a more amenable ruler in a Sarai suddenly become vulnerable.

Like Tamurlaine himself, Toktamish seems to have been created out of pure militarism. He showed now a soldierly resilience, regrouping, even contracting an alliance with the Mamluk sultanate, before striking south again. Once more Tamurlaine marched to face him. Toktamish's alliance with the Egyptians proved empty; the support he had engineered from the rulers of Lithuania was not forthcoming; the Grand-Prince of Muscovy sat within his walls and collected the taxes he had been permitted; the Ottoman Turks squatted on their holdings in Asia Minor, a fearful eye on Tamurlaine's fury. Beside the River Terek, in 1395, that fury swept Toktamish aside and demolished his ambitions. Again it seemed as though appalling history was about to be repeated: Tamurlaine marched into Russia, smashed his way into Yeletz on the upper Don, then swung away to the south, ravaging Astrakhan, the Crimea and the Bulgar lands, decimating the Alans and Circassians, and burning down the tarnished beauty of Sarai.

In effect this ended the unity and power of the Golden Horde. For something like another century the campaigns of its decline, the battles of its long disintegration, would continue to be fought. It would retain something of its importance within Russia and its khanate would continue to call to the ambitious. But Tamurlaine's victories had relegated it to the periphery of history, had brought it indeed to the first shadows of oblivion.

In 1399 Vytautus of Lithuania marched to place Toktamish back on his throne, but, intercepted by the armies of the Khan's principal rivals, was utterly defeated. But the rivals, too, suffered a cutting-back – the survivor, Edigu, a commander of the nomad Mangkuts, now became the strong man of a weakened state. For a short while it seemed as if Toktamish, once Tamurlaine's protégé, now a fugitive, would be able to call upon the power of Samarkand to make him Khan a second time; but abruptly, somewhere in Siberia, he died.

There now is heard the cacophonous rise and fall of names, a wilderness of heroes; their swords are high for a moment, their claims loud, before they are hacked down into oblivion. Kepek, Devlet Berdi and Said Ahmed, sons of Toktamish; Ulugh Mahmed and Barak, their cousins; Kuchuk Mahmed; Ulugh Mahmed's son, Mahmudek; and the King of Poland's protégé, Hadji Girai, who established himself and his heirs in the Crimea. All these fought, made alliances, marched and counter-marched, won and lost vast areas of land, an endless turmoil of hope, ambition and sudden death, a wickedly bubbling, blood-red brew in that vast cauldron, interestedly stirred and sampled by the Princes of Moscow, the Dukes of Lithuania, the Kings of Poland. The Golden Horde itself divided into the Crimean Horde and the Great Horde, the former supported by the Ottoman Turks and allied with Ivan of Muscovy, the latter tied in a brittle union of self-interests with Lithuania and Poland.

At the end of the fifteenth century the leader of the Great Horde was Sheikh Ahmed, that of the Crimean, Mengli Girai. As Mengli waxed, so Sheikh Ahmed waned. His brother, Said Mahmed, deserted him; Alexander of Poland became evasive, inactive. With twenty thousand men the Great Horde faced the confident ranks of the Crimeans. They had the advantage of fighting from their own fortifications, but their power was spent, their hour long over. Sheikh Ahmed fled from defeat, seeking sanctuary. In Astrakhan the rulers would not take him in; they knew where power lay. He turned west, sought aid from his self-serving ally, Alexander. Understanding the realities as well as anyone in Astrakhan, this monarch had him killed. The year was 1505 and the Great Horde had come to an end. It took another 270 years before the Crimean khans gave up their fief, although by then they had long been not Mongols but Ottoman Turks.

So, in dispute and petty murder, in the swift spilling and the slow dilution of blood, the grandeur of the Golden Horde slipped almost unnoticed away. What remained was its effect on the development of Russia, a country they had encouraged into despotism and restrained from development over three centuries. Throughout the years of their suzerainty, their tyranny, they drew from its principalities enormous sums in tax and tribute. At the same time they cut it off at least partially not only from the burgeoning cultures of the West and the fading marvels of Byzantium, but also from its own magnificent past. In a sense the history of Russia ever since has been the desperate attempt to catch up those lost centuries. It may be that, despite leaders from Peter the Great to Lenin, that gap has always been too wide – and that today, as the West declines, it has become irrelevant.

Timur Lenk, known to us as Tamurlaine. The Transoxianan ruler, in attempting to re-establish the empire of Genghis Khan, smashed the power of the Golden Horde.

# 9  THE ILKHANS OF PERSIA

**A**baqa, the son of Hulagu, ascended to the throne of the Ilkhans after his father's death in 1265. His lands stretched from the Oxus to the Euphrates, but to the north lay the ambition of the Golden Horde, to the south the hostility of the Mamluks. Of all the great fiefs into which the unity of Genghis Khan's empire had divided, that of the Persian rulers was the weakest. Thus beleaguered, criss-crossed by trade routes and under threat even from his covetous cousins to the east, Abaqa made sure that his authority should rest firmly on that of the Khaghan; his *yarlik*, his licence to rule, came directly from Kubilai. With a Muslim alliance ranged against him, it seemed politic that he should seek, not only legitimacy from the Great Khan, but security from alliances with Christians. He too married a daughter of the Byzantine emperor, Michael Palaeologus, he made overtures to the Armenians and other Christian people of eastern Europe and Asia Minor, he took the Nestorian patriarch under his protection and, when hard-pressed in 1274, he sent a deputation to Pope Gregory x, then presiding over the Council of Lyons.

By that time Abaqa had suffered almost ten years of warfare, a decade of tenacious defence and brittle counter-attack. From the east Barak Khan, a descendant of Chagatei and by then an ally of Kubilai's rival Kaidu, came trampling over the Oxus, occupying large tracts of Khorasan. It was not until 1270 that Abaqa was able to repel his forces; three years later he went briefly over to the offensive and sacked Bokhara, but was unable to hold it. That great river, the Oxus, the Amu Darya, remained the frontier between the khanates. In the north Berke's death eased the pressure applied by the khans of the Golden Horde, but Borak's venture in the east seemed to the Mamluks a diversion they could exploit. While Abaqa was busy along the Oxus they struck.

They did not merely strike at Mongol holdings in Asia Minor, however; Baibars was now, after all, the strong arm of the Cairo Caliph and as such the personification of Muslim vengeance on the infidel. He overran crusader Antioch and Jaffa as delightedly as he did any Mongol stronghold, and howled through the lands of the Armenians as much because they were Christians as because of their friendship with the Ilkhans. Thus Abaqa's proposal of a two-pronged attack upon Egypt, the Mongols striking from the north, the Christians from the west, seemed to many of the European powers an attractive idea and for a while was deeply pondered by the Kings of France, England and Aragon. But Baibars understood more than the bludgeonings of warfare; the delicate dance of interest and alliance that is diplomacy came to him as easily. Venice and Genoa preferred trans-Mediterranean trade to any Crusade against the Mamluks; Byzantium was their rival. For Charles of Anjou, later King of Sicily, Byzantium again, with her barbaric eastern Church, was Catholicism's true enemy. The emperor in Constantinople, meanwhile, was interested only in maintaining a balance of relationships in the Eastern Mediterranean; his own ramshackle empire was too fragile to be committed to any cause other than its own survival.

And then, Abaqa was after all a Mongol, a pagan, a traditional enemy of limitless ambition and inhuman cruelty – Europe knew all about the Mongols. The crusader nations had already shown their reluctance to interfere during Hulagu's reign, and now they again stood aloof from the internecine conflicts of the Middle East. They did mount an attack on the Bey of Tunis, but disease picked them off; among those who died was Louis IX of France (later canonized), who in his militantly saintly way had been perhaps the most enthusiastic supporter of a Mongol alliance. With his death all hope of concerted action between Abaqa and the Crusaders vanished; left to flourish unhampered the Mamluks were now able to strangle the remaining western strongholds along the coasts of Syria and the Holy Land.

In 1277 Baibars died and when the Sultan Kilawan succeeded him, he discovered opposition to his rule in Syria. These divisions among his enemies greatly encouraged Abaqa and, in 1280, he marched to take advantage of them. Soon his men were rampaging about the streets and markets of Aleppo in the age-old

Acre, its plan as it was in 1291 here reconstructed, was
the last Crusader stronghold on the eastern Mediterranean
seaboard. The refusal of the Crusaders to co-operate with
the Mongols may have contributed to their defeat by Islam.

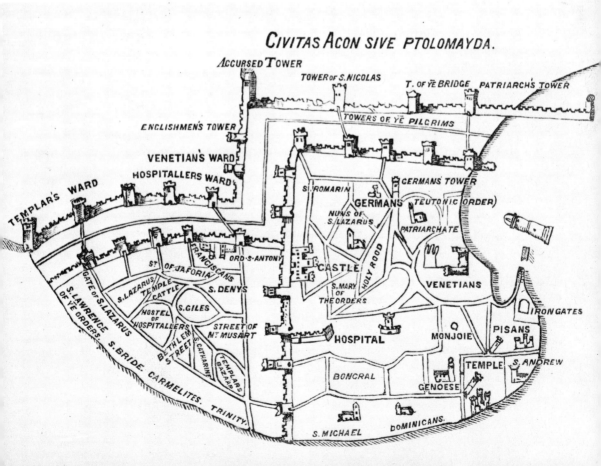

gratifying manner. The following year, however, a further assault southwards was halted near Hims. The Mongol army, with their Christian allies from Georgia and Armenia, were put to flight, and what had briefly looked like a new invasion had been revealed as no more than another raid. Thus thwarted, the Ilkhan seems to have sunk into the compensations of alcohol – according to Rashid, he travelled to Hamadan in 1282, arrived in the middle of March 'and took up residence in the palace . . . The whole time he gave himself over to drink and pleasure.' About midnight on 1 April, 'he met that which changes everything, the predetermined hour of his death, in the shape of a black bird. . . .' No one but he could see this bird, however; suddenly, 'seated on his golden chair, he gave up his cherished soul'.

Despite Abaqa's wishes – he had preferred his son Arghun – it was his brother Taghudar who by threats and intrigue wriggled his way to the throne. In order to establish peace in the whole region, he now embraced Islam, despite having been baptized and brought up as a Nestorian by his Christian mother. With Abaqa's hoped-for Christian alliance thwarted by the Christians themselves, this change of direction was by no means illogical. It made the Mamluks potential allies instead of enemies, and conversely it drove a wedge between the Mamluks and the Golden Horde, whose khans had not yet decided whether they ought to follow Berke's religious example with any enthusiasm. But the Mamluk sultan was lukewarm in his responses to Taghudar's overtures – it may be that, like many others in history, the Ilkhan overestimated the value of belief, underestimated the importance of political and economic rivalries. Mongol power and the power of the Mamluks, glowering at one another across the Euphrates, would not have the logic of their enmity confounded by an alteration in one man's prayers.

While Kilawan in Cairo might be in two minds about Taghudar's conversion, many of Persia's Mongol aristocracy were not. Observing Taghudar change his name to Ahmed, his title to Sultan, suffering his persecutions of the non-Muslims in his realm – a desperate and bloody expedient to convince the Islamic world of his sincerity – they came to the conclusion that only revolution would reverse these trends and expel such impurities from the nation.

This unrest was Arghun's opportunity – which is not to say that he did not himself share the convictions that caused it. Taking care to complain to Kubilai of his uncle's wayward abandonment of the ancient ways, he marched west from Khorasan, the province of which Taghudar had made him governor. The Ilkhan Taghudar – or the Sultan Ahmed – came out to meet him, at first with fair success. But the disaffection of the conservatives had eaten deeply even into his most immediate support. His own generals turned on him and by their mutiny made certain of his defeat. Arghun, pausing only to have his shifty uncle executed, clambered over his dead body to the throne.

Thus in August 1284, the Persian territories of the Mongol Empire saw the rulership once more in the hands of a traditionalist. At home Arghun favoured the Buddhists, as his father and grandfather had before him; abroad, in the same way, he sought security by alliance with the eastern Christians. He attempted to revive the idea of a joint assault by the Mongols and the western powers against Egypt, now itself rent by dynastic dissension as the disinherited family of Baibars tried to wrest from Kilawan their birthright. In a letter to Philip the Fair of France, Arghun stated categorically that the Mongols had decided, 'after reporting to heaven, to mount our horses in the last month of winter in the Year of the Tiger

[1290] and to dismount outside Damascus on the fifteenth of the first spring month . . . and if, by the authority of heaven, we conquer those people, we shall give you Jerusalem.' But such a stupendous gift was never to be, the rendezvous that might have made it possible was never to take place. By the beginning of the fourteenth century the recapture of Jerusalem by Christendom was more acceptable to European monarchs as a future commitment, a pious ambition, a dream of possible glory, than as an action to be undertaken with any sense of immediacy.

Thus Arghun's letter, carried by the Genoese Buscarelli – Arghun writes it 'Müsqeril' – was the final effort in a diplomatic campaign that had involved many embassies and letters, but not a single concerted campaign. At the beginning of March 1291, Acre fell to Mamluk assault; the last Crusader bridgehead in Palestine had been removed. By then Arghun himself was on his death-bed, the last weeks of his reign made over-turbulent by the resentment his *sahib-divan*, his finance minister, had aroused among the people. This man, Sa'd al-Dawla, of Jewish origin, had incurred the hatred of the nobility by limiting their thefts from the exchequer, of the military by subordinating them to the political power, and of the pious by his ancestry. As the Ilkhan lay, snared by death, his minister was seized and beheaded; six days after the fall of Acre ended forever his policy of cooperation with the Catholic West, Arghun himself died.

On the wings of a military conspiracy there now came to the throne Arghun's younger brother, Kaikhatu, a gentle, self-indulgent man, weak, improvident, fond of alcohol and beautiful boys, who apparently without a second thought appropriated the resources of his state's exchequer to pay for his own dissipations. Unlike most other Mongol monarchs he never ordered an execution, but one has the feeling that it was indolence and lack of resolution rather than true humanity that lay behind this uncharacteristic restraint. An idea he did take up nearly ruined his people – at the suggestion of one of his princes he decided to issue a paper currency, like the Chinese. Neither he nor his adviser seems to have understood that such a currency needs backing – Kubilai's notes were supported by silver to half their face value – and all gold and silver coins were immediately withdrawn. On 12 September 1294 these notes, or *ch'ao*, each with its Muslim affirmation, 'There is no God but God and Mohammed is His Prophet', were flung abruptly into circulation. Within a week peasants had ceased to supply the towns and cities; within a month all trade had ceased and the country faced stagnation, bankruptcy and famine. For a while the truth was kept from the Ilkhan – when he noticed a closed bazaar he was told that in that place the bazaars never opened on that particular day – but in the end the unrest, the riots, the attempted assassinations began to penetrate even the haze of self-indulgence in which he lived. The paper money vanished – but only a short while before Kaikhatu himself.

In April 1295 a new conspiracy put forward the claims of his cousin Baidu. Kaikhatu marched against him; the quarrel between Khan and claimant was personal, for, while drunk, Kaikhatu had belittled and insulted Baidu. Now this minor folly, and all the greater ones, came home to roost. Near Hamadan his army was broken by the insurgent forces, he himself was captured and executed by strangling. Baidu seems to have had strong Christian leanings; since he wore a cross round his neck he may even have been a Christian. In any case, his patronage of churches and their priests immediately aroused the dedicated hostility of the orthodox Muslims. In the spirit of the times they cast about for a claimant who

might advance their cause, a man whom they might install as their faction's ruler. Such a man was available.

Rashid says of Ghazan, the son of the Ilkhan Arghun and his intended successor, that despite his Buddhist upbringing 'he was able, with his sharp eye and correct attitude, to see through the mysteries of these idolatrous practices. He reflected on the different faiths and . . . became enlightened through the light of the religion of Mohammed streaming into his radiant inner being.' It is more likely, however, that the decision to proclaim himself a Muslim was taken upon somewhat cooler considerations. He was a man of intelligence at a time, and in a family, where intelligence had for a while been in short supply. As a provincial governor he had been alone in resisting the introduction of the infamous paper money – pleading that the dampness of the climate made the use of paper unsuitable, he had had the presses burnt on arrival. Now, as a would-be claimant, he at once saw the wisdom in the advice of his general, Nauwaz, to capture the Muslim cause by a public conversion. In June 1295 Ghazan announced himself as, so to speak, the Muslim candidate; by October Baidu was dead and he was the head of his country.

For two years there followed a persecution of Christians and of Jews, while the Buddhists were forcibly converted to Islam and their temples destroyed. Ghazan himself was less fanatical than such behaviour seems to suggest; it was Nauwaz who led this onslaught on the religious minorities within the realm. Perhaps Ghazan felt that it was necessary to let the gales of bigotry blow themselves out, perhaps he grew tired of the unrest in his kingdom. In the spring of 1297 he turned on his adviser and minister, executed those who most closely followed him, forced Nauwaz from sanctuary in Herat and had him, with Mongol cold-bloodedness, cut in two. He then issued a decree commanding from his subjects that tolerance in religious matters that had been Mongol policy since the days of Genghis; he himself took a leading part in attempting to heal the split, already centuries old, between Sunni and Shia sectarians within his borders.

At the same time he was a firm, even despotic ruler. He took the processes of government out of the hands of the ministers, the viziers and the emirs, who had been given the responsibility during previous reigns. These, caught between the rapacity of the aristocracy, the legitimate demands of the Khan and the needs of the people, had without exception succumbed either to these pressures, their own greed or the unpopularity that was the price of rectitude. The Khan himself, on the other hand, had the right to quell the emirs or to reward them, the ability to succour the people or force them to obedience. Ghazan certainly understood how to quell the emirs – in a single month his executioners dispatched thirty-eight of them, as well as five full princes – but his most important legislation concerned his state's finances.

Not only the introduction of paper money had reduced the Ilkhan's exchequer to a haphazard state of fantasy. Rashid tells us that the imperial treasury did not have even a tent to store its ingots and coinage. The treasury officials had to 'put down the treasures in the open, and covered them with felts'. Chaos was compounded by the greed of the notables: 'Every time a treasure was brought in,

A page from the thirteenth century Chronicle of Alfonso X of Castille, showing Crusaders in battle against the forces of Islam.

ABOVE A nineteenth-century view
of the ruins of Ghazan Khan's
mosque in Tabriz.

OPPOSITE Ghazan, the great Ilkhan of Persia,
vigorously engaged in one of his many reforms:
the pruning of both the numbers and
the powers of the state messengers.

emirs and friends of the treasurers arrived to claim a share and the treasurers
would give them something according to their rank.' Minor officials, the guards,
the treasurers themselves, 'everyone of them took something home. In this way,
every year eight-tenths of these treasures were squandered. . . .' Ghazan and his
executioners put a stop to all this.

Ghazan also regulated the taxes, which before his time had been gathered with
hardly any supervision by the provincial governors. Some of these might take a
cattle-tax from the peasantry as often as thirty times a year. Very little of this
money found its way into the state treasury, being kept by the governor, his
cronies and anyone powerful enough to threaten them with exposure. He also saw
to it that the abuses that had overtaken the ancient system of state messengers were
eradicated; officials in charge of the posting routes had requisitioned food and

fodder wildly in excess of the original demand, but as time passed the numbers of such messengers, the *ilchis*, grew until, in Rashid's words, 'even if fifty thousand mounts had been stationed at each mail stage, they would not have been enough.' As a symbol of status, as people with influence in their own right, these messengers began to be almost a state within the State. They 'began quarrelling among themselves . . . they also robbed the people of turbans, clothes and other possessions. While on their travels they sold the excess of food they had requisitioned with such skill and craftiness that they even outshone the Chinese and Indian merchants. They tormented, flogged, hanged and tortured people in every way. . . .' Meanwhile men pretending to be *ilchis* turned to theft on the highway.

It was a situation that threatened the communications structure by which the State was run and on which it depended; Ghazan reformed it, just as he made the highways themselves secure, partly by reviving the ancient cooperative practices for the mutual protection of wayfarers, but more importantly by establishing a reliable body of guards for law enforcement. In the private sector he limited or totally eliminated the usury that had, through the levels of interest demanded, begun to threaten the economic viability of both husbandry and commerce; at the same time he introduced humanitarian measures for the care of the sick and the aged.

He supported enterprise among the peasantry by permitting anyone to take over untilled land and to cultivate it without suffering taxation for the first difficult years. When taxes did have to be paid, they were regulated by the level of output. And once the level of taxes had been decided on, it could not be altered; prominently inscribed on stone or metal, the local governor's decree on taxation remained as witness against him should he unlawfully attempt to raise their level, or collect a tax a second time. This security for the peasantry was reinforced by the construction of new irrigation systems, by the development of villages and by the Ilkhan's interested patronage of the country's crafts. It is no wonder that Rashid, who watched all these developments and worked for Ghazan himself, as had his father before him, was able to write: 'With all these measures, prosperity was restored, those who had left their homes returned of their own free will and the finances of the provinces today flow more freely even than what is given out by the Imperial Mint. Two or three times each year, without delay, tax revenue flows into the Imperial Treasury. Nobody needs to pay a single coin, load of straw or grain, ram, wine or chicken by way of an "extra" of any kind.'

It seems fitting that, for all his awareness of his ancestry, Ghazan was the first Mongol ruler of Persia to leave off his coinage all mention of the Great Khan. He tried to steer his realm towards internal stability with his equable laws, humane taxation and religious tolerance. Externally he was perhaps less successful, for he would dearly have liked to impose his will on the base-born Mamluks. His efforts in Syria, however, which had included yet another sack of Aleppo in 1299, came to an abrupt end in 1303 when his army, despite the steps he had taken to ensure that they were properly paid and provisioned, failed to respond to his concern with victory. He was already in ill-health, though not yet thirty-five; as his captured soldiers marched through the jeering crowds of Cairo, the severed heads of their fallen comrades slung from their necks, he sank dispiritedly towards death. In May 1304 he died, having succeeded no more than any of his predecessors in pushing aside the Mamluks and forcing an outlet to the Mediterranean.

Mongol overlordship, bringing with it
a confluence of cultures, led in Persia to
a continued development of the skills of
painters, architects, writers, scribes and
metalworkers. This bronze candlestick inlaid
with silver dates from the thirteenth century.

Despite his change of religion, itself perhaps more politic than convinced, Ghazan always saw himself as a guardian of Mongol traditions. Probably more than any other ilkhan, he would have liked to continue and complete the work his ancestor Hulagu had attempted fifty years before. At the same time, for all his recognition that it was he and not the Khaghan who was supreme in Persia, he did all he could to bring together again the scattered interests and conflicting ambitions of the Ghengisite heirs. He realized that the future of Mongol imperialism could lie only in Mongol unity, reviving in this grasp of the obvious the straightforward clarity of Genghis Khan himself. But the unity of which he was able to help lay the foundations, although praised by his successor and instrumental in raising to the remnants of the khaghanate Kubilai's grandson Timur, was a brittle thing; even as it seemed to be building, the corrosive tides of time were sweeping it away.

In the ilkhanate territories themselves meanwhile, this involvement in the Mongol tradition was compromised by his acceptance of Islam. The resentment of conservatives was reinforced by his use – his necessary use – of outsiders such as Rashid ad-Din as his ministers and advisers. The result was that he always had to contend with a disaffected aristocracy, precisely those who should have supported his taking the lead, as a matter of principle and not simple ambition, in the factions that formed against him. This aristocracy, powerful and in its nomadic heritage contemptuous of both the urban bureaucracy and the land-tied peasantry, was always difficult to control; its members were the absolute masters of those who followed them and as such able to reject even the claims of the crown to keep them in check.

The patricians of the cities too, for all Ghazan's valiant efforts at control, used their positions to carve out for themselves enormous fortunes, either by exploiting the corruption in provincial and central government, or by squeezing the peasantry on their inherited estates. Money acquired in this way they invested in the highly profitable international trade of which Persia was the centre, using the resultant wealth to obtain yet more land and more tied peasantry – so beginning the cycle again on an even larger scale. Meanwhile the great lords of the Mongol ascendancy made their annual migrations north and south, as they had always done, cutting a swath of depredation across the countryside as they passed. And all the time the peasants in particular had to run an endless gauntlet of taxation – the *kubchur*, theoretically levied on meadow-land, in fact drawn from all who lived off herding; the *kharaj*, which was a simple land-tax; the *ushr*, which took a percentage of what the land produced; the *tamgha*, which was a sort of profits tax on all transactions, no matter how small; and for non-Muslims – the Jews, the Christians, the Buddhists, the Zoroastrians – there was a special tax as well, the *jizya*.

All this fell with some weight on the cities, but it must have been a devastating burden on a countryside hardly recovered yet from the ravages of Genghis Khan's original assault. By the time it became Ghazan's capital, Tabriz had a population of well over a quarter of a million, suggesting either a high level of urban wealth or the kind of desperation in the country that causes its people to flee to the towns for work or charity. In the towns and cities, however, they found themselves even more

Mongols used the hunt as a military training ground.
For the delicate art of the Persian miniaturist,
it made a magnificent subject.

in the power of the rich than they had been while still on the land. The tax-exempt *mullah*, the absentee landlord, the corrupt official and the profit-hungry merchant formed between them a cabal that neither the unrest of the people nor the displeasure of the Khan could undermine. All that Ghazan could manage was to reorganize what was within his power, to lighten here and there the burden that lay on the people. But the contradictions in his own position as an alien ruler divided from his Mongol nobles by the change in his religion meant that underlying the new stability of his realm there were the flaws and faults of the earthquake to come, the beginnings of an incipient chaos.

Ghazan was succeeded by his brother Uljaitu, who seems to have been content with this inheritance of brittle stability and to have imagined that it would continue without his supervision. The responsibilities of State slipped once more into the hands of ministers (one of the most powerful was still Rashid ad-Din), the governors of the several provinces took up again the profitable privileges Ghazan had partly cropped from them, and slowly the State slipped back into that condition of evident laxity from which the previous reign had begun to drag it. Uljaitu altered his capital to the new city of Sultaniya in 1307, without in any way altering the direction of his rule. In the twelve years that he was Khan, the work begun by his predecessor was undermined, set aside, countermanded or forgotten.

As might be expected from a ruler elsewhere so traditionalist, however, Uljaitu tried to revive some of the military glories of his dynasty. On the shores of the Caspian the people of Gilan, protected by the tangled forests of their low hills and the heavy swamps of their flatlands, had long maintained a detached independence from the affairs of the Ilkhan's subjects; now they were forcibly subdued. In 1312 Uljaitu went the route of ancient aggression and crossed the Euphrates, but a month of skirmishing brought no result and little glory; he withdrew again behind the natural boundary of the river, his brief incursion into Mamluk lands the last round in the long struggle begun half a century earlier by Hulagu.

The Emir Choban, governor of Khorasan, became during these years the true upholder of the throne, the single unifying power of the realm. The viziers struggled for the privileges accruing to those who stood close to the Ilkhan, but the advice that actually modified the sovereign's decision was usually Choban's. The only power to vie with his was that of Rashid, particularly after his great rival, Sad-ad-Din Saweji, had been put to death – the penalties for failure in these struggles were extreme and almost always final. When Uljaitu died and was succeeded by his son Abu Said, the influence of Emir Choban, who had shepherded him to the throne, was greatly increased. Rashid was now entangled in rivalry with another minister, Taj-ad-Din Ali Shah; this time it was the great Rashid who fell – and paid for his fall with his life. The new Ilkhan, as pleasure-loving as any of his predecessors, was content to let Emir Choban take the difficult decisions of statecraft.

It was perhaps no more than a fit of royal petulance that caused Choban's downfall. Abu Said desired the Emir's daughter, but was refused by her father on the grounds – doubtless ridiculous even to a decadent descendant of Genghis – that the girl was married. It is not clear whether Choban's son Temur-Tash compounded this recalcitrance by the private indiscretion of making love to one of the

Courtiers await the pleasure of Uljaitu, successor as Ilkhan to his brother Ghazan. The painting comes from the sixteenth-century India of the Moghuls – hence the respectful attendance of two elephants, unlikely to have been present in Uljaitu's capital, Sultaniya.

Khan's concubines, or by the public one of proclaiming himself an independent prince – it may be that one folly followed the other – but what is certain is that Choban had too many enemies to survive such a crossing of the Khan's will. He was, moreover, engaged in a minor campaign in Khorasan; in his absence there were voices enough to turn the monarch against him. When he heard that he had fallen from grace, he tried to rise against Abu Said in armed rebellion; his was no attractive cause however; his followers deserted him and in the end, bereft of ambition, he fled to Herat. It was not far enough for safety – in 1327 he was executed.

With his passing the true centre of the realm had vanished. When Abu Said died in 1335, aged only thirty-one (poisoned, some said, by a jealous concubine), it was, despite his interest in the opposite sex, without an heir. The dynasty of the Ilkhans had come to an end: the great Ghazan's severity, the summary nature of his justice and the industry of his executioners meant that there were no direct successors left in Hulagu's blood-line. The lands that Hulagu had united fell apart and, in the provincial capitals that had for a while lived and even grown rich under Mongol rule, princes of a quite different ancestry now sat in rulership.

Paradoxically the alien Mongols had both revived and added impetus to the development of Persian culture; architecture and painting flourished while they reigned and in supporting the literature of their adopted land they helped in establishing the mellifluous Persian as the central language of Islamic culture (though not, of course, the religion) instead of the harsher Arabic. In connecting Persia by the strands of blood as well as commerce to the rest of Asia, they opened it to a wide range of cultural influences; they looked benignly upon mathematicians and scientists. Yet the culture of Muslim Persia and Iraq had been established long before their arrival and would continue long after they had vanished from Khorasan, Tabriz and Baghdad. In the end, with the exception of a handful of buildings, of artifacts, of words and phrases, it was almost as though they had never conquered, never swaggered into domination, never slashed and bludgeoned their bloody way to power: it was almost as though they had never been.

# 10 THE SONS OF HEAVEN

After the death of Kubilai, there was perhaps little to be expected from the Yuan dynasty except that it should keep the angle of its decline as gentle as possible. At a *kuriltai* in 1294 his grandsons decided that of their number the resolute Kamala was the best suited to hold together the empire. He, however, preferred, it is said, the ruder life of khan and guardian of the northern borders; beyond those frontiers Kaidu still lurked and the task of watching for him was one of great responsibility. (Rashid on the other hand tells us that Kamala was passed over because a stammer made it hard for him to repeat the maxims of Genghis, a skill deemed essential in the ruler.) In consequence, his brother Timur was elected. Supported by the respected commander Bayan, conqueror of the Sung, his position seems to have been secure, but little is remembered of his achievements.

This reticence on the part of history must be because he seems to have had none of Kubilai's touchy impatience. Not for him campaigns begun at the instance of a hair-trigger pride; on the contrary, he called a halt to the campaigns that Kubilai had already begun. Only the last eruption of Kaidu's hopeless ambition in 1301 hurried him into war. Soon afterwards, however, Kaidu died; with the passing of this standard-bearer of Ogadei's house, it and the house of Tuli were finally able to reach understanding. Despite Timur's relative passivity, he held to the possessions and the place of Kubilai; his troops made his continued overlordship clear to the semi-dependent rulers of Annam, Champa and Burmese Mien, and he always received the stipulated tribute from these and other territories.

Timur died in 1307, lamented by the chroniclers, who praised him for buildings put up in honour of Confucius, and for his benign clemency; he was only forty-two and it may be that his death so early was a greater loss than one can now imagine. China after its adventures and sufferings needed an emperor happy to consolidate the work done by his more energetic predecessors. He was succeeded by his nephew, Khaishan, who found himself with a dynastic struggle on his hands. While on the one hand the threat from Kaidu's line had ended when Chapar, Kaidu's son, made his formal submission, on the other the claims closer to home of another grandson of Kubilai, Ananda, seemed likely for a while to disturb imperial serenity. The clash of these two men was also a clash of religions, for Khaishan had leanings towards Buddhism, was a patron of the Confucian scholars, protected Christianity and welcomed its missionaries, while Ananda was a deeply orthodox Muslim, steeped in the Koran and thus impelled to use any position of power he might achieve to propagate his faith. It may be that by his death in internecine battle China was spared the disruptive effects of prolonged religious dissension. As it was, the country soon returned to the serenity of Mongol tolerance.

Thus during Khaishan's reign, John of Montecorvino, come from the West to spread Catholicism, established himself in Pekin; he had earlier managed to convert Timur's son-in-law, but after this prince's death he set up a Franciscan mission as the focal point for a community of Alans. These Caucasian people, Greek Orthodox by birth, had been brought east many years before to serve in Kubilai's armies. Now John became their spiritual director – as it were, their parish priest. He built two churches for them, both within the walls of Pekin and one only a little way from the imperial palace. He also claimed to have baptized six thousand people, despite the intrigues and hostility of the Nestorians; such conversions may not have meant quite what he thought them, since they were in the minds of those who underwent them not inconsistent with a weather-eye adherence to other faiths. In Avignon, Pope Clement v was sufficiently pleased with his efforts to appoint him Archbishop of Khanbaliq, the name by which Pekin was then known.

Such religious activity may have seemed significant to western Christians; to the people of China it was only one strand in the complex pattern of beliefs that were available to them. Important among these, much more so than any Christians, were the Lamas of Tibet, students of Sanskrit, philosophy and magic. The name of the claimant Ananda (Sanskrit for 'bliss') suggests that his parents may have come under their influence; another such was the new emperor, Ayur Balibatra, who after only four years succeeded his brother when the latter died at the age of thirty-one.

Known more appropriately by his Mongol name of Buyantu, he continued what Khaishan had begun, supporting the traditional Confucian studies and, as a result, opening some of the higher echelons of the administration once more to the Chinese. It was they who most assiduously pursued those studies and it was such studies that after 1313 were again put to the test in the various examinations held by the civil service. Proficiency led to promotion; for the first time since the Mongols had ascended the imperial throne, Chinese scholars once more took their traditional place in society. Buyantu's son Shuddhipala, known to the Mongols as Gegen, continued this policy, but varied it by his adherence to Buddhism. He thus managed to antagonize both Mongols and Chinese; at the age of twenty-one he paid for his heedlessness by becoming the first Mongol ruler to fall to the political assassin. Yesun Timur, his cousin, succeeded him in 1323, for he had been too young – and perhaps too preoccupied with his religion – to have sons of his own. This great-grandson of Kubilai ushered in a decade during which Khans came and went with a pitiful regularity.

Yesun Timur himself died in 1328; Khaishan's son Kushala reigned for a year, being followed by his brother Togh Timur. In 1332 a baby succeeded to the throne, a child named Irinchinbal who was then seven years old and survived at this eminence for only two months. When he died the throne passed to his elder brother Toghan Timur; and with him it seemed for a while as though this mortal rot had been stopped. But the centre of government in Pekin had been fatally weakened by each succeeding emperor's insecurity of tenure.

The invasion of China was perhaps Genghis Khan's one really premeditated campaign. Here he fights in a mountain pass; in a battle like this above the rich plains of Shan-si, the Mongols destroyed a Chinese army said by some to have numbered half a million men.

بوشيد بلاد حيدان باد
گوى وكوى كمى كرد دى نيك
شهشاه و از ورك كرد دى
بجشيذار اكه وبد

يكباره از ملك وبوشه
شاد ذام شيران سرى
بيد كرد ورى نشانيت
ردا نيت كاذنيانىيت

جاكه كرذكران جنواد
بحشد بروستان سرب
ذك كف ازدخان جاكرى
شيندوراذغديناوى

سراسيه دشزاد شه
دنده تزاباذ برخ
تواذ بانثنت اكردى
نديدكرده بى ياركى

بنكام بيانت رخ ازبرز
يكباذ كباره ازنوكا
بشير ونينه مجديينى
كشيد درشب دكوش

كرف صوار اعواز ذكرد
شهر نيده بندكشيد
دوره دخان بذ زبارد
كرى كش كشد ازذبكاله

The division between what had been the Kin lands of the north and the Sung lands of the south had never been healed. What both ends of China had in common, however, was the sufferings of the peasantry. Kubilai's grandeur had been paid for out of their taxes and built by their coerced hands. In the north it was the new Mongol overlords who, by taking over the peasants' cultivable holdings for pasture, forced them off the land. Thus they were driven into either the military or the gangs of half-starved labourers who put up the buildings of the empire, the monuments and follies of its government, its princes, its magnates and its priests. In the south the old Sung hierarchies had been kept largely undisturbed; the passing of their own emperors, however, left no intercessionary power between the peasantry and the lords who controlled their existence. Precisely because the Mongol rulers needed the cooperation of the administrators and aristocrats who had run the southern state for the Sung, they did not take the place of that defunct dynasty, nor use their authority to curb that of magnate, landlord or bureaucrat. This reluctance to involve themselves did not, however, help the successors of Kubilai to gain the respect or even tolerance of the Chinese aristocracy. The contempt that these had always felt for foreigners, outsiders, newcomers, was in no way diminished by Mongol conciliation based on weakness. At every level, therefore, from the abused, over-taxed and poverty-stricken peasantry to the ambitious, arrogant and luxury-loving landholders, the Chinese had learned, or had never forgotten, to detest their overlords.

Travellers, who saw only the wealth, the obvious grandeur and industry of the empire, believed it to be stable and imagined it to be fortunate. The roads were safe and they carried a complex commerce. To the west they led away to Persia and Europe; the southern ports heaved with ships bound for the Philippines, the East Indies, southern India, the Persian Gulf. A vast trade was carried on across the Gulf of Tonkin with the wealthy kingdoms of Indo–China. Everywhere merchants, happy in their official tax exemptions, packed their bales on horseback or ship, on camel, wagon or mule, and sent them off to the ends of the earth. Unfortunately for China many of them were foreign – Muslims from western Asia, Venetians, Genoese, Armenians – and the profits they made flowed, like their goods, out of the emperor's realms. It was not paper money that these shrewd entrepreneurs sent to their homelands, but useful metal coinage. Perhaps this helped to accelerate the inflation that had always been, as it were, built in to China's issue of paper money, an issue never fully backed by the resources of the imperial treasury. Now more and more money was being printed at a time when there was a steady outflow of gold and silver coinage. Thus the instability of the empire and its ruling house was matched by that of its currency, a development that could only arouse a resentment in the mercantile class as great as the contempt of the aristocrats and the distress of the peasantry.

In 1325 the first open resistance to the existing state of things came thrusting up through the brittle surface of contentment. From then on, sometimes with greater ferocity, sometimes half-curbed, there was a constant rebellious nibbling at the

A sixteenth-century Moghul painting shows Genghis Khan besieging a Chinese city. The guns are almost certainly anachronistic, but not the enormous catapults. It was in order to destroy Chinese resistance that Genghis Khan made his soldiers learn the techniques of siege-craft.

RIGHT Mongol authorities remained tolerant of most religions and philosophies, and the Yuan emperors of China were no exception. This stone rubbing of Confucius walking with a disciple dates from the century of their rule.

LEFT A bronze coin from the mints of the Yuan emperors. They also issued paper money which, supported by gold and silver to half its value, remained stable over several decades. Inflation at last undermined it, a factor in the Yuan collapse.

BELOW The patronage of the Yuan emperors permitted the traditional crafts of China to flourish. This stoneware jar decorated with phoenixes dates from early in the fourteenth century.

夫子之像

得於聖人之家

仰之彌聖人之教

人之教而衣而不

而屬咸其小而不

安若天台其小子

德有如言其小子

未有政名如土

而日政知言土

四十九政知十九

security and institutions of the empire. The forces of the emperor – at that point, briefly, Yesun Timur – like those of his successors, soon proved themselves unable to cope. They were no longer the hard armies of the original Mongol generals, disciplined, used to the barest subsistence and reared on victory. Nor were their leaders like those in the past, men who shared the meagreness of their soldiers' lives and so demonstrated the unity they at the same time demanded; these were great barons, separated from the men they led by wealth rather than by ability or inherent power. There was never any hope that this army – like every established force at a disadvantage when faced with guerrillas – would provide the empire with the security it had to have.

One result was that the wealthy, those with property to protect, began to raise their own troops of vigilantes and militia. Every such detachment contributed its weight to the break-up of the accepted social structure. As the unrest grew, Toghan Timur's chief minister, Bayan, reacted in a manner that confirms that the Mongols' detestation of the Chinese was equal to any that the Chinese bore their masters. In 1337, it is said, he proposed a policy of extermination against everyone named Chang, Wang, Liu, Li and Chou – a policy which if successful would have left the country with more rulers than ruled. Unable to proceed with so drastic a counter-attack, he reversed the policy begun by Khaishan. The higher levels of the civil service were again closed to Chinese and, since the Mongol bureaucrats and court officials carried on their business in the Mongol script, he commanded that no Chinese be allowed to learn it. He restricted Chinese ownership of weapons and horses. Such measures came too late: the time when a Mongol could enforce them

A pottery figure of an actor, modelled in the days of the Yuan dynasty. The theatre was always a particular delight of the emperors.

were long over. Bayan's nephew Toghta forced his fall and took his place; he attempted conciliation again, reopening the bureaucracy to Confucian scholars, creating public works to aid the unemployed poor, wooing the Chinese by manifest admiration and patronage of their culture. In vain: in 1356 he died by poison.

If the opposition to the Mongols was widespread, it was by no means unified. Indeed it was not always directed against the Mongols as such, but rather at all those who ruled the country, taxed its poor and enslaved its destitute. The appearance of a genuine revolutionary during the middle decade of the fourteenth century began to draw together the threads of revolution. This man, Kuo Tsu-hsing, was the leader of the insurgents in Honan; his successes attracted to him great numbers of the desperate and disillusioned. His was a genuine class movement, directed at Chinese landlords as well as Mongol governors, but he died in 1355. He was followed as revolutionary leader by Chu Yuan-chang, a villager, the son of peasants, although himself educated in the cloisters of Buddhism and once destined to become a monk. His name, Chu, is also the Chinese word for pig, and perhaps because of this, perhaps because of his appearance (but the pictures we have may be caricatures based on the name), he was later known to his enemies as 'The Pig-Emperor'. It was he, with a shrewd far-sightedness, who altered the class basis of Kuo's revolutionary movement. No longer directed against the rich, but specifically against the foreign overlords, it was now open to the patriotic members of the middle classes and the aristocracy, in China so wealthy in experience and expertise.

Meanwhile the centre of Mongol ascendancy, the very core of rulership, was rotting within its walls. Reality was kept at bay by distance, by false information and soothing counsel, by flattery and the magnetism of pleasure. Orgasm is easier to achieve than organization – the Emperor amused himself with pretty boys, with dancing girls; he distracted himself with the simulated battles of the hunting field while elsewhere incompetent commanders lost his real battles and his realm; he surrounded himself with the magic-working lamas of Tibet instead of practical-minded ministers of State; he shut out the distant sounds of strife, despair, fury and collapse with the harmonious clatter of his eleven-piece orchestra. While in the far south his ports were being lost to Chu Yuan-chang's revolutionaries, on his palace lake floated a magnificent toy, a dragon ship with nodding head and waving tail and superbly worked, beautifully balanced feet that paddled in the water.

In 1365 Chu Yuan-chang captured Nankin. This success signalled his forth-coming victory; his own conciliatory policy drew to him the prosperous gentry, while the discipline of his forces won the approval of the peasants, for so long terrorized by every passing band or faction. In Nankin he set up a government, its authority an increasingly plausible alternative to that so weakly administered from Pekin. By controlling southern agriculture, southern ports and the routes between the two halves of China, he was now able to begin squeezing the north in a sort of economic blockade. At the same time he fought his own internecine struggles to gain control of the whole insurgent movement. One by one the other rebel leaders were either defeated or incorporated in his own forces. Within four years he was the undisputed lord of what had once been the Sung lands; the time had arrived to take the northern half of the country and drive the Mongols back into the wilderness from which they had come.

On the face of it this must have seemed a gigantic task. A century and a half had passed since the victories of Genghis Khan had settled the Mongols in northern

Two views of Chu Yuan-chang, the
revolutionary leader and later the first
Ming emperor. That Chu means 'pig'
in Chinese was almost certainly the reason
for his being given the nickname 'Pig-
Emperor'. Caricaturists were not slow to
seize the opportunity this gave them. On
taking power, he changed his name to
Hung-wu.

China. Everywhere they had garrisons, estates, posting stations, administrative centres. The land was theirs and they had long been established on it. In the south their hold had always, and deliberately, been kept weak, but on the north it seemed to be clamped as tightly as ever. Nevertheless Chu Yuan-chang issued a proclamation – 'Barbarians like this were made to obey and not command a civilized people!' – and marched. As rumours percolated faintly through the musky corridors of his palace with tales of losses in the South, the Emperor Toghan Timur ordered that the rebels should be halted on the Yangtze. It was too late. They had already crossed it. Some quarter of a million men, it is claimed, were now advancing under Chu Yuan-chang's orders on Pekin.

Concerted action, a united front, some sign of resolution, might still have saved the Mongol dynasty. Among the Chinese there must have been many with as much to lose through revolution as the Yuan emperors themselves. But there was neither unity nor resolution. The Mongol generals quarrelled among themselves: as in the days of the Kin, two of them successively occupied the capital itself, jackals disputing over a corpse. As what defence there was collapsed, so did imperial morale. Toghan Timur fled when Chu Yuan-chang reached the plains before Pekin. With his family and his immediate court, he halted briefly in the summer capital of Shang-tu, then hurried on to Jehol (now Chengteh). In 1370 he died there, even his misery beyond his comprehension. In this bewilderment and despair the dynasty of Kubilai, the family of Genghis, ended its governorship of China.

The great service the Mongols had done the world was to open China to the other cultures of Asia and the West. Gunpowder, printing, such minutiae of pleasure as playing cards – all these probably flowed over the land-bridge uniting that distant Cathay with Europe. In return China received from the outside world one of its later staples, sorghum, several important medical herbs and, again among the world's listed pleasures, the wine of the grape and the art of refining sugar. And the abacus, long considered indispensable to the minor arithmetic of Far Eastern commerce, was introduced to China during this period. These, however, are only the measurable influences, the artifacts and skills, spread by contact. More intangible were the cultural connections. The religions of the West penetrated China, though in the end they did not survive, and brought with them tales of distant gods and new philosophies. The Mongol tolerance of conflicting beliefs made such ideas available without hindrance, and so helped to enrich the cultural heritage of succeeding generations. Within China itself the arts were encouraged by Mongol rule, though not perhaps directly: the suspension of the civil service examinations made literature the scholar's most likely route to success. The later Yuan emperors, however, often looked kindly on scholarship and certainly under Kubilai the more flamboyant of builders and painters must have been encouraged by imperial patronage.

With the victory of Chu Yuan-chang much of the openness of the previous century vanished. Establishing the dynasty he called the Ming and ascending the imperial throne himself in the name of Hung-wu, he strengthened Chinese nationalism by internal encouragement and external control. Under the Ming emperors, China became once more a mysterious land, a place of legend and marvellous riches that had been glimpsed for a while, as though between the clouds of history, before being obscured again to everything but memory and rumour. As for the

ABOVE Most of what the Yuan emperors constructed was torn down
in the revolutionary and nationalistic fervour which
followed their downfall. This relief panel
on the Chü-yang Gate
in the Great Wall is one of the few examples of
Yuan dynasty sculpture to have survived.

LEFT Life for the wealthy was always gracious in China, except
when war or revolution disrupted it. Here a lady sits
at her toilet before a mirror; two maids attend her,
another sweeps the outer courtyard and a fourth approaches,
smiling, with a bowl of tea.

Mongols, three months of near-lunatic ferocity saw them and all their works almost extirpated from the soil of China. Every Mongol landlord or bureaucrat, every official associated with, or bound to, the Mongols, everyone with the slightest pretensions to authority under the Yuan dynasty stood in danger of being butchered wherever found. Those with houses and holdings fled before the fury of the peasants, almost always in vain. They died in the anguish of the tortured, the despair of the cornered, the bewilderment of the very young, the very old. Only the military were here and there retained, whole units, unconcerned about who paid them, being taken on contemptuously as the mercenaries of the new regime. What had been constructed under Mongol rule – the palaces of Kubilai, the pleasure gardens of Toghan Timur, the great houses of the lesser khans, the very walls of Pekin – was smashed to the ground. Whole areas of the country were emptied of people and had to be repopulated by government-sponsored migrations. The unconcerned arrogance of fifteen decades of Mongol tyranny was balanced by these three months of bloodshed. When they had passed – and their fury been extended far beyond the Great Wall until, in 1388, Karakorum itself crumbled to ash in a fire lit by Chinese torches – the Mongols of eastern Asia were again what they had been before the days of Genghis Khan: an inconsequential tribe quartering the bleak plains that border the Gobi Desert.

# 11 THE HEARTLANDS

East from the Oxus, towards the very heartlands of the Mongol nation – somewhere on those plains lay the borders of the realm ruled by the house of Chagatei. It was an inland realm, an empire of grasslands, of long caravan trails, bisected by the silk route itself, its eastern hills a nomad's paradise unhampered by the intrusion of cities. Its western territories were the more civilized, settled by Muslims and once under the unifying influence of the Khwarismian empire. Samarkand stood here, and Bokhara, trading centres devastated by Genghis Khan but, once rebuilt, too well positioned not to flourish.

For the early Mongol Khans, Chagatei and his immediate successors, it was the basin of the Ili, a river flowing west into Lake Balkhash, that was the centre of their activities. Lake Balkhash itself and the stubborn slopes of the Altai Mountains were the northern boundaries of their influence; in the South the Pamirs and the great ranges guarding Kashmir and Tibet hemmed in their rule. Here there was always a strong, frequently a dominant, faction determined to preserve the traditional ways of the Mongols. There was, except in the western areas, little inducement to change; foreign influences were few and transient, for people passed through these uninviting steppes, these hills and wide, grassy valleys, on their way to the enticements of China in one direction, Persia in the other. The preservation here of the ancient mobile existence was aided by the long governorship of Transoxiana itself by the intelligent Mahmud Yalavach, a merchant trusted early by Genghis (but mistrusted and dismissed, like so many others, by that ambitious dowager, Turakina), and his sons.

Chagatei himself was succeeded by his grandson, Kara Hulagu, but Kuyuk Khan replaced him by his uncle, Yesu Mangu. The Great Khan, Kuyuk, however, did not spend long on that throne his tenure had made so gloomy; in the dynastic struggles following his death, Yesu supported the claims of Ogadei's sons. It was an error; Mangu became the Khaghan and one of his first acts was to punish the Chagatei ruler by removing him and setting up Kara Hulagu for a second reign. It was the first time, though by no means the last, that the ambitions of the Ogadei line would have their repercussions in the affairs of the Chagatei khanate.

Kara Hulagu died in 1246 only a few months after Mangu had replaced him on the throne. For a while there was confusion in the house of Chagatei; the western provinces threatened to drift away under the strong governorship of Masud Beg, Mahmud Yalavach's son, destined with his brother to be in control throughout the old Khwarismian lands for more than another forty years. In Karakorum Mangu died; Arik-Buka, in local charge, made his bid for supreme power and, as one

LEFT A coin struck in the days of Kuyuk Khan, whose intervention in the Chagatei succession helped to produce a chaos of claimants.

RIGHT From these bleak plains the Mongols burst out upon an outraged world and, their brief empire in ruins, to these bleak plains they finally returned.

aspect of this, appointed Kara Hulagu's brother, Alghui, as Khan in the Chagatei territories.

It had been the intention of Arik-Buka to extend his power-base westward and build a strong land-link with the territories controlled by Berke, Khan of the Golden Horde, who was no supporter of Kubilai and disputed the latter's claim to become the Great Khan. Alghui, however, had ambitions of his own and did not think much of Arik-Buka's chances of success. He withdrew his support from the young claimant and was rewarded, as those are who read the currents of history aright, by the support of the surviving mighty. After Arik-Buka had submitted to his elder brother, Kubilai gave his full recognition to Alghui as khan of the Chagatei horde, despite the fact that it was his rival who had first appointed him.

Such dynastic struggles leave bitter enmities behind them, however; Berke, the Kipchak Khan, refused to recognize Alghui, while an even more powerful enemy of Kubilai, that hero of the Ogadei house, Kadai, considered him as much his enemy as the Khaghan himself. In 1265 Alghui died; his successor was Kara Hulagu's son, Mubaraq Shah. As his name implies the new Khan was a Muslim; perhaps for this reason, perhaps to establish his own power – Mubaraq had not taken the precaution to gain his consent – Kubilai sent a punitive expedition against him. It was led by his cousin, Borak, whose success in driving out the proclaimed Khan may have gone a little to his head. As *de facto* ruler, he too proclaimed himself the Khan; unlike his defeated predecessor he was able to consolidate his position by flinging back the column Kubilai now sent to bring him down.

This complicated and destructive power-game aided in the end only one man, the ambitious Kaidu. If these central lands were lost to Kubilai in Pekin – though to the west the Ilkhans of Persia continued in at least nominal allegiance to the Khaghan for several generations – they might come under Kaidu's control as legitimately as that of anyone else. And Kaidu was able, a clever general and a competent administrator; above all he was the grandson of Ogadei and confident in the claims he made. By the time he died in 1301 he was, as far as Borak and his people were concerned, much more clearly the Great Khan than Kubilai.

For the Mongol empire as a whole the consequences of this were severe. Although the lands left to the house of Chagatei had neither the brilliant history nor the complex civilization of those to the east and west, although they were not as

Borak Khan, who
in 1264 was sent
by his cousin,
Kubilai, to oust
the legitimate
descendant of
Chagatei,
Mubaraq Shah.
Borak proceeded
to annex the
Khanate for
himself, and in
this miniature he
is being
recognized as
their ruler by the
notables of the
Chagatei lands.

wealthy nor able in the same way to draw the attention of the world, they were central to the whole imperial structure. Once Kubilai had set himself up in Pekin, it was essential that there should be swift, open and secure communications between his capital and those of his royal cousins if the eastward tug he had given to the balance of the administration were not to distort and finally destroy imperial unity. Yet it was precisely this ease of communications which the establishment of Kaidu's power from Karakorum to the Oxus made impossible. Nor did the disruptive effects of his ambitions stop there: his battles against the Ilkhans of Persia, against the Golden Horde and, above all, his endless and bitter war against Kubilai himself, all helped to break down the already shaky unity of the Mongols' transcontinental rule. By the beginning of the fourteenth century, therefore, the factual empire, as against its piously accepted myth, had already come more or less to its end.

Nevertheless in the next generation legitimacy was again imposed for a while. Borak's son Tuwa, and much more comprehensively his grandson Kebek, between them reinstated the Chagatei line as rightful Khans in their inheritance. Kaidu's son Chapar attempted to keep his hold by diplomacy, proposing to Pekin a loose federation of equal states bound in a sort of free-trade union – the idea, though over six centuries old, remains familiar – but had not the power or the generalship of his father. He had to give way before the renascent vigour of the Chagatei princes.

After Tuwa died in 1307, his son Esen Buga became Khan. It was, however, Kebek who held the effective power and, when his younger brother died in 1318, it was he who succeeded him. He was a man somewhat different from his immediate ancestors. It may be that the powerful presence of Kaidu to the east had forced the Chagatei princes to seek shelter in the west. Whatever the reason, Kebek, although not a Muslim, preferred the douce life of the cities to the harsher and more barbarian splendours that surround a nomad chief. He built himself a palace, as Ogadei and Berke, Hulagu and Kubilai had done before him.

His successor was again a brother, Tarmashirin, who came to the throne in 1326. He was a Muslim – he took the name Ala ud-Din – and he used the strong basis of power he had now inherited to begin once more the ancient Mongol games of conquest. He understood the realities of his situation, however; attempts to break out westward into the lands of the Ilkhans, the last under his brother in 1316, had always ended in failure. To the north lay the watchful armies of the Golden Horde. To the east lay a wilderness, and beyond it the great fortresses of China, governed by the nominal head of the empire of which he was a prince. To the south, however, lay India, neither Mongol nor powerful; it was to the south that he led his armies.

Under Tarmashirin Mongol forces appeared once more on the banks of the Indus and, either less debilitated by the heat than their predecessors or better at picking their seasons, crossed that river and reached out into the plains beyond. Multan and Lahore felt the weight of their armed avarice on several occasions, they plunged across the fertile flatlands of the Punjab, in 1326 even reaching the outskirts of Delhi. But the weight of rulership had rested too long in the western provinces; in

Sultan Bayazid, one of the early leaders of the Ottoman Turks and a general of genius, met his match in Tamurlaine and was captured outside Ankara. He died a few months later from, it is said, his mortified pride.

1334 there was an uprising directed against their urbanized, Muslim ruler by the traditional conservatives, Mongol in custom and belief, still based on the Ili Valley. In Tarmashirin's place they set up a new Khan, Jenkshi, dedicated to preserving the ancient values and the law of Genghis.

Jenkshi, as befitted his regenerative purpose, left the western cities and made his headquarters at Almalik, on the River Ili. There, partly in pursuance of the Mongol tradition of tolerance, but more particularly to spite the Muslims, he welcomed Christian missionaries. Benedict XII, from his own exile in Avignon, made Almalik one of the Far Eastern bishoprics in 1338 and to that dangerously distant see appointed Richard of Burgundy, of the Franciscan order. With considerable missionary effort a church or two had been consecrated and a number of converts been made, one of them a prince of the Khan's own family – Catholic Europe could be forgiven for its renewed optimism. The very success of the Christians, however, in a country already so polarized by religious conflict, had in it the causes of its failure. Before Richard had been a bishop more than two years, an affronted mob of Muslims had hacked him, five other friars and an Italian merchant named Gilotto unpleasantly to death.

There had always been an inner incompatibility in the Chagatei lands. The sophisticated, urbanized and Muslim West, the barbaric, conservative and animistic East – these had tugged in different directions. Khans had lived some-times in one centre of power, sometimes in the other. Now the time for such shifts and compromises was over. In a turbulence of armed disagreements, superficially religious but as much political as anything else, the old khanate broke up. The eastern sections withdrew into an age-old sullenness, into a dour refusal to accept any alteration or modification to the manner of their lives. With their horses, their wagons, their felt tents, their sheep and their goats, they turned their backs on the complexities of history and returned to the near-anonymity of their ancestral restlessness.

In the west, meanwhile, weak Khans rose to power, waxed fat and waned abruptly at the will of great emirs. One of the greatest of these, Emir Khazghan, pushed back the frontiers of what had been the Persian Ilkhanate as far as Herat, the prince of which recognized the Chagatei suzerainty. In 1357 this strong man was assassin-ated and another self-made war-lord, Tughluk Timur, claimed the throne of all Transoxiana. By 1360 he had been accepted as the new Khan. He had a son, Ilyas, whom he made governor of Samarkand. But Ilyas was still an untried administrator and needed able lieutenants; his father appointed as his minister and adviser a man, equally young but already, despite his wanderings, of proven capability in battle, a man who might be trusted since, like the Khan, he claimed descent from Genghis himself – Timur Lenk, whom Europe was to know as Tamurlaine.

What of the heartlands themselves, the river valleys where nearly two centuries earlier the whole improbable adventure had begun? It was there that the eastern Mongols, expelled from China, made their last attempt to rally. Karakorum was a ruin, a crumbling reminder of an already vanished vigour, of pretensions no longer

Tamurlaine's forces besieging
a fort like many along their
route from Georgia and Armenia
and through Asia Minor.

撂秧

晨雨麥秋潤午風槐
夏京溪南與溪北笃
歌撂新秧抛擲不停
手左右無亂行我教
撂秧馬代勞民莫怠

With the victory of the Ming, the Mongols of Central
Asia reverted to what they had been in the days of
Genghis Khan, raiders intermittently plundering the
riches of the Chinese empire. Ming defences were stout,
however; peasants like these – shown in a contemporary
woodcut planting rice – were able to cultivate their
fields without fear.

sustainable by the diminished successors of a previous century's giants. The son of Toghan Timur, the last Yuan emperor, accepting the logic of his circumstances, reverted to the strategy of his ancestors and began a series of plundering raids on China. He was not now, however, facing the cumbersome China of the Kin, a place of fluttering indecision and damaging blunder. In Chu Yuan-chang – now the first Ming emperor Hung-wu – the Mongols faced an adversary as resolute as they, and a thousand times more powerful than they had become.

In 1388 a Chinese army of some hundred thousand men marched decisively against the Mongols; with little opposition they hammered their way into Kara-korum and burned what remained of its imperial grandeur. Then they set them-selves to grim pursuit, following the Mongols as they drew back and back along the line of the River Kerulen, finally cornering them beside the ruffled waters of an upland lake, Buyur Nor. The battle smashed the last pretence of Mongol power. They lost their camp with all its tents, they lost their herds, they lost their menfolk – it is estimated that seventy thousand were taken prisoner – and they lost almost all their ruling family. Their Khan, Tokur Timur, may himself have escaped the Chinese; if he did, he was not as swift as the disappointment of his own followers. Bitterly, it was these who probably killed him. His successor, Elbek Khan, died in battle against the Khirghiz; Elbek's son Aljai Timur attempted once again to out-face the might of the new dynasty in China and met his expected defeat at the hands of the emperor Yang Lo.

In 1412 Aljai Timur was decisively smashed by a new power in Mongolia, that of the four-tribe confederation, the Uirat. Their Khan, Mahamu, was succeeded by a line of powerful rulers, one of whom, Esen Taiji, was to win great victories against the Ming and even take one of their emperors, Ying-tsung, prisoner. Theirs, however, was a new power, perhaps that of cousins to the true line of Genghisite Mongols, but separate, different. For all the care Genghis Khan had taken to ensure the survival of the empire he had created out of the bloody segments of two continents, it had not stood longer than a couple of centuries. What remained of his people and his family were, by 1450, almost exactly what they had been in 1200. They had memories, tales of an ancient ferocity and of a world cowering to the whiplash of their ambition, but year by year these were becoming legends, fossilizing into a mythology, offering only a momentary pride to the young, a com-forting satisfaction to the old. 'Once, long ago, when Genghis Khan. . . .' But their world had contracted, that name too great for it now; one sees them staring for a while into the fire, then wordlessly making their way one by one towards their tents. . . .

# Book Four
# AFTERGLOW
# AND NIGHTFALL

# 12 THE LAST ASSAULT

**W**ith the collapse of Chagatei rule, the eastern areas of steppeland ceased to be of interest for a while to either conqueror or historian. The richer western provinces, however, still provoked the dreams of adventurers. Emirs made their thrusts for power, often using some remnant of the Chagatei line to cloak their ambitions in legitimacy. Most of them by now spoke Turkish or some closely related language; all of them were Muslims. To the west of them again, across the Oxus, the ruins of the Ilkhanate too were fought over by a succession of empire-builders, the most successful of these being the Jalayirids, a family that succeeded in establishing itself across Iraq, Kurdistan and Azerbeijan. To the south, there were the Mamluks, secure in their hold over a prosperous Syria, an energetic Egypt. Yet in many places there was a hidden tension, a threatening though as yet hardly noticeable split between the classes. Rulers had often arrived later on the scene than ruled; it was the explosion of Islam, the wars against the Crusaders, the aftermath of Turkish or Mongol victories, the spread of Mamluk power, that had swept them across the borders of Western Asia and deposited them as the governors of peoples alien to them by blood and heritage. Islam seemed to unite them, but there was throughout this huge area a brittleness caused not only by the disruptive consequences of this endless whirl and swing of power, the meaningless rise and fall of princelings, but also by the suspicions of the native-born for those come from elsewhere to claim a throne. Prosperity disguised but did not diminish these suspicions – and only increased the lure of power.

It was in this general climate that there came thrusting into the light not only of history but of legend that lame warrior, Timur Lenk. Born in the arid lands south of Samarkand, in a valley, itself green, but dominated by the white and barren peaks of the Hindu Kush, by the time he was twenty he was the leader of a band of nomad villains whose success was beginning to draw to itself the rebellious, the rootless and the disaffected. That he himself was noted for his personal piety made him acceptable to many who might have rejected a mere robber chieftain.

When Tughluk Timur appeared from the east determined to conquer Transoxiana, Timur Lenk by courage and cunning served him well. Forced to return to put down a revolt among his chiefs, he left his son Ilyas as regent in Samarkand and, as we have seen, Timur Lenk at his shoulder as adviser. A secondary position did not suit the great Timur; he tried to set off the violence of an uprising, but had not realized that such an attempt is useless if popular support has not been organized. The people were unhappy, certainly, and quite prepared to rise, but not for a stranger, a man about whom they knew nothing except that he hinted at descent

from Genghis Khan (as who among the ambitious did not?), was probably a bandit and had helped Tughluk Timur to power. Isolated, the young Tamurlaine fled from his death-warrant into the mountains. For three years he skirmished, raided, hid and fled again. Slowly he built a reputation, then a power; it was during these years that he got the wounds that left him lame for life. By a mixture of subtlety and daring – once he had fires lit on distant hills to make his enemy think himself surrounded – he defeated the forces of the regent, Ilyas.

It was now the turn of his allies to suffer one by one the audacious complexities of his tactical wiles. They had hoped for a free confederation of equal lords; slowly they were forced to submit to the one among them with the intelligence and the force to take the rulership for himself. It was less than ten years after Tughluk Timur's triumph in 1360 that Timur Lenk was proclaimed Emir el Kebir or The Great Emir. Despite his occasional claims to be descended from Genghis Khan, however, he too now felt the need to lend legitimacy to his own power by appointing a true Genghisite, Syurhatmish, as Khan. He was, indeed, never to rule in his own right, which suggests that his doubts about the link between himself and Genghis were as strong as ours.

At the age of thirty-five, illiterate, but a most sophisticated chess-player, a lover of literature and the arts, a man of great cunning, great diplomacy, great insight, great endurance, already, it is said, white-haired, Timur Lenk had established his base. From it he would for a while recreate the greatness of Genghis Khan's empire – for, whether by blood or not, Genghis Khan was every Mongol and Turkic nomad's true ancestor.

He reinforced his own position by giving greater authority than before to the Muslim *mullahs*, and by stretching out into the surrounding lands the tentacles of an espionage system as complete as any the world had seen. Like Genghis Khan, he understood that it was information that led to victory. He now fought a succession of campaigns against his minor neighbours, establishing his local supremacy with greater and greater emphasis. He threatened Herat and Khorasan, and in turn saw their rulers accept his suzerainty. The Shah of Isfahan, an old man with a long experience of survival, sent him the gifts of vassalage. For a moment it seemed as though the old Ilkhanate would fall without effort into his hands, but when he turned to continue his work of conquest in the mountains of Afghanistan that overhung his birthplace, the people of eastern Persia rose against him.

His response offered the world its first evidence that a cruelty as extreme as that of Genghis Khan and Hulagu was loose again. Towns crumbled at his touch, under the sword of his executioners dynasties disappeared; when he had captured the chief city of Khorasan, he took two thousand of his captives and walled them up alive in a windowless tower, monument to their unwisdom and their slow, appalling death. In Afghanistan he was soon able to continue the work to which he had now set his hand; it was here that for the first time he built the pyramids of skulls so often set up beside the cities he destroyed, grisly cairns to mark the passing of whole populations. Satisfied by his gains in the high mountains, he returned once more to the plains. From the base he had now established in eastern Persia, he set out to

A city falls. The dead lie in appalling heaps. At Tamurlaine's order, the heads of the massacred are struck off. They make a gruesome decoration for the conqueror's memorial tower. The legend of terror which surrounds his name has a new addition.

reduce the rest of the country. He smashed his way into Ghazan's city, Sultaniya; he drove great emirs before him like a gale drives leaves; he began to overrun Azerbeijan in pursuit of Ahmed, the western Sultan.

It was now, in 1391, that he was first distracted by the out-matched ambition of Toktamish, his one-time protégé, Khan of the Golden Horde. Those skirmishes, however, did not hold him long. He sent his son Miran Shah to deal with them; he meanwhile struck westward again, waging holy war in Georgia, unholy war in Muslim Turkestan, holy war again when he reached the Christians of Armenia. What finally brought him back was the reluctance of the new rulers in southern Persia, the sons of the old Shah of Isfahan, to accept him as their overlord. He took their capital without a fight, but the demands he made of its people roused them in their own defence. Tamurlaine, however, had a genetic inheritance of fury; when he learned that three thousand of his men had been killed in the rebellion, he returned to Isfahan with an army of seventy thousand. On the house of every scholar, every artist and every holy man he placed a guard. Then he let his soldiers loose with only one order – that each of them was to bring him one severed head. Some murdered, others bought the fruit of their bloody labour: heads changed hands for a while at a gold piece each, but a glut on that market soon altered the price. In a short while they were worth nothing; a little later, picked clean by crow and worm, they lay in white piles beside the silent ruins.

Now, from the north, came news that Toktamish was again on the attack. With horses dying under him in exhausted relays, it is said, Timur sprang across the width of Persia. Toktamish was repulsed, pursued, destroyed, At the end of this campaign, Toktamish was for a while a distracted fugitive, a prince lost to dignity, and Tamurlaine confronted Europe from the banks of the Volga. Yet already behind him, in Asia Minor and in Persia, the empire he hoped to build was rattling into insecurity, its various parts dropping all pretence of allegiance to him.

As always, Timur could not impose the legitimacy of his rule on those he conquered. He moved too swiftly for that – speed was how he built his victories, but imperial administrations need time and patience. Genghis Khan had had brothers he could rely on, had known how to pick advisers, ministers, generals. He had conquered, then consolidated; when he had moved further, he had left behind local rulers almost as gifted as he. He had been able to inspire a personal loyalty even in men who had fought as his enemies. For all his gifts, his subtlety, his pleasure in art and music, the great feasts with which he celebrated his victories and the glories with which he decorated his cities, Timur Lenk, the fearsome Tamurlaine, never had followers of such quality. Though his intention was empire, his *métier* was war. As a Subatei to someone else's Genghis Khan, he might have been a marvel – but whom would he ever have allowed to be his commander?

Soon, with eighty thousand men, he was once more in southern Persia, this time intent on smashing Mansur, that highly competent, highly courageous shah. He had collected an army in the mountains, come down while Timur was engaged in his struggle with Toktamish, and had set up Shiraz as his capital. Timur Lenk thrust at Mansur three-pronged: one column blocked his retreat to the mountains, one reduced his upland fastnesses, the third attacked him head-on in Shiraz. The fight was drawn-out and hard, for Mansur was a fighter as courageous and almost as able as Timur himself. At the end, with the remains of his guard about him, Mansur came at the head of a murderous wedge for Tamurlaine himself. It is said

Timur Lenk, Tamurlaine the Great,
accoutred for war even on his throne.

that he struck him, twice, but his sword was turned away by Timur's helmet. If he died then, he did so at the very feet of the conqueror, brought to a final subjugation by mortality.

Having forced Ahmed to flee from Baghdad to the security of Cairo, Timur Lenk turned away towards the Caucasus. Here no power could withstand him. His task was subjugation, his method terror, murder the outcome. Small detachments, independent armies roved the lands east of the Black Sea. Where they passed, not enough were left alive to mourn the dead. He would have obedience, and if the living would not give it to him, he would change their condition. By the time he set Miran Shah on the throne once occupied by Hulagu, he had halved the populations of Georgia and Armenia. And it was then, in the full flow of his triumph, that Toktamish, his forces regrouped, emerged again through the passes east of the Caspian. He thought he had alliances; as we have seen, he had none he could rely on. Beside the River Terek he brought Timur Lenk close to defeat, it is said came near to killing him, but was at last forced to flee. Once running, he was given no chance to rally, neither along the Volga nor in the forests nor, later, on the Dnieper; the armies of the Golden Horde were destroyed and scattered, the tribes that made it up fled about eastern Europe, western Asia. Timur Lenk rampaged through the Russian principalities and dukedoms almost to Moscow, then swung away again, plundered the Genoese in their Black Sea foothold, then smashed through Astrakhan until, on the Volga once more, with the great wand of his fury he made Sarai, that great city, vanish for ever. Today the learned may pick over the pieces – a glazed tile here, a pin there, a stretch of conduit under the soil, the brickwork of a canal, a piece of cloth, a trace of coffee, a cluster of pots – but the twenty square miles of bright water, tall mosques, workshops, palaces and winding streets of Berke Sarai were destroyed for ever. And Toktamish, who had ruled here and thought, in pride, to measure himself against Timur's elemental strength, had vanished too, wandering far to the east, across the Siberian steppes, dying in the end at the hands of a minor chieftain, a man named Shadibek.

Now, at the age of sixty, it seemed as though Timur was prepared to settle his quarrel with the world. He had great lands, had cowed the great princes who ruled them or killed those who would not be cowed. Beyond the borders of his rule he had destroyed his most immediate enemies. Between Oxus and Jaxartes he could live in immense, if endlessly suspicious, state. No bridges crossed those rivers except the temporary structures by which his armies advanced against the world. Without a pass no one might take the ferries which, to west and east, provided the only way out of his domains – though entry was free to anyone who came. In the south of these domains, Samarkand stood as his monument, a city loud with trade, bright with mosaic, cool with fountains and gardens, sonorous with poetry and music. Having destroyed its rivals, he diverted to it almost all the trade of the eastern world. From Novgorod and Nankin, from Delhi, Hamburg, Alexandria or Venice, merchandise and merchants threaded their laborious way to where, in this city of endless lanes and squares, of shaded arcades and sudden flamboyant minarets, the energy of Tamurlaine had decreed the existence of the world's central market.

But it was not only merchants who came here. Painters arrived, and scholars, leaders of religion, philosophers; architects built monuments to his victories, those very victories in which the work of their predecessors had been razed or burnt to the ground; the books in which the learning of a universe was preserved were

Like Genghis Khan, Tamurlaine sharpened
his warrior skills and those of his men
on the hunting field.

brought by pack-train to the city – while the libraries that had once contained them were demolished beyond hope of repair; the carpets, the miniatures, the manuscripts of the brightest Asian civilizations were carried here with all the care of love, while the civilizations themselves lay scattered, broken, wrenched from the grasp of those who had created them.

Here in Samarkand this great destroyer became a builder, forcing up constructions with the same ferocious energy he brought to their destruction everywhere else, this great scatterer of order became a collector, gathering with a helpless greed the best examples of that epitome of order: art. It was as if, having once been poor, a wanderer, he now demanded an endless compensation for that early deprivation, as if an insatiable hunger was in him which no amount of accumulation would ever allay. Yet, having created Samarkand, alive with half the languages of earth, ablaze with the turquoise and azure, the gold and the alabaster of mosaics, he himself spurned it. It was what he had made; it was not where he lived. For him there was only the tent, the great pavilion of a khan, sign of his inexorable ambition, symbol of his nomad inheritance.

Nothing would hold him in one place. There were still riches out of his grasp and he had to reach for them. To the south lay India, the vast plains beyond the Indus stretching away into a haze of gold-flecked fable, that Hindustan that had for generations been a raiding ground for the warrior princes of Islam. He now had grandsons to command his armies; one set out from Kabul, the other followed the line of the Himalayas. Tamurlaine himself, tempted by the impossible simply because – like a local mountain to another generation – it was there, scrambled his way into and through the high mountains of the Hindu Kush, half-subduing mountain tribes no conqueror had bothered with before. Then, with one grandson in Lahore and the other in Multan, he fell upon the cities of the Punjab.

There was dissension in India between the Muslim rulers and the Hindu princes, especially the warrior Rajputs. This, allied to the speed of his campaign, prevented the mounting of any real opposition to Tamurlaine – though one doubts that any opposition now could have halted him. He was sixty-two, had been ill, understood that death was creeping closer and knew that what still had to be done must be crammed into time too short, by anyone's standards but his own, for its achievement. Northern India then was ruled by Sultan Mahmud of the Tughluq dynasty, founded by Ghazi Malik as a consequence of his efforts against Genghis Khan in the wars fought two centuries before by Jelal ud-Din. He could do little but watch and wait as Tamurlaine's columns carved their way through the dust and the blood towards his capital at Delhi. Everywhere the stink of corpses was curtained by the acridity of smoke. In Bhatnair the desperate population set their own city on fire and flung themselves into its flames. Plunder loaded the great wagons of Tamurlaine's advancing army, the shuffling feet of the enslaved lifted a permanent column of dust into the air. In the end there were too many captives, some say a hundred thousand men, women and children, others think even more; they made the war machine unwieldy, too slow. Outside the walls of Delhi Tamulaine ordered that they be killed. An hour later their corpses lay across that plain like the fruits of some appalling harvest.

Tamurlaine leads his army through the Katur Mountains and down to the northern plains of India. The viceroy he set on the throne in Delhi was to be the precursor of the Moghul dynasty.

وصاحبطران عصای بدست مبارک کرفته یک قدمه پیاده میرفت وچند اسپ خاصه را بطناباز کرده فرو

کداشته اکثراشوانشمده کناه داشت وملف شد و اسب بسلامت رسید و انخضرت سوا شره امراولشکریان

پیاده درر کاب میرفتند تاآنکه بقلعه ان کراهان رسیدند که برکناراب ودامان کوسی بلند واقعاست واثبان قلعه

Samarkand, where Timur the Destroyer
turned builder. From every corner of
the lands he conquered he brought back
treasures to enrich the city – yet he
never lived in it himself.

Mahmud came out of the city to fight, his weapons gleaming, his shambling war elephants ranged in front. No might availed him, nor his sophisticated missiles, naphtha bombs and metal-tipped rockets, a military technology learned from the Mongols. He was swept aside by the imperious necessity of Tamurlaine's lust for more land, more objects, more vassals. Four months after crossing the Indus, the ruler of Transoxiana was sitting on the throne of the Tughluqs, smiling with the easy benevolence of the victor at the line of nawabs and emirs and petty sultans vying with each other in the expression of their profound and unshakable allegiance. Had he wanted to spare Delhi? It is supposed so, since he arranged these festivals of conquest. Yet to him there might have been something humorous in accepting this civilized homage while already, in the outer suburbs, his men were striking down the innocent and carrying off what valuables they owned. The gates of the inner city were closed against the looters, but opened again. The march had been too long, the war too hard, for the men to turn away from plunder. It was what they had suffered for. They turned on those who tried to stop them: looting turned into mutiny. Lost to all discipline, greed their only commandment, Tamurlaine's army fell upon the inner city like some heaven-decreed vengeance. They killed the population wherever it fled or cowered, in the streets and lanes, in the cellars, in the very mosque itself, that magnificent mosque of a thousand pillars where, only a few hours before, prayers had invoked the blessing of God on the conqueror. Those who were not killed were driven through the gates in chains, there to be selected as the slaves of this or that patrician. The gold and jewels, the silver and the pearls, were carried off for ever on the bent backs of jubilant soldiers. As always the artists and the craftsmen were treated more gently than the rest; workers in stone were picked out to serve Tamurlaine himself – he still had Samarkand to finish, extend, beautify.

When he left Delhi, it faced nearly two centuries of desolation. Half depopulated, it became one town among others, not for generations to be again the capital of a rich people secure in their pride. Tamurlaine himself struck eastward, crossed the Ganges, his men now killing and plundering without opposition or relief, already gorged yet still unsatiated, pillaging the country like an enormous robber band, neither strategic nor diplomatic sense in their long march. By the time they turned for home, they were so burdened that an army once renowned for its speed of movement could manage no more than three or four miles in a day. It wound its way slowly through the gathering heat of the Indian summer towards the Indus, the cool of the mountains and the exultation of a victorious home-coming. Behind him, Tamurlaine left as ruler of a devastated country Khizr Khan Sayyid, governor of Multan, who would be viceroy in his name. Later, he would found his own ruling house in India; in time this fact, too, would have its consequence.

In Samarkand Timur Lenk discovered that his son Miran Shah had begun to behave like a fool. He drank, he wasted the State's money, he ignored his duties. Now and then what must have been his frustration at his inability to surpass, even to match, the masterful exploits of his father, burst out in a wild destructiveness. In Tabriz, in Sultaniya, he tore down great buildings, defaced monuments, struck beauty into dust, despoiled tombs, stole the collected funds of the imperial treasury. His father for a while wanted him dead; in the end he deposed him from his Persian throne and made his younger son Khalil regent. Then he turned westward, his face once more towards war.

In Asia Minor the Turkish confederation that had gathered under the Ottoman ruler, Osman I, and his son Orkhan, had been reaching out north and west, building a new empire, a new and rival force in the world. Beyond them Byzantium, half-surrounded, sagged towards collapse. It paid the Turks an annual tribute; other states combined to try to thwart these successors of the Mongols. At the battle of Kosovo in 1389, Orkhan's son Amurath defeated an army brought against him by an alliance of Serbs, Hungarians, Bulgars, Poles and Albanians. He himself died in that battle; at Nikopoli, a town on the Danube, his son and successor Bayezid smashed a Christian army gathered from much further afield, a European force brought out in the crusader spirit to force back yet another enemy of Christendom. This was in 1396; two years later, while Tamurlaine was grabbing bloody-handed at the wealth of India, Bayezid – now nick-named *Ilderim*: 'The Lightning' – was thrusting his eastern frontiers forward to the Euphrates. One may believe that, choosing between evils, the border princes were glad to turn to him as a protector against the known ferocity of Timur Lenk.

As for that Lame Timur, he must now have been searching for some reason to deal with this threatening upstart. It was Sultan Ahmed of Baghdad who gave him the excuse he needed. Tamurlaine marched westwards from Tabriz and, like a piece in a game of chess moving to avoid a long-term danger, Ahmed turned to flee. This time it was not to the Mamluks that he went for sanctuary, but to the Ottoman sultan. It looked as though, by this action, he had at last bound together an alliance against the Transoxanian ruler that had a chance of victory – Egypt, Syria and the forces of Bayezid I together could in theory place formidable power in the field.

Tamurlaine, as always, moved at an unexpected pace. He already had an army out, punishing the unfortunates in Georgia and Armenia who had fought in rebellion against his son, Miran Shah. Now he demanded that Bayezid should give up Ahmed and those who had fled with him. The Turkish sultan refused. Tamurlaine swung through Asia Minor, smashing his way into two of the Osmanlis' strongest fortresses; before Bayezid, busy about Constantinople, could march against him, however, he had thrust southward into Syria. The captured forts held back the Turks; he was free to face the Egyptians on their own. Outside Aleppo, scene of such Mongol triumphs as this part of the world had ever witnessed, he hacked down the Mamluk army led by Sultan Faraj, clambered into the city and once more destroyed it. Then he marched on Damascus. As that city hesitated on the brink of surrender, he heard that among those within was the great philosopher and historian, ibn Khaldun. Timur sent a message over the walls, asking to see this sage, and down those walls ibn Khaldun was lowered, to spend seven weeks in the conqueror's company. From him Tamurlaine wanted information, especially details of North Africa. Was he intending to march on, past the Nile Delta, westward towards Algeria? Not yet, perhaps; but he listened avidly to ibn Khaldun and had read to him the written report this obliging intellectual prepared.

Meanwhile Damascus surrendered; again it may be that Tamurlaine wanted it spared. It was here that he discovered that finely curved dome, the splendid proportions of which, noted down then at his order, would appear again and again on Asia's most magnificent buildings, copied in their turn from the copy he had erected in Samarkand; not least, it can be seen in the lines of the cupola of the Taj Mahal. But what Tamurlaine stole from the beauty others had created never prevented him from destroying it once he had taken what he desired. Perhaps it was after he

Tamurlaine, who tried all his life to revive the glories of Genghis Khan's empire, emulated his predecessor on the battlefield, yet never matched him as an administrator.

had left that the soldiers, as at Delhi, insisted on taking the plunder they thought their due; perhaps it was then that the population died and the buildings tumbled, then that the great mosque, monument of the Omayyad Caliphs, split and sagged under its burden of flame: but ibn Khaldun saw Damascus sacked and he was Tamurlaine's companion, had asked from him before that last blow fell a safe conduct for the civilian officials, but only travelled back to Egypt when the smoke was fading from the Syrian sky.

And the Caliph's town, Baghdad? Forty days of resistance ended, as had so many vain attempts to bar Tamurlaine from victory, in massacre. With his slightly sickening selectivity, the sentimentality of the self-taught, of those who care nothing for people but are enraptured by the abstractions of religion and art, he ordered every dwelling house destroyed, every mosque and school preserved. He opened the gates for the poets, the scholars, the designers of mosaics, the painters and illuminators and calligraphers, gave them horses, sent them to the safety of cities he would not attack. Every other human being died, ninety thousand men, women and children, their heads hacked from their bodies and piled in the grisly hillocks that proclaimed his triumphs, a range of a hundred and twenty rotting peaks of flesh and bone. Then he moved on to where Bayezid waited for the necessary confrontation between these uncompromising forces of the known world's central lands.

In his mid-sixties the military inventiveness of Tamurlaine was as quicksilver as ever, his moves executed with the same speed as they had always been. He moved to Sivas, one of the strongholds he had taken before his campaigns in Mesopotamia. Bayezid built his camp at Ankara, waited a while, then moved forward. On favourable terrain he halted, prepared his lines, sent out probing patrols. Everything had

been done well and according to established rule. When his scouts returned, however, they brought bewildering news – Tamurlaine had disappeared. He was not
in the city of Sivas nor anywhere between it and Bayezid's army. It was not until
news came that he was approaching Ankara that Bayezid realized he had been
out-flanked. Keeping the River Kizil Irmak between himself and the Osmanli
army, Tamurlaine had made a long southern detour, and was now preparing to
storm the walls of Ankara.

Bayezid hurried back. Already the morale of his men, used to victory, must have
been lowered. For the first time they had met an enemy who thought more pene-
tratingly and moved more quickly than they. What they discovered when their
forced march had brought them back to their starting point cannot have encouraged
them. Tamurlaine was in their camp, the half-forced walls of Ankara left to await
the outcome of battle. Between them and the camp should have been a stream, but
all they could see was the black-streaked, pebble-strewn earth over which water
had flowed only a few days before. Tamurlaine had built a dam, diverted the water;
it now flowed behind him, was under his control. His own wells had been filled.
On that high plateau of central Turkey, in the relentless heat of mid-July, Bayezid's
men had to face not only Tamurlaine, but their own thirst.

Like the desperate men they had now become, they fought for the whole day;
whole armies seemed to disappear into the maw of battle; kings and sultans fell,
humbled by death; that proud elite, the Janissaries, were cut down in swathes,
reaped by the huge energy of Timur Lenk. As the waterless horses flagged, so
Bayezid's mounted archers lost mobility. The Turcoman battalions Bayezid had
forced into his ranks now turned against him – their King rode with Tamurlaine.
Bayezid stood and fought, when flight might have proved the wiser. By nightfall,
he was Tamurlaine's prisoner – honoured by his undesired host, given his own tent,
but dishonoured in his own esteem. Pride shattered, he died within months.

His son, Suleiman, fled across the Bosporus and, from the relative security of the
European shore, sent the abject messages of a vassal to Timur. In Byzantium there
was jubilation, rich gifts were sent to the victor, for the siege of Constantinople had
been raised, the city had been saved, the successor of the Mongols had become the
saviour of Christendom. It was another fifty years before a later Turkish generation
would finish the work Bayezid had begun; Tamurlaine had by half a century
postponed the final fall of the Roman Empire.

Almost blind now, unable to walk or ride, having to be carried in a litter to super-
vise the continued building in his capital, Tamurlaine struggled to fill in the details
of his destiny. To the east, China stood, a huge empire once governed by his fore-
bears. Hung wu, the first Ming emperor, had sent envoys to him, in the name of
adopted Mongol myths of world supremacy demanding Tamurlaine's homage.
Tamurlaine had imprisoned them, but other matters had taken his attention and
he had later released them. In time, embassies had been exchanged and, since such
relations were always in the Chinese view those between ruler and vassal, it is
almost certain that Tamurlaine had politically accepted his secondary role. Now,
in despite of age and winter, he gathered a new army, nearly a quarter of a million
men, and led them eastward at last to expunge the galling memory of even so
meaningless a vassalage. He crossed the frozen Jaxartes and progressed as far as
Ortrar. But however swiftly he travelled, sickness and death were swifter. He was
sixty-nine years old, he had used up all the energy of his life and there was no

more left to call on. His fevers overwhelmed him; weakness swept him off his feet. On the night of 18 February 1405 he died. Outside his pavilion, rising above the calling of imams and the lamentations of his court, a bellowing thunderstorm yelled across the world.

So this contradiction vanished, this builder-destroyer, this defender of Islam with his trail of wrecked mosques, this conqueror who dreamed of empire and left behind him ten thousand miles of devastation. He was a man of agreed piety who used religion like the most cynical of modern propagandists: when he attacked Khorasan, he said it was because it belonged to the Shia faction in Islam, supporters of Ali, Mohammed's son-in-law, as the Prophet's successor; but when he swooped on Syria, it was because the Syrians had sided with Caliph Mu'awiyah against Ali; he attacked the Christian states of the Caucasus because they were infidel, the Ottoman Turks because they had not fought Christians with sufficient vigour, the Muslims of Delhi because they had not reduced the idolatry of Hinduism. Yet he destroyed Sarai out of pique – though it was the pique of a monster – and he used the victories of his endless campaigns to enrich himself, his family and his land. He killed hugely, his massacres sending shudders of horror through the world for generations; yet everywhere in his domains new irrigation channels were dug, dams were built, the land was persuaded to bear fruit. Wherever his armies marched, great cities tumbled into ruin; it was as though his touch was disaster to brick and mortar, stone and wood. Yet in Samarkand he laid the foundations not only of his own buildings and of a city the marvels of which astonished the world, but also of a new style of architecture, a delicate blend of some of the dominant strains of Asiatic design, which was to become the hallmark of many of the great buildings of Islam.

Perhaps the kind of greatness that he craved was that of the nomad chief who had made the whole earth his meadow. When he was last in Samarkand, already preparing the war he intended against China, he laid out on the open steppe the plunder of his many wars, the tribute of his many vassals, the gifts of his distant peers. There they all were, spread for the contemplation of his people, like the booty displayed beside his tent by a warrior chief. From France and Spain in the west, from the banks of the Volga, from Berke Sarai and Damascus, from Baghdad and Delhi and Ankara, from Byzantium and Cairo, there lay the proof of his greatness, visible to all. It gleamed and glittered, its fabrics swayed in the wind, its outrageous animals – ostrich, giraffe – drew the bemused eyes of passers-by; and in a babble of languages craftsmen and artists and scholars took their places too beside the casks and caskets in which the artifacts he desired had been brought to Tamurlaine. And then, again like a nomad chief, the feast was ordered and the drinking began. It was the effects of that, some believe, and not old age, which killed him, that last monumental celebration which summarized his life. He had collected a vast pile of heterogeneous objects, each one of them witness to the awe and terror his name aroused. But they did not add up to a civilization, these priceless gewgaws gathered with jackdaw intensity: he had failed to collect an empire, for all his constant victories.

As is fitting his sepulchre is magnificent, powerful yet delicate, a summary of Islamic architecture. His body was placed under an enormous jade slab and there it lay for nearly five and a half centuries. Then, in 1941, the inquisitive entered it, their justification the indiscriminate curiosity covered by the word 'scientific'.

They found the bones of a tall man, his right arm maimed, his right leg lame. His bearing had been, they said, imperious. Almost touchingly, the last hairs of a chestnut moustache adhered to the skull. On this basis, the Soviet Archaeological Commission reconstructed the shape of the flesh that may have lain upon those bones. Now we have his bust, probably one of astonishing accuracy. He himself, with his greed, his wilyness, his energy, his cruelty and his bewildering contradictions, continues to elude us.

His conquests, never unified by very much more than his own personality and will, now became the objects of a scramble for power. Shah Rokh, Timur Lenk's youngest son, finally emerged from this bloody scrummage as the strongest. He rejected Samarkand, however, making his capital in Herat, in Khorasan. His eldest son, Ulugh Beg, acted for him in Samarkand, and seems to have followed at least one tradition of his grandfather in his zeal to add to the city's buildings. To the north of Samarkand he built his circular observatory and in it placed a giant sextant. With this he busied himself in drawing up astronomical tables later to be widely used. He built a school of religious philosophy, as though to proclaim that his grandfather's piety had not been forgotten, and in his rule of nearly forty years made Samarkand a sort of university town, tranquil, beautiful, devoted to science, mathematics and the arts.

He founded a dynasty in Samarkand, just as other members of the family did in Bokhara, in Khorasan – where flourished under their care a magnificent series of painters, creators of some of the most sparkling miniatures in Persian history – in Balkh and in the Farghana valley, where in his early days Timur had had his own base. Under these Timurid princes, literature developed, both in Persian and in the Turkic language known as Chagatei; everything seemed to point to civilized rule, a period of calm after the gigantic storms of the fourteenth century. Unfortunately the rivalries within the family now matched the rage with which Timur himself had faced the outside world. They quarrelled, fought and fell. From the south came the Uzbeks, descendants of the Kipchaks, led by men of the blood of Genghis Khan (the tribe's name derived from that great Khan of the Golden Horde, Uzbeg), and slowly drove Tamurlaine's clan into obscurity. By the time the Uzbeks' greatest leader, Mohammad Shaybani, died in battle in 1510, they had established themselves in those much-disputed lands between the Oxus and Jaxartes. From there no one was ever able to oust them.

One of the rulers flung from his throne by the turmoil of this invasion was Zahir ud-Din Muhammad Babur, Khan in Farghana. He had been a ruler since the age of eleven, had learned the tricks of warfare, had discovered the value of gunfire in battle. Driven out from his ancestral lands, he looked about for others – on his father's side, he was five generations from Timur Lenk, and on his mother's fourteen from Genghis Khan. True to his blood he gathered an army and, hemmed in by Uzbeks and by Persia, struck out in the only direction open to him, the south. In India there ruled a dynasty descended from Khizr Khan Sayyid, who had been placed on that throne to govern in Timur Lenk's name. It was time that one of Timur's blood checked on his inheritance.

Babur marched, like his predecessors and ancestors, across the plains of the Punjab, attracting the disaffected, the over-zealous, the ambitious. Sultan Ibrahim Lodi brought his army out to face him and for eight days the two forces faced one another. On the night of 20 April 1526, Babur sent out a patrol, perhaps mounted a

The tomb of Tamurlaine in Samarkand. His empire, never a cohesive
entity even while he was alive, did not survive his death.
He is remembered not as the founder of a dynasty, but as perhaps
the most comprehensively destructive monarch in history.

full-blooded attack; with hindsight one sees it might have been no more than a feint.
Provoked, the Sultan ordered his attack the following morning. But Babur had not
wasted that week of inactivity: his men had built defences, a breastwork, behind
which they stood ready to repulse attack. Seeing this the Sultan's forces lost their
impetus; some slowed, others halted, a few turned to run. During that moment of
hesitation, as the Indian army hung like a sea between tides, Babur struck. To
support his charge, he had guns, weapons the Sultan's troops had never seen. There
was a long confusion, a hoarse babble punctuated by the flash and explosion of
gunpowder. The Indian army broke; the way to Delhi lay open.

In March 1527, having aroused in his men a religious fervour that would find
dangerous echoes in the centuries to come, Babur drove them forward against the
Hindu warrior princes of Rajputana. He broke their power on that field once and
for all; their earlier exploits became legends, folk-lore – his own now manufactured
history. On the banks of the Ganges, near where the River Ghagra flows into it
after crossing Uttar Pradesh, he defeated the wild bands of the mountain tribes,
men come down from Afghanistan and the high valleys of the Pathans. He had made
himself lord of northern India. With a Genghisite mixture of cruelty and concern
he and his descendants formed it into a great realm. In the dynasty of the Moghul
emperors, the blood-line of that great conqueror who had come howling out of
obscurity three centuries before was preserved in power for another two centuries.

# 13  THE BENEFITS OF FAILURE

It had been the intention of Genghis Khan to conquer the world and to found an empire that would survive down the generations. In both these intentions history thwarted him. The consequences of the Mongol campaigns, therefore, although considerable, were not those expected by the Mongols themselves. In the main their activities have become synonymous with a senseless cruelty, a violation of all security, all boundaries; for centuries they were regarded as the epitome of human destructiveness. It has taken the cold ingenuity of the twentieth century to match and even outstrip the heinous crimes that both legend and true recollection have placed at their door. Yet the turmoil they created in central Asia was bound to have results; the alteration they caused to the distribution of cultures, peoples and religions in the lands to which their power stretched was crucial in the development of the whole world.

The most immediate effect of the Mongol surge westward was the sudden influx of Turkish tribes it caused in western Asia and even eastern Europe. There had been an intermittent and sometimes violent migration of these peoples westward from the steppelands of Asia for several centuries, but by the time Genghis Khan and his successors had finished hurling the populations of two continents to and fro this process had been enormously accelerated. The Seljuqs had been just ahead of them and these they had smashed, but Genghis in particular, and all his family out of necessity, had relied on Turkish assistance. Early on Kereits and Naimans had joined him, and from then until the empire's collapse they and their cousins had rallied to the Mongol cause. Indeed without them that cause would have been lost, since the Mongols alone, for all the speed of their attacks and the versatility of their tactics, never commanded the numbers necessary to achieve the domination they craved.

Once the empire had begun to take shape, Genghis recognized, in a way that later Tamurlaine never seemed to, that he had to give his attention to its administration. It was then that the Turks above all began to come into their own for, outside China, it was they who provided the basic manpower of the bureaucracy. It will be remembered that it was the Turkic Uighur script that was adopted by Genghis as the written language of his administrators. The Mongol victories emphasized the importance of the Turkic languages and this in turn added to the importance of the people who spoke them. These people by far outnumbered the Mongols themselves and, over the decades, the weight of this majority began to alter the very structures of Mongol society. The Kipchak khans of the Golden Horde were considered to be Turks; Tamurlaine, for all his boasted Genghisite ancestry, is always referred to as

Turkish. It was as Turks – again despite their Mongol ancestry and their Persian culture – that the first Moghuls ruled in Delhi.

This was on the whole a purely demographic consequence of the Mongol invasions, but the vast scope and swift break-up of the Genghisite empire meant that the political developments that arose from it cut across these tenuous links of racial cousinship, or occurred well outside their influence. For example the effect of the Mongol presence, brooding in Berke Sarai, on the development of Russia led to the rise of oppressive dynasties in Moscow and a tradition of despotism never perhaps to be shaken off. It may well be that the shifting of Russia's centre of political gravity so far to the east did not have the long-term effects that have sometimes been claimed for it. Mongol suzerainty did not mean the end of Christian art, Slavonic literature or the Orthodox religion. Indeed, it may even be that oppression brought to the subject race an unprecedented and accelerated unity. The momentum of the culture's true development, however, must have been retarded: the anxious and self-seeking stewardship of the Muscovite princes, the economic consequences of ruthless taxation, the damage done by the ceaseless wars fought both to the west and to the east, and the siege mentality developed by the Church in response to the Kipchaks' conversion to Islam, must between them have placed a weight upon Russia so heavy that not only the burden itself but even the effort to remove it will have distorted centuries of the country's history.

In China, on the other hand, inhabited by a people whose culture was already millennia old, the Mongols could not destroy or hold back from development social, administrative or artistic processes. Indeed so powerful were these that the Mongol dynasty, the Yuan, succumbed to them almost from the beginning, never accepting them less than whole-heartedly from the time of Kubilai on. Thus, once the Mongols had been driven out, it was from these points of view almost as though they had never existed. Politically, however, and in religion, the results of Mongol intervention were longer-lasting and, on the whole, beneficial. The great gift the Yuan made to China was unity. Over four decades they struggled to impose their will from Korea to Yunan, from the Yellow River to Han-chou. As a result, from the time they drove the Sung dynasty from southern China, through the rise and fall of emperors and the whirling fortunes of modern revolution, the country has always been one. Despite the differences of language and even culture existing between provinces, despite the near autonomy achieved at one time or another by specific areas, that identity, that underlying interconnection, established during the time of Mongol overlordship – perhaps even in reaction to it – has now survived for seven hundred years.

In western Asia, where the Mongols were perhaps most active over the longest period, there were several unexpected effects. One was, as we have seen, the collapse of the western, Christian effort to retain a crusader foothold along the eastern coast of the Mediterranean. The inability of the kings and commanders of Catholicism to accept the Mongols as their allies meant that they were left vulnerable to a Mamluk power with which no accommodation was possible. It may be that they would have become the victims of the Mongols in the end, in just the same way, but the fact is that Genghis Khan and Hulagu were after temporal power. They had no religious quarrel with the Christians, as the Muslims did, and were indeed rather sympathetic to their faith. It would have been possible, theoretically, for the crusaders to cede some political power to the Ilkhans in return for their protection;

in practice, of course, their own struggle was as much temporal as religious and they were prepared to cede nothing to anyone. Their isolation should have led them logically to the solution of alliance, and that in turn should have induced them to make terms with the Mongols, but they are not the only ones in history who have turned away in pride from the only course that might have saved them.

Of greater importance to the world as a whole was, as has been mentioned, the long-term effect of destroying the Seljuq Turks. For a while the Mongols themselves were able to take their place, allied with or subduing the Christian people of the Caucasus, holding down or containing the shattered sultanates of Asia Minor. With the nagging border warfare between the Ilkhans of Persia and the Golden Horde, however, and the establishment of Mamluk power in Syria, an opportunity arose in Asia Minor for a new force to develop. The break-up in due course of the great Mongol fiefs into smaller khanates, an anarchy of princelings, permitted this new force to flourish, to put down roots that even the fearful jealousy of Tamurlaine could not destroy. Once his descendants, the Timurid princes, had begun to tear down their inheritance in dynastic rivalry, the way was clear for this new force – now not so new, beginning to be known and feared in its own right – to expand, and

flourish, and thrust out to the north, the west, the south, in due course to build the complex conglomeration of vassal dynasties and governorships that, as the Ottoman Empire, would dominate western Asia and eastern Europe over four centuries.

Further east the structure of modern Persia derives from that imposed upon its provinces by the heirs of Hulagu. It was the ilkhanate that established its borders and imposed on it a homogeneity which, for all the long skein of its history, gave it the shape and character it bears today. Under the Ilkhans' patronage Persian literature and Persian art not only continued and in some cases advanced from the culture the Mongols had inherited, they also became the central expression of the Islamic sensibility. The architecture of Persia now seems the archetypal statement in arch and cupola and mosaic-covered wall of Muslim culture; the delicate line and decorative detail of its miniaturists appears again and again in the paintings of Muslim Turkey, Muslim India.

Polo, played by Mongol horsemen and depicted in water-colours by Li Lin, a fifteenth-century Chinese artist. This game is almost certainly one of the minor legacies left to the world by the Mongol conquests.

Above the curved roofs of Canton rises
a thirteenth-century Muslim minaret.
One effect of Mongol rule across the whole breadth
of Asia was the spread eastwards
of both Islam and Christianity.

Indeed, the effect of Mongol ambitions on Islam was profound. The fact that in their western realms it was this religion that the Mongols adopted altered in various ways its future development. That they did adopt it need not surprise us. Riding out of the wide grasslands, the vicious summers and bleak winters, the simple and often bloody recreations of their nomadic past, the Mongols in their western thrust were suddenly confronted with the wealth, the beauty, the complexity of Isfahan, of Samarkand, of Bokhara, of Tabriz. They reduced these cities, smashed them down, as though their very elegance had excited their greatest fury. Yet the cities lived again and the people, sustained by the two poles of mosque and market-place, survived. Beyond the limits of Mongol advance the Muslim armies of the Mamluk sultans kept a watchful guard, theirs a power even the Mongols were forced to respect. The disunited vassal princes of western Russia, however, the helpless kingdoms of the Caucasus regions, the jealously combative Genoese and Venetians and the doomed Crusaders of the Syrian coastlands – these offered a collective spectacle no warrior people could admire. Even the Christian advocates who arrived at the Khaghan's court – Catholic, Nestorian, Greek, Syrian, Armenian – could not speak with a united voice. The Mongols knew of course that there was a pope and a clutch of great powers somewhere to the west, they even sent envoys to the courts of European kings, but they had no direct experience of them, they never felt the weight of their anger. All the Mongols knew of them was that they had been unable to defeat the Muslims, that they hesitated when offered an opportunity to do so through an alliance with the Mongols themselves, and that they disagreed endlessly among themselves.

Not all the interest Genghis and the others felt in the ideas and beliefs of distant peoples could alter the fact that this made a less attractive picture than did the steadfastness of Islam. Once the western parts of the empire were released, as it were, by the fading power of the distant Khaghan, it was inevitable that their rulers would go the way of the large majority of their subjects and abandon their shamanistic past or the tenets of a Buddhism, their adherence to which made them a tiny minority, and accept Islam. A fact that thoughtful rulers seem always to have understood is that a profound difference in belief between themselves and those they govern causes difficulties and often leads to princely downfall.

One action that had an important short-term effect on Islam was the extirpation already described of the Ismaili sect, its servants the Assassins, and the threat they represented to Sunni orthodoxy. But there was another, less easily definable result, also to the gain of the orthodox. The arrival of the Mongols did for a while drive Islam on the defensive. Threatened by so monumental a power, trapped, in west-central Asia at least, into a struggle for its survival, it lost for ever some of the early brilliance of its culture. Not all the patronage of the Mongols could bring back the swiftness of thought, the penetration of metaphor and image, the dazzling leaps and jumps and trapeze flights of the earlier Muslim philosophers and poets. Besieged, Islam like any other ideology looked to its unity. It could no longer afford an anarchistic fringe of questioners, nor the unquiet and disquieting band of Sufi mystics who searched for new ways of thinking, of feeling, of sensing God. It was Persia above all that had provided these (though Moorish Spain offered a variety of intellectual flourishes) and it was Persia above all that suffered both the first advance and the last internecine struggles of the Ghengisites. Elsewhere, too, the Mongol influence would modify religious and cultural development. In India the existence of their dynasty as late as the eighteenth century meant, for Hindus, a subjugation to emperors whose beliefs were totally alien to their own. The Mosaic God of Islam, eternal, personal, singular, did not find it easy to co-exist with the pantheon of Hindu deities, altering in importance from place to place and epoch to epoch, nor with the impersonal Brahman which lay beyond them. Thus a division in the people was perpetuated that, exploited by the later colonial overlord, continues in hatred and suspicion in our own times. More happily, the Mongol introduction of Buddhism to China proved less disruptive, a fact perhaps due more to Chinese tolerance than any quality in Kubilai and his successors. On the other hand, it was not achieved without damage or difficulties – it was the Taoists above all who suffered the consequences. When that champion of Buddhism, Kubilai himself, ordered in 1281 the burning of all the Taoist books in China, he struck an almost crippling blow at the continuity of the country's culture. Yet Taoism survived; Confucianism under the later Yuan again began to take its ancient place. With the downfall of the Yuan Buddhism lost its political significance, but its religious influence was too deeply embedded to be much disturbed.

In western Europe, which never felt the direct arrogance of Mongol power, the consequences of that empire's rise and fall were, paradoxically, perhaps more momentous than anywhere else. For one result of the generations of war suffered by the countries east of the Euphrates, and of the defensive orthodoxies encouraged in Islam by Mongol successes, was that the swiftly developing culture of those lands was abruptly halted and even, for a while, curtailed and stunted. Unchallenged, therefore, the Catholic-based art, science and philosophy of western Europe could ripen at its own unforced pace. The influence emanating from Byzantium, however, accelerated that pace as scholars, books, artifacts and works of art all rooted in the ancient classical world made their way to safety before the Turkish threat. It may be that here Tamurlaine's interruption of the Ottoman pressure and the fifty years this won for the population of Constantinople proved decisive, for all through the first five decades of the fifteenth century a stream of erudite refugees brought to Italy and the West the materials for that gorgeous unfolding of a dormant spirit, that slowly spreading wonder of image and invention, the Renaissance. Thus one may conclude that it was partly the ferocity of the Mongol conquerors that made possible the most extraordinary moment of cultural regeneration Europe ever experienced.

Those conquerors, however, did not neglect the administrative consequences of their victories. By the time they had reached the furthest limits of their advances, under the khaghanate of Kubilai, what has been called the *Pax Mongolica* stretched from the source of the Volga to the mouth of the Yangtze, and under its sheltering concern the caravans and pack-trains of the world moved for the first time with ease across the broad back of Asia. China, which had been a fable, at best a rumour, unknown, forbidding, suddenly stood open. Trade flourished, merchants ranged far and wide, missions passed to and fro, religious, diplomatic, mercantile. Then, abruptly, Islam slammed shut that gate. China withdrew behind its walls. The Ottoman Turks stood astride the trade routes. Once more whatever came from Asia had to be carried laboriously up the Red Sea, transhipped, and re-exported from Alexandria. This time, however, Europe had information to work on. The Far East was memory now, not myth. Almost at once the search for the sea routes to India and Cathay began, supported by new geographical theories that would change for ever humanity's idea of the planet it inhabited.

Yet, for all the manifold difference the Mongols made to the development of a variety of civilizations, they never established their own. Genghis Khan had set out to dominate the world; for all his understanding, even his wisdom, he never realized that it is not by warfare that one dominates vast populations, nor even by firmly benevolent administration – it is by ideas, by beliefs, by the intangibles of human communication. When the Arabs broke out of the meagreness of their history and the aridity of their ancestral lands, they carried with them their faith and the words in which it was enshrined. It was this which made their conquests permanent; their subject peoples were altered by what they brought, they ceased

Buddhist grottoes at the Chi Hsia Monastery
in South China. Under the patronage
of several of the Yuan emperors, Buddhism
enjoyed greatly increased power during
the years of Mongol control.

Travellers like Marco Polo – on whose description of Khanbaliq or Pekin this fifteenth-century map is based – made China a reality to Europe. As a result, the closing of the caravan trails to the east stimulated the seaborne expeditions which led to the discovery of America, and of the route to India and the Spice Islands.

to be the same people they had been before the arrival of their Muslim conquerors.

The Mongols brought nothing, could offer nothing. They could destroy, or they could take. Did they sense at some level of their beings this emptiness? Was it for this reason that Genghis, Ogadei, Kubilai, all in their turn listened so intently to the missionaries of the world's religions? Was there a word they hoped to hear, some messenger they hoped to recognize? Had they done so, had they brandished such a word or the commandments of such a messenger before them, they would have been not merely invincible, as they nearly were, but successful in their larger intention, which they were not. They took on the ideas and cultural priorities of the people they had defeated – in China the Chinese, in Persia the Persian – and hoped in these borrowed rags to pass for fully dressed. But those whose clothes they had knew where they had come from. The formidable impartiality of their law, upon which the peace they imposed was based, hardly survived its founder, Genghis, and certainly not his grandsons. Rule of law, in any case, has never been a cry to enthuse millions. The Mongols could always force from the people they ruled a sullen acceptance of their presence; except on a personal basis they could never win their respect.

In the end, therefore, it may be that the popular belief about them is the true one. They contributed to the sum of human cruelty, they murdered, plundered and destroyed on a vast scale; then they vanished. What they hoped to achieve they did not achieve; what they did achieve they achieved by accident or in the name of some other authority – Buddhism or Islam. They were barbarians, come slashing out of their own darkness to smash the light that so attracted them. And they were the last of their type; by the sixteenth century gunpowder had made war a matter of technology. From then on armies needed the support of complex economies, developed industries, an urban sophistication. For a while it was believed that this had brought about the end of barbarism; the twentieth century has demonstrated that it had only extended its scope. Afraid to acknowledge this, we can always look down the eight centuries that divide us from Genghis Khan. At such a distance monsters are safer to contemplate than when they stare back at us from our mirrors.

# Chronology

| | Western Europe | Eastern Europe | Western Asia |
|---|---|---|---|
| 1162 | | | |
| 1197 | | | |
| 1202 | | | |
| 1204 | Crusaders sack Constantinople | | |
| 1206 | | | |
| 1207 | | | |
| 1208 | | | |
| 1209 | | | |
| 1211 | | | |
| 1215 | Magna Carta signed | | |
| 1217 | | | Kara-Khitai invaded |
| 1218 | | | Kara-Khitai defeated |
| 1219 | | | Khwarismians attacked |
| 1220 | Frederick II crowned Emperor | | Bokhara, Samarkand fall |
| 1221 | | Subatei defeat Georgians | Shah Muhammad dies |
| 1222 | | Battle of Kalka | Jelal ud-Din defeated |
| 1223 | | | |
| 1224 | | | Jelal returns |
| 1225 | | | Jelal attacks Caliph |
| 1226 | St Louis crowned | Jochi dies | Jelal takes Tiflis |
| 1227 | | | |
| 1228 | Sixth Crusade | | |
| 1229 | | | |
| 1230 | | | Mongols attack Jelal |
| 1231 | | | Jelal dies |
| 1232 | | | |
| 1233 | | | |
| 1234 | | | |
| 1235 | Spain recaptures Majorca | Georgia ravaged | |
| 1236 | | Armenia invaded | |
| 1237 | | Volga crossed | |
| 1238 | | Vladimir, Moscow, etc fall | |
| 1240 | | Kiev falls | |
| 1241 | | Wahlstadt. Hungary falls | |
| 1242 | | Sarai founded | |
| 1243 | | | |
| 1245 | | | |
| 1246 | | | |
| 1248 | St Louis's Crusade | | |
| 1251 | Death of Frederick II | | |
| 1252 | | | |
| 1254 | | | |
| 1255 | | Batu dies | Hulagu starts campaign |
| 1256 | | | Assassins destroyed |
| 1257 | | Berke Khan | |
| 1258 | | Nogai invades Poland | Baghdad falls |
| 1259 | Treaty of Paris | | Syria invaded |
| 1260 | | | Mamluks defeat Ked-Buka |
| 1262 | | Berke attacks Hulagu | Hulagu attacks Berke |
| 1263 | | | Battle of Terek |
| 1264 | | Nogai attacks Byzantines | Hulagu dies |
| 1265 | Battle of Evesham | | Abaqa Khan |
| 1267 | | Berke dies | |
| 1268 | | Mangu-Timur Khan | |
| 1269 | | | Borak invades Transoxiana |
| 1270 | | | Borak repulsed |
| 1271 | | | |
| 1272 | Edward I crowned | | |
| 1273 | | | Abaqa sacks Bokhara |
| 1274 | | | |
| 1277 | | | Baibars dies |
| 1279 | | | |

| Heartlands | Eastern Asia | |
|---|---|---|
| Genghis Khan born | | 1162 |
| Toghrul restored | | 1197 |
| Tatars massacred | | 1202 |
| Keraits defeated | | 1204 |
| | | |
| Genghis proclaimed Khaghan | | 1206 |
| Jochi subjugates steppe tribes | | 1207 |
| | Invasion of Hsi-Hsia | 1208 |
| Uighurs accept Mongol rule | | 1209 |
| | Kin attacked | 1211 |
| | Pekin falls | 1215 |
| | Mukhali commands against Kin | 1217 |
| | Kin counter repulsed | 1218 |
| | | 1219 |
| | | 1220 |
| | | |
| | Mukhali–Sung alliance | 1221 |
| | | 1222 |
| | Mukhali dies | 1223 |
| | | 1224 |
| Genghis Khan returns | | 1225 |
| | Hsi-Hsia invaded | 1226 |
| Genghis Khan dies | | 1227 |
| | | 1228 |
| Ogadei Khaghan | | 1229 |
| | | 1230 |
| | Kin attacked | 1231 |
| Tuli dies | Kin defeated at Kum-chou | 1232 |
| | Kai-fung falls | 1233 |
| | End of Kin dynasty | 1234 |
| | Sung attacked | 1235 |
| | | 1236 |
| | | 1237 |
| | | 1238 |
| | | 1240 |
| | | 1241 |
| Ogadei dies | | 1242 |
| Turakina regent | | 1243 |
| Carpini mission arrives | | 1245 |
| Kuyuk Khaghan | | 1246 |
| Kuyuk dies | | 1248 |
| Mangu Khaghan | | 1251 |
| | Kubilai attacks Sung | 1252 |
| Rubruck mission arrives | | 1254 |
| | | 1255 |
| | | 1256 |
| | | 1257 |
| | Kubilai controls south China | 1258 |
| Mangu dies | | 1259 |
| Arik-Buka claims Khaghanate | Kubilai proclaimed Khaghan | 1260 |
| Kubilai defeats Arik-Buka | | 1262 |
| | | 1263 |
| Arik-Buka surrenders | | 1264 |
| | | 1265 |
| | Kubilai's final assault on Sung | 1267 |
| | | 1268 |
| | | 1269 |
| | | 1270 |
| | Yuan dynasty proclaimed | 1271 |
| | | 1272 |
| | | 1273 |
| | Japanese repulse invasion | 1274 |
| Kaidu attacks Karakorum | Lin-an falls | 1277 |
| | Sung dynasty ends | 1279 |

|  | Western Europe | Eastern Europe | Western Asia |
|---|---|---|---|
| 1280 |  | Mangu-Timur dies | Aleppo sacked |
| 1281 |  |  | Mamluk victory |
| 1282 |  |  | Abaqa dies |
| 1283 |  |  |  |
| 1284 |  |  | Arghum Ilkhan |
| 1285 | Philip the Fair crowned |  |  |
| 1288 |  | Poland repulses Golden Horde |  |
| 1289 |  |  |  |
| 1290 |  | Nogai makes Toktu khan |  |
| 1291 | Acre falls to Islam |  | Arghum dies |
| 1292 |  |  | Gaikhatu Ilkhan |
| 1294 |  |  | Paper money issued |
| 1295 |  |  | Gaikhatu dies; Ghazan Ilkhan |
| 1297 |  |  | Ghazan executes Nauwez |
| 1299 |  | Toktu defeats Nogai | Aleppo sacked |
| 1301 |  |  |  |
| 1303 |  |  | Syria invaded |
| 1304 | Pope moves to Avignon |  | Ghazan dies; Uljeitu Ilkhan |
| 1307 | Edward I dies |  | Sultaniya founded |
| 1308 |  | Kaffa sacked |  |
| 1312 |  | Toktu dies | Uljeitu leaves Syria |
| 1313 |  | Uzbeg Khan |  |
| 1314 | Battle of Bannockburn |  |  |
| 1315 |  |  |  |
| 1316 |  |  | Uljeitu dies; Abu Said Ilkhan |
| 1318 |  |  | Rashid executed |
| 1325 |  |  |  |
| 1326 |  |  |  |
| 1327 | Edward II dies | Ivan Kalita prince in Moscow | Choban executed |
| 1328 |  |  |  |
| 1335 |  |  | Abu Said dies |
| 1336 | Hundred Years' War begins |  |  |
| 1340 |  |  |  |
| 1341 |  | Uzbeg dies |  |
| 1348 | Black Death in England |  |  |
| 1352 |  |  |  |
| 1355 |  |  |  |
| 1356 | Battle of Poitiers |  |  |
| 1357 |  | Ottomans take Gallipoli |  |
| 1360 |  |  |  |
| 1368 |  |  |  |
| 1370 |  |  | Samarkand Timur's capital |
| 1377 | Edward III dies | Toktamish khan |  |
| 1380 |  | Battle of Kulikovo Pole | Timur invades Persia |
| 1381 |  | Toktamish crushes Russia |  |
| 1388 |  |  |  |
| 1390 |  |  | Timur takes Sultaniya |
| 1391 |  | Timur defeats Toktamish |  |
| 1393 |  |  | Timur takes Baghdad |
| 1395 |  | Timur again defeats Toktamish |  |
| 1398 |  |  |  |
| 1399 | Richard II dies |  |  |
| 1400 |  |  | Timur takes Damascus |
| 1402 |  |  | Timur defeats Bayazid |
| 1405 | Papal schism ends |  | Timur dies |
| 1406 |  | Toktamish dies |  |
| 1412 |  |  |  |
| 1510 |  |  | Timurid dynasty ends |
| 1526 |  |  |  |

| Heartlands | Eastern Asia | |
|---|---|---|
| | | 1280 |
| | Japanese repulse invasion | 1281 |
| | | 1282 |
| | Champa falls | 1283 |
| | | 1284 |
| | Tonkin falls | 1285 |
| | Annam falls | 1288 |
| Kaidu defeated | | 1289 |
| | | 1290 |
| | | 1291 |
| | Java repulses invasion | 1292 |
| | Kubilai dies | 1294 |
| | | 1295 |
| | Burma falls | 1297 |
| | | 1299 |
| Kaidu dies | | 1301 |
| | | 1303 |
| | | 1304 |
| | Timur dies | 1307 |
| | | 1308 |
| | | 1312 |
| | | 1313 |
| | | 1314 |
| | Odoric mission arrives | 1315 |
| | | 1316 |
| Kebek Khan | | 1318 |
| | Peasant revolts begin | 1325 |
| Kebek overthrown | | 1326 |
| | | 1327 |
| | Chagatei horde invades | 1328 |
| | | 1335 |
| Timur born | | 1336 |
| Christians massacred | | 1340 |
| | | 1341 |
| | | 1348 |
| | Kuo Tsu-hsing revolts | 1352 |
| | Chu Yuan-chang leads revolt | 1355 |
| Tughluk unites Chagatai Khanate | | 1356 |
| | Chu takes Nankin | 1357 |
| Timur vizier to Ilyas | | 1360 |
| | Yuan emperor flees Pekin | 1368 |
| | Yuan dynasty ends | 1370 |
| | | 1377 |
| | | 1380 |
| | | 1381 |
| Chinese destroy Karakorum | | 1388 |
| | | 1390 |
| | | 1391 |
| | | 1393 |
| | | 1395 |
| | Timur invades India | 1398 |
| | | 1399 |
| | | 1400 |
| | | 1402 |
| | | 1405 |
| | | 1406 |
| Uriat defeat Algai Timur | | 1412 |
| | | 1510 |
| | Moghul dynasty founded | 1526 |

# ACKNOWLEDGMENTS

Photographs and illustrations are supplied by or reproduced by kind permission of the following:

Bibliothèque Nationale Paris 2, 26, 36–7, *49*, *50*, *67*, 80–1; British Library 179; British Museum 14, 29, 35, 44, 57, *68*, 86, 89, 129, 138, 154, 155, 181, 186, *197*, 200 (above), 206, 210, *215*, *216*, 218, 229; Camera Press 8–9, 13, 18, 47, 61, 90, 93, 96–7, 220–1; Robert Harding Associates 200 (below), 202; Paolo Koch 157, 247; MAS, Barcelona 184; Metropolitan Museum of Art, New York 52–3; National Palace Museum, Taipei 204 (both); Novosti Press Agency 114, 116, 119 (both), 122–3, 164–5, 168, 170, 174, 176, 232; Osterreichische Nationalbibliothek, Vienna 124, 132; Outlook Films Ltd. 102; Josephine Powell 239; Radio Times Hulton Picture Library 24, 104, 189, 191, 227, 235; Snark International, Paris 71; Topkapi Palace Museum, Istanbul 111; University of Edinburgh 22–3, 76; Victoria and Albert Museum 40, 54, 143, 149, 224, 231; H. Roger Viollet 211; Warburg Institute and the Asiatic Society of Bengal 65, 78, 99, 136–7, 145, 150–1, 212–13; Werner Forman Archive 32, 112, 134, 141, 162, 187, 192, *198*, 207, 244

*Numerals in italics indicate colour illustrations*

Picture research by Pat Hodgson

Maps and genealogical trees by Tony Garrett

# INDEX